Michael Lewis is Head of Portable Antiquities & Treasure at the British Museum. An expert on the Bayeux Tapestry, he is the author of *The Real World of the Bayeux Tapestry*. He is a member of the Bayeux Tapestry scientific committee that is advising Bayeux Museum on the reinterpretation and redisplay of the embroidery.

David Musgrove is Content Director of the HistoryExtra.com website and podcast, plus its sister print magazines *BBC History Magazine* and *BBC History Revealed*. He is also the author of the bestselling *100 Places That Made Britain*.

David Musgrove

Michael Lewis

THE
STORY
OF THE
BAYEUX
TAPESTRY

UNRAVELLING
THE NORMAN CONQUEST

With 22 illustrations

For Felicity

ON THE COVER
Details from the Bayeux Tapestry, 11th century,
with special permission from the city of Bayeux.

First published in the United Kingdom in 2021
by Thames & Hudson Ltd, 181A High Holborn,
London, WC1V 7QX

This paperback edition published in 2024

The Story of the Bayeux Tapestry:
Unravelling the Norman Conquest
© 2021 and 2024 Thames & Hudson Ltd, London

Text © 2021 David Musgrove and Michael Lewis

Designed by Lisa Ifsits

British Library Cataloguing-in-Publication Data
A catalogue record for this book is available from
the British Library

ISBN 978-0-500-29765-0

Printed and bound in the UK by CPI (UK) Ltd

MIX
Paper | Supporting
responsible forestry
FSC® C171272

Be the first to know about our new releases,
exclusive content and author events by visiting
thamesandhudson.com
thamesandhudsonusa.com
thamesandhudson.com.au

CONTENTS

INTRODUCTION · A Remarkable Survival 7

CHAPTER 1 · Putting the Conquest in Context 13

CHAPTER 2 · A Unique Embroidery 31

CHAPTER 3 · The Story Begins 53

CHAPTER 4 · Captive in France 70

CHAPTER 5 · At the Court of Duke William 91

CHAPTER 6 · The Brittany Campaign 105

CHAPTER 7 · A Sacred Oath 118

CHAPTER 8 · Harold Becomes King 125

CHAPTER 9 · William Raises an Army 148

CHAPTER 10 · The Lull Before the Storm 167

CHAPTER 11 · The Great Battle 180

CHAPTER 12 · The Bayeux Tapestry and Its Legacy 204

Timeline of Key Events 217
Further Reading 222   Acknowledgments 234
Sources of Illustrations 235   Index 236

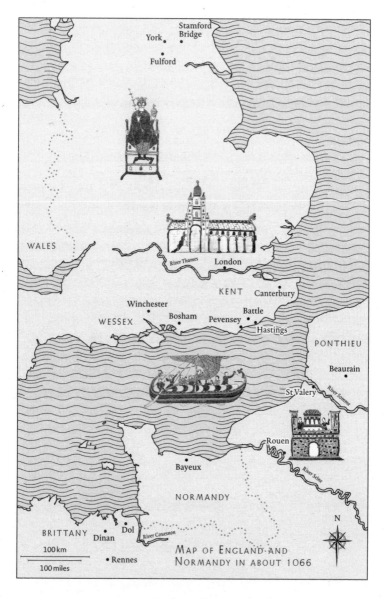

York

Stamford
Bridge

Fulford

WALES

River Thames   London

Winchester

WESSEX   Bosham

KENT   Canterbury

Battle

Pevensey

Hastings

PONTHIEU

Beaurain

St Valery

River Somme

Rouen

River Seine

Bayeux

NORMANDY

BRITTANY   Dinan   Dol

River Couesnon

100 km

Rennes

100 miles

MAP OF ENGLAND AND
NORMANDY IN ABOUT 1066

N

At the time of the Norman Conquest, England was a relatively new,
but wealthy, kingdom, and Normandy found itself in a position of strength.

A REMARKABLE SURVIVAL

Political intrigue, extreme violence, graphic nudity – the Bayeux Tapestry has it all. Most people probably know that it shows the stricken Anglo-Saxon king Harold II (Godwinson) dying on the battlefield of Hastings in 1066 amid a shower of arrows, while the mounted knights of Duke William of Normandy mow down his closest followers. Axes clash against helmets, swords slash and spears fly, fallen warriors are trampled beneath charging hooves and have their armour stripped from them, leaving their naked bodies lying on the ground. All this is shown on a strip of linen around 68 m (223 ft) long, with an intensity and gory vividness that still has great power and immediacy today, nearly 1,000 years after the Tapestry was created.

The scene of high drama is the climactic moment of this most famous of battles, providing the breakthrough William needed to conquer England and forever change British history. Leading up to this final bloody act, the Tapestry shows the full fury of the Battle of Hastings, from the first manoeuvres and troop deployments, through the Norman cavalry assault on the shield-wall of the Anglo-Saxons, as they sturdily defended their hilltop position – despite the death of Harold's brothers – and then the tactical success of the Norman archers coming into play to weaken English resolve and finally allow the invading horsemen to gain the upper hand.

So, on the surface at least, the Bayeux Tapestry tells the dramatic tale of how the last Anglo-Saxon king of England was killed in battle and was replaced on the throne by his Norman adversary. However, there is much more to this remarkable historical and artistic treasure than that. While the battle itself may be the most familiar and famous episode depicted, the Tapestry devotes much more space – almost three quarters of its length – to the run-up to this clash. Before it gets anywhere near the battlefield, it charts the political machinations on both sides of the Channel in the years leading up to the Conquest, introducing key characters in the story and showing the moments that led to Duke William's decision to launch his assault to claim the English crown.

The story of 1066 has been drummed into British schoolchildren for generations – in part because it is such a dramatic tale, but no doubt also because it has such a fantastic artistic accompaniment in the form of the Bayeux Tapestry. The fact that the embroidery tells the story through images more than words, apart from the terse captions, lends it an air of approachability that a standard medieval documentary source, typically written in Latin in challenging handwriting, simply cannot match. Most of all, perhaps, it is famous because 1066 was undeniably a turning point in British history. The remarkable achievement of Duke William over the English is noted also in France, although it perhaps does not have such a hold on the public imagination there as the history of the French monarchy. Whereas for the English 1066 is a key moment that marks the end of Anglo-Saxon England, for the French the major historical year of note is 1789 – the beginning of the French Revolution. But both the English and French recognize that the Conquest also bound together the history of the two countries in a profound way, perhaps never again to be repeated until the two world wars of the twentieth century, and specifically the liberation of Normandy by the Allies in 1944. Even though the Conquest was of England (not Britain) and was by Normans (not the French), it had major long-term repercussions for the rest of Britain and Ireland too. The different ways in which the British and French, or more specifically the English and the Normans, have responded to the story of the Conquest have influenced how the Bayeux Tapestry is appreciated and understood.

Dispelling some myths

The first thing that should be said in any book about the Bayeux Tapestry is that it is not a tapestry at all and it probably wasn't made in Bayeux. Leaving aside for now the question of where it was produced, the Bayeux 'Tapestry' should in fact more accurately be described as an embroidery, where a design is stitched on to fabric – in this case on linen using woollen threads – rather than a tapestry.

The confusion dates back to 1729, when a French monk and antiquarian, Bernard de Montfaucon, published engravings made from a drawing of part of the Bayeux Tapestry in the first volume of a substantial work he produced on the historical monuments associated with the French monarchy (see pl. 2). The original drawing had been made some years earlier and came from the collection of another Frenchman, Nicolas-Joseph Foucault (see pl. 1), along with a detailed description. In his account, Montfaucon used the word *Tapisserie*, and from then on, the label 'tapestry' has stuck.

Until Montfaucon published his book, the Bayeux Tapestry was barely known about – in fact it was through his efforts to trace the textile shown in the drawing, and then have a full, accurate copy made and published, that it was rediscovered. The Tapestry is recorded in an inventory listing the treasures of Bayeux Cathedral of 1476 (see pl. 5), which says it was 'hung round the nave of the church' once a year at a certain time and was otherwise stored in a chest, so it was certainly there then. It had probably been there for centuries before that; one theory is that it was sealed in the crypt of the cathedral when it was blocked up in the early twelfth century and only saw the light of day again in 1412.

Some references have been unearthed in the last few years which reveal that from 1396 to the 1420s a tapestry that sounds similar in content to the one in Bayeux today was in the possession of the then French king, Charles VI (r. 1380–1422), and that the same embroidery might subsequently have passed into the hands of John, Duke of Bedford (1389–1435), and then on again to Philip (the Good), Duke of Burgundy (r. 1419–67). Whether this was the same textile as the one described in the Bayeux Cathedral inventory (and thus surely the one we know today), and if so how it might have got from Burgundy to Bayeux in the mid-fifteenth century, are difficult questions to answer. However, if it is the same work of art, then it could not have been sealed up in the crypt of Bayeux Cathedral until 1412 while simultaneously being in the French treasury in 1396, so it is unlikely.

The survival of this fragile textile through the centuries is remarkable. It came through fires in Bayeux Cathedral, and after its rediscovery by Montfaucon was saved for the nation during the French Revolution. Increased interest from people wanting to see the Tapestry did not always ensure its protection. In 1817, the visiting English antiquary Hudson Gurney described the mechanism used to roll out the embroidery for visitors as resembling something that 'lets down the buckets to a well', so by the time another English antiquary, Dawson Turner, viewed it a few years later he observed that it was 'much rubbed at the beginning, torn towards the end, and some portions of it are even missing'. In the course of the nineteenth century some restoration work was undertaken, and in 1842 the Tapestry was put on display fully extended in a specially made case in a room in the library in Bayeux. It was moved again during later crises and conflicts, but always returned.

Nowadays it is straightforward to see the Tapestry first-hand, as it still resides in Bayeux, Normandy, in northwest France, under the custody of this small city. The embroidery is owned by the French state, and even though as far as is known it has been in Bayeux almost continuously since at least the late fifteenth century, it was only in 2017 that an official convention was signed between the French government and the city formalizing its status. In 2007 it was included in UNESCO's Memory of the World register as an object of global value. From 1983 it has been displayed in a museum housed in a seventeenth-century seminary (where priests were trained), close to the heart of the medieval town centre. This building will be refurbished to enable the Bayeux Tapestry to be better displayed and presented, and in a way that will ensure its long-term safety. This also creates the opportunity for the loan of the Tapestry to the UK, most suitably to the British Museum, where it could be displayed in a single length, as was announced by the French president Emmanuel Macron in January 2018.

So, because it is now in Bayeux, and has been for centuries, and because an eighteenth-century French monk was a little loose with his language, it is known as the Bayeux Tapestry (La Tapisserie de Bayeux). There is an argument that it should now be more correctly and accurately referred to as an embroidery, but in this book we are going to follow tradition.

Scholarly debate

There are a few things that are broadly agreed on by the majority of researchers who have studied the Bayeux Tapestry, and many things that are not agreed on at all. As might be imagined, there is a wealth of literature to absorb to understand these varying points of view – over a thousand scholarly books and articles. These studies not only explore the history of the Tapestry itself, and where, when, why and for whom it was made, but also investigate numerous details of its imagery and take more theoretical approaches to this most famous of embroideries. One researcher, writing in 1935, wondered whether 'everything had already been said' about the Tapestry, so he would perhaps be surprised to discover that people are still finding new things to say about it over eighty-five years later.

Clearly, the Bayeux Tapestry is an important historical document in its own right, a primary source for the Norman Conquest and pivotal in our understanding of the politics of the day. Detailed investigation of the Tapestry itself as a physical artifact, in terms of the materials and techniques used, has been reasonably instructive in establishing a date and location for its manufacture, but yet more could be revealed by proper scientific analysis and study – a tantalizing prospect in the context of its redisplay. Furthermore, looking at it as a piece of artwork helps us to appreciate the context in which it was produced and its place in the cultural story of the period.

It has also been mined by a plethora of researchers over the years as a resource for the social and artistic history of the time to which it belongs. The pictorial richness of this unique source has enabled academics to further our understanding of many aspects of the contemporary eleventh-century world, even if some of the Tapestry's illustrations are based on details found in late Anglo-Saxon art. Architecture, including castle design, military techniques and strategy, arms and armour, shipbuilding and carpentry, and dress and fashion are just a few of the areas that have been explored to good effect.

Many uncertainties and mysteries remain, but with a greater knowledge of what to look for when examining the Bayeux Tapestry much more can be discovered than might be apparent at first sight. In this book we hope to offer a guide to both the story it tells and the surprises it contains. Obviously, to do this we have drawn heavily on the work of the multitude of scholars who have researched the Tapestry over many years, but we have tried to distil the key themes of these studies in our text so that the story can be followed without undue distraction from detailed academic debate. We hope you will be encouraged to delve further into the topic by following the reading suggestions at the end of the book, where the major studies on the Tapestry are acknowledged – and also of course to see the Tapestry first-hand.

CHAPTER 1

PUTTING THE CONQUEST IN CONTEXT

The Bayeux Tapestry, put simply, depicts the story of the conquest of England by Duke William of Normandy and the demise of King Harold II, previously Earl Harold Godwinson of Wessex, at the Battle of Hastings on 14 October 1066. This occurs in the aftermath of the death, in early January 1066, of King Edward (later named 'the Confessor' after his canonization as saint in the mid-twelfth century), who had been king of the English since 1042, but who had notably failed to produce a son and heir. The Tapestry famously shows the action of the battle in great detail, but it also recounts the events leading up to it, from about 1064. To understand the situation fully, and how this conflict arose, it is necessary to look back even further, at the complex politics and history of this part of northern Europe.

Setting the scene

Normandy today occupies a large coastal area of northern France, with Brittany to its southwest, and, across the narrow Channel, England to the north. The various polities are well established now, but in the eleventh century things were not so simple. For several centuries travellers, raiders and merchants from Scandinavia (today generally conveniently grouped together under the name Vikings) had been using the North Sea and English Channel to plunder, trade with and settle in Britain and Ireland and other parts of northern Europe. They caused great difficulties for the Anglo-Saxon rulers of England and also disrupted life and politics in what is now France and the Low Countries. At the start of the tenth century, the king of West Francia, Charles the Simple, unable to defeat the Vikings, granted lands around

Rouen to a 'North-man' named Rollo, and this is deemed to mark the beginnings of the Duchy of Normandy.

Around 150 years later, by the time of the events recorded in the Bayeux Tapestry, Normandy was an established entity, with its dukes technically owing homage to the king of France but regularly at odds with both their nominal overlords on the French throne and their various neighbours. Throughout this period, both Normandy and Anglo-Saxon England were very much part of the same maritime culture of northern Europe, which also included the counties of Flanders (broadly in modern-day Belgium but also parts of what is now France and the Netherlands) and of Brittany, plus smaller entities such as the counties of Ponthieu and Boulogne.

The perceived ethnicities of these various groups of people are worth examining. Several hundred years of Scandinavian attacks on Britain and Ireland meant that by the eleventh century the area that was to become England had an Anglo-Scandinavian character to it. This was especially true in the north and east, the area once known as the Danelaw, where the inhabitants may have felt strong affiliations to Scandinavia. Throughout the land at this time, people seem to have referred to themselves generally as *Angli* or *Saxones*, so while there was a sense of Englishness, England was a relatively new concept. Æthelstan, grandson of Alfred the Great, was the first king to unify the English peoples, in 927. The label Anglo-Saxon has long been used as the historical term to define this period of English history up until the Norman Conquest, and indeed as an ethnic determinant for the people occupying the area that roughly makes up modern England today. In this book, 'Anglo-Saxon' is used, along with 'English', to describe the inhabitants of the kingdom of England, as it remains the most widely understood term, and also because it was in contemporary usage, with Alfred, Edward the Elder and Æthelstan all styling themselves kings of the Anglo-Saxons.

Despite a similarly strong Viking influence in Normandy, across the Channel there was a sense of a cultural or ethnic divide, highlighted no doubt by linguistic differences. The Normans almost certainly did not see themselves as French, in the way that other inhabitants of what is now the northern part of France perhaps more easily accepted as an identification, but they had more or less embraced French culture by the eleventh century.

Edward the Confessor became England's king over a century after Æthelstan, in 1042, when in his late thirties, though only after a complex power struggle. He was the son of King Æthelred II the Unready (r. 978–1016) and his second wife, Queen Emma, who was the daughter of Richard I of Normandy. Most of Edward's early years were spent in his mother's Norman homeland, in exile, after Danish invaders led by King Swein Forkbeard and his son Cnut had conquered England in 1013, the culmination of a series of raids. Æthelred, Emma and their family were forced to flee to Normandy. Swein did not occupy England for long, however, as he died in 1014. Æthelred returned and drove back the Danes under Cnut, until his own death in April 1016 from natural causes. Edmund Ironside, Æthelred's son by his first wife, took up the fight against the invader. Despite his defeat at the Battle of Assandun (also known as Ashingdon) on 18 October that same year, a treaty was agreed which formally divided the kingdom, with Edmund taking the south and Cnut the rest of the country. When Edmund suddenly died just a month later, Cnut claimed the crown of England as sole ruler.

Queen Emma acted swiftly after the passing of Æthelred and soon married her deceased husband's rival, Cnut. She even sidelined her sons by Æthelred, Edward and Alfred, and began a new dynasty with the birth of another son, Harthacnut. Cnut died in 1035, to be succeeded by one son, Harold Harefoot, and subsequently in 1040 by Harthacnut. It was under Harthacnut's short, and seemingly unpopular, reign (1040–42) that Edward, of royal Anglo-Saxon stock, was invited back to England, possibly to help shore up support for his half-brother. Harthacnut seems to have reached an agreement with King Magnus the Good of Norway that if either of them died without an heir, his kingdom should go to the other. However, when Harthacnut did die childless, it was Edward and not Magnus who used the opportunity to take the crown, supported by Earl Godwin of Wessex. As can be seen, not many people survived long in power at this time, and Anglo-Scandinavian-Norman interests were closely entwined in the upper echelons of society.

Feuding families

King Edward came to the throne at a time when the English kingdom was relatively weak and vulnerable to foreign aggression. That meant he had to play his hand carefully to maintain the support of his nobles, particularly the key figure of Godwin, Earl of Wessex, who held extensive lands across southern England and had made his name during the period of Scandinavian rule. Godwin had been on the political scene for several decades and was involved in various machinations and power-plays in that time. Despite personal bad blood between the two men – Edward had blamed Earl Godwin for the blinding and murder of his brother, Alfred, when the latter returned to England on a mission from exile in 1036 – Godwin gave his backing to Edward's claim to the throne. As a reward for his loyalty, the new king dealt out lands and titles to Godwin's sons, Swein and Harold, and his nephew Beorn. Edward also married Godwin's daughter Edith, which all meant that the Godwin family were never far from the action during the Confessor's reign.

The relationship continued to be an uneasy one, however: Edward and Godwin clashed repeatedly over the dishonourable behaviour of the latter's eldest son, Swein. He was a man who seems to have been able to find trouble easily in life – his catalogue of misdemeanours includes the abduction of an abbess and the murder of his cousin. He was outlawed more than once. Edward and Godwin also disagreed over who should be the next Archbishop of Canterbury after the incumbent died in 1050. Importantly for this story, Godwin accused Edward of favouring men from the continent (including Normans) over those of Anglo-Danish stock when it came to positions of power. The two men identified themselves with opposite sides of this cultural divide, which was to define not only their relationship but also the future direction of the English kingdom.

Things came to a head in 1051 with an altercation in Dover between Godwin's men and those of a visiting dignitary, Eustace II, Count of Boulogne, the former brother-in-law of King Edward. Eustace complained about the incident to Edward, who then ordered Godwin to deal with the townsfolk since Dover was in the region under his control. Godwin refused, and the situation escalated into an armed stand-off, bringing England to the brink of civil war. Ultimately, Godwin and his sons backed down, were declared outlaws and fled into exile. A rapprochement came about a year later when the Godwins returned in force to England, and all their lands and titles were reinstated. As part of the peace deal, Edward was forced to banish some of those 'foreigners' whose presence had so annoyed Godwin and other members of the English nobility. At this distance in time, it is hard to fully appreciate the importance of these events, but Edward was clearly weakened, for he was now somewhat beholden to England's Anglo-Scandinavian nobility, and to Earl Godwin in particular. Given this situation, Edward was unlikely to have been overly distressed to witness the death of Earl Godwin, who appears to have suffered some sort of stroke while dining with the King the following Easter. The Godwin family power base was not diminished by this event, though, as the Earl's son, Harold, succeeded him in Wessex. Harold's elder brother, the reckless but latterly penitential Swein, had died the year before his father on the return leg of a pilgrimage to Jerusalem.

By this time, across the Channel in Normandy, Duke William had managed to establish through force of arms and strength of personality firm authority over his lands, despite having been born outside Christian wedlock to Robert I, Duke of Normandy (r. 1027–35). Whether his illegitimacy mattered much within Normandy is not completely certain, as it was common for the nobility at that time to have concubines. In 1051, when Godwin and his sons were briefly in exile, Duke William possibly visited England. Some later sources say that this was when an alliance was agreed between the two rulers, and, crucially, when King Edward made William his heir. While some scholars see no reason to doubt that this visit took place, others dispute whether it happened at all. Whatever the reality, such a promise from Edward to William is the basis for the Norman view that William was Edward's rightful successor, and it certainly seems from William's actions in 1066 that he believed it also.

It is easy to see why such a deal would have been in King Edward's interests in 1051. He needed allies against his over-mighty subjects, particularly Earl Godwin, whom he had just banished and whose ongoing intentions no doubt remained a cause for concern. Godwin had fled to Flanders, while some of his sons, including Harold, went to Ireland. Ironically, the exile of the Godwin family, and the power vacuum it left behind, created an opportunity for previously less influential aristocrats in England to flex their muscles, and some of these (especially in northern England) possibly preferred to pledge allegiance to Scandinavian rulers, who themselves might have their sights on England. On top of that, the King, who had Norman blood himself through his mother Queen Emma, would have been well aware of the military and political prowess of Duke William.

But even if William did visit England in 1051, it is far from certain that an offer of the crown was made, and if so, it would anyway have been superseded by events following the return of the Godwin family a year later. Edward has a posthumous reputation for being frivolous and capricious in his offers of the English crown, but perhaps he changed his mind to reflect changing circumstances, and against the backdrop of having no children of his own. Earlier Anglo-Saxon kings had created problems of succession by having too many sons (Edward the Elder, r. 899–924, had about fourteen), but for Edward the Confessor it was the opposite situation. He was also on the wrong side of middle age, which at this time would be anything over thirty, and apparently dedicated to a marriage that was not productive. Furthermore, the decision as to whom Edward could designate as his heir was not his alone, despite his personal wishes and whether or not he wanted it to be William. Although the oldest surviving sons did tend to follow their fathers on the throne in this period, it was a principle that was far from set in stone. English kings before Edward had to have the support of the Witan (a council of the highest echelons) to rule, and Edward's successor would have needed the same endorsement. By 1064, when the story in the Bayeux Tapestry opens, the Anglo-Saxon nobility probably had a clear idea of who they wanted to be the next king, and it was not going to be William.

The closest living lineal descendant to Edward was Edgar, the grandson of the King's long dead half-brother, Edmund Ironside (see pl. 3). After Edmund's short reign of just a few months and his death in 1016, his kin had fled abroad for their safety. In 1057, Edward the Confessor sanctioned an English expedition (which seems to have included Earl Harold Godwinson himself) to seek out the old king's children, known to be living in the Hungarian royal court, and bring them back to England, presumably to secure the succession. How 'English' these royal relatives might have seemed after their long time out of the country is debatable; they probably did not even speak their native tongue. It was unfortunate that Edmund's son, another Edward, died as soon as he set foot in England (even before meeting the King), but with him was his own young son, Edgar, perhaps only five years old. Edgar survived and was considered by King Edward as *ætheling*, meaning throne-worthy, designating him as a prince of royal stock who was fit to be king. However, given Edgar's youth and Edward's advancing years, there was undoubtedly a significant question mark over whether such a boy could hold together the English kingdom after the Confessor's death. Even so, boy-kings did rule successfully in other parts of Europe at this time, including Philip I of France (r. 1059–1108), who was just eight years old when he became king, and Henry IV of Germany (r. 1053–1105), who was only five.

Indeed, it has recently been argued that young age was not such an impediment to kingly succession, and that these European examples would have meant that it was not at all far-fetched to think that Edgar could have taken the crown. Further, a recent biography of Edward the Confessor has stressed the importance of the royal blood in the pre-Conquest English kingly succession, with those who could trace their lineage via the male line back to the semi-legendary Cerdic, founder of the West Saxon dynasty, having a higher standing than those around them. Edgar Ætheling had such blood.

It is not known when Harold Godwinson's ambitions to seize the crown crystallized, but it is not impossible that he was prepared to serve as regent to Edgar until the latter was old enough to rule for himself. By late 1065, it might have been clear that Edward's demise was near. That same year Harold's brother, Tostig, Earl of Northumbria, had been banished from England, and immediately sought help from foreign powers, including King Harald Hardrada of Norway, to regain his earldom. The year before, in 1064, Harold Godwinson had, on a trip to Normandy, witnessed first-hand the audacity of Duke William of Normandy in his dealings with rebellious Bretons, as shown in the Tapestry. Thus by 1066 the situation was hotting up for a great clash, and England needed an experienced warrior leader.

This might not justify Harold's actions in taking the crown, but on the eve of the Confessor's death, it seems Harold's mind was made up that only he had the strength to rule and keep foreign wolves from the door, and in this determination he was probably supported, even encouraged, by the English aristocracy. As a result, Edgar Ætheling was sidelined, and Harold took the throne. After Harold's death at the Battle of Hastings, Edgar did not disappear but lived on for many years, becoming involved in several rebellions against the Normans. Somehow, he reached an accommodation with King William and returned to his court in the 1070s. Whether that was a case of the Norman keeping his enemies close, or because by then he no longer regarded Edgar as presenting a threat to his crown, is hard to say.

Writing history

Immediately after the Battle of Hastings, chroniclers began to attempt to explain the story of 1066 and to justify the various actions and individual motives from either a Norman or an English perspective. Some later writers attempted to be much more impartial, or at least to suggest that was their aim. Once the Bayeux Tapestry was rediscovered it became a major source for understanding the Conquest, adding a visual dimension to extant written sources. Earl Harold takes a prominent role in the embroidery, and his interplay with Duke William is a key theme of the storyline. The Tapestry is not categoric – indeed, it takes an enigmatic stance on most things – but its narrative seems to dance around the question of whether Harold perjured himself by swearing an oath to support William's claim to the English throne, before then taking the crown himself after the death of King Edward. The story is very complicated, and hard to unravel, but a brief review of the nature and approach of the written sources is helpful in trying to get to grips with it.

With any source, it is necessary to consider the intent of the person behind it in order to interpret what it says. On the Norman side are two Williams – of Jumièges and of Poitiers. William of Jumièges's work is among the earliest of the literary sources that deals with the Norman Conquest. His *Gesta Normannorum Ducum* (Deeds of the Norman Dukes) was originally written in the 1050s and 1060s, while he was a monk in the abbey of Jumièges in Normandy. His account was then extended, probably at the request of Duke William, who visited the abbey in the summer of 1067. At the beginning, the author dedicates the work to the Conqueror in fawning terms that clearly reveal where his loyalties lie. This gives a taste of his style: 'Many have shown in many ways how the vigour of that rare genius bestowed upon you as a gift by the Heavenly Steward prevails with wondrous effectiveness, whether by leadership in war or in all those matters which you propose to undertake or accomplish.'

Jumièges's report of the Conquest itself is brief, and he is notably not as hostile towards Harold as later writers. He states that Edward the Confessor sent Robert of Jumièges, then Archbishop of Canterbury, to Normandy to Duke William to nominate him as his heir. No date is given for this, and the whole incident is questioned by some historians, but if it did happen it is thought to have occurred in the spring of 1051. William of Jumièges then says that Edward also later sent Earl Harold, as the greatest of his earls, to William to 'swear fealty to him concerning Edward's crown and confirm it with Christian oaths'. A journey by Harold to William with echoes of this story is shown in the early part of the Bayeux Tapestry.

William of Jumièges also records that Harold, having crossed the Channel, was captured and imprisoned by Count Guy of Ponthieu, in whose territory he had landed, and only reached Duke William after having been freed on William's orders. Harold then 'swore fealty concerning the kingdom with many oaths, before being sent back to the king [Edward] laden with gifts'. Jumièges goes on to relate that, after Edward's death in early January 1066, Harold immediately usurped the throne, perjuring himself in the process. Consequently, Duke William, 'who himself by right should have been crowned', built a fleet and invaded England. In this account, the Norman Duke's justification for the Conquest was fully grounded in Harold's perjury, committed after solemn oaths.

William of Poitiers's work, the *Gesta Guillelmi Ducis Normannorum et Regis Anglorum* (The Deeds of William, Duke of the Normans and King of the English), was written in the 1070s, most probably between 1071 and 1077. According to near contemporaries, the author was in the Duke's service as a knight before he became his chaplain. Poitiers's account, like that of Jumièges, is written with a clear bias towards Duke William – it aims to justify his acts and stress the legitimacy of the Conquest and William's right to the throne of England. Poitiers reiterates and expands on the key points found in Jumièges's account, but he directs much more opprobrium at Harold, describing him variously as 'insane', 'pernicious' and 'a perjurer'. Typical of his vivid, declamatory language is the following short quote, which relates to the end of Harold's sojourn in Normandy with Duke William, when he had been, according to Poitiers, well treated, rewarded and honoured by his host: 'We address these few words to you, Harold. After these things, do you dare to rob William of his inheritance and wage war upon him whom by sacred oath you have recognized as of your race, and to whom you have committed yourself by hand and mouth?'

Then there is the *Carmen de Hastingae Proelio* (Song of the Battle of Hastings), an epic poem which has been ascribed to Guy, Bishop of Amiens, and is thought to have been written in 1067. The dating and authenticity of this poem have been challenged, but most historians now see it as a contemporary account of the battle. It is addressed to William the Conqueror and seemingly written to garner some favour from him, perhaps for Bishop Guy himself or on behalf of Eustace, Count of Boulogne. Eustace had fought alongside William at Hastings, but then fell from grace the following year and might have wanted to restore good relations. The *Carmen* records an exchange of ecclesiastical messengers before the Battle of Hastings, as does William of Poitiers, and also describes how King Edward had declared William his heir, and that Harold had witnessed this. This version also alludes to the possibility of Harold having visited Normandy, because it says that it was Harold who took some of Edward's royal regalia to the Duke, but it does not specifically describe the voyage: 'King Edward with the assent of his people and the advice of his nobles, promised and decreed that William should be his heir; and you [Harold] supported him. The ring and sword granted him, and, as you know, sent to him through you, stand witness to this.' Although Harold is described as a perjurer, he is not dealt with in quite such vitriolic terms as in the account of William of Poitiers.

Of the so-called English sources, the *Vita Edwardi Regis* (Life of King Edward) was also written in about 1067. There is no named author, but it was probably written by a monk from the monastery of St Bertin in Saint-Omer, then in Flanders; recently the case has been made that this was Folcard of St Bertin. An account of the reign of Edward the Confessor, it is dedicated to his widow, Queen Edith, and was probably commissioned by her. Edith was the sister of Earl (later King) Harold, and there is a considerable amount of detail about their family, the Godwins, within this text. The book recounts the various conflicts that took place between the Godwin family and King Edward in the years running up to the Conquest, particularly focusing on the actions of Harold and Edith's father, Earl Godwin, who had a notably fractious relationship with the King. It does not include any reference to Harold visiting Normandy, whether under Edward's direction or anyone else's, but it does record various other travels of the Godwins, including a visit by Harold to Rome on pilgrimage – so the omission is noteworthy.

It also refers, in another context and with dismay, to Harold being 'too generous with oaths', which perhaps alludes to the stories of oath-swearing already witnessed in the Norman chronicles. There is no mention of any promise of the English crown being made to William by Edward, instead it records Edward entrusting the kingdom to Harold on his deathbed. Indeed throughout, the *Life* takes a very positive attitude towards the Godwin family and has been seen as an early attempt to revive their reputation after the Norman Conquest.

Slightly later in composition is Eadmer's *Historia Novorum in Anglia* (History of Recent Events in England). Eadmer was an English monk in Canterbury, writing between about 1093 and 1119, and he appears to have taken the view that the Norman conquerors of England were destroying Anglo-Saxon culture. He is not afraid to take a critical tone in relation to the new Norman king, William I, nor to express his view that he was a particularly heavy-handed ruler, especially regarding matters of the Church. In Eadmer's words, for instance, 'He [William] would not allow any one of his bishops, except on his express instructions, to proceed against or excommunicate one of his barons or officers for incest or adultery or any other cardinal offence, even when notoriously guilty, or to lay upon him any punishment of ecclesiastical discipline.'

That said, Eadmer is not overly positive towards Harold either. He does describe the Earl's trip to Normandy, but claims that Harold's aim was to free some of his relatives who were being held as hostages by the Duke, rather than having been sent on the orders of King Edward to offer William the English crown. According to Eadmer, the King specifically advises Harold not to go, and predicts that it will bring misfortune upon the kingdom. Harold goes anyway, is shipwrecked and captured. While Harold is in Normandy, Duke William tells him how he was long ago promised the crown by Edward. Since 'there was danger whatever way he turned', the English Earl is forced, so Eadmer says, to support William's claim through the swearing of oaths. On his return to England, Harold is berated by Edward for going. King Edward then dies and, 'as he had before his death provided', Harold succeeds him. When Duke William sends a messenger reminding him of their agreement, Harold's reply is that he cannot be held to it because it was not in his gift at that time to grant: 'As for the kingdom, which was not yet mine, by what right could I promise it?'

There is also the Anglo-Saxon Chronicle, which was originally initiated by Alfred the Great (r. 871–99) and consists of a series of annals offering a year-by-year account of Anglo-Saxon history. Several different versions exist (named by letter in the Victorian era), each with its own variations, omissions and additions, and they have a regional bias, reflecting what is seen as important from a local perspective. The C, D and E versions are the most instructive on the Conquest period. The tone is fairly terse, generally concentrating on facts and listing events, though now and again individual chroniclers become a little more excited. One version (D) does refer to Duke William visiting Edward in England in 1051, but makes no mention of any promises or nominations: 'Then forthwith Count William came from overseas with a great force of Frenchmen, and the king [Edward] received him and many of his companions as it suited him.' None of the versions records Harold's visit to Normandy in 1064, but they do include a description in poetic terms of King Edward committing his kingdom 'to a wise man, Harold himself, a princely earl, who at all times loyally obeyed his superior'. They also relate the fact, which the Norman sources (and the Bayeux Tapestry) do not, that Harold fought his brother Tostig and King Harald Hardrada of Norway at the Battle of Stamford Bridge near York on 25 September 1066, before racing south to fight and lose the Battle of Hastings less than a month later.

Later still are accounts that are sometimes bracketed as Anglo-Norman in approach, given the passage of time between when they were written and the events they describe. The Chronica Chronicarum (Chronicle of Chronicles), written by John of Worcester, is one example of these. It charts the history of humanity from the very beginning up until the 1140s and includes a fair amount of detail on the Norman Conquest.

Orderic Vitalis, whose *Historia Ecclesiastica* (Ecclesiastical History) dates from the first half of the twelfth century, certainly knew, and borrowed from, the chronicles of William of Jumièges. The *Gesta Regum Anglorum* (Deeds of the Kings of the English) by William of Malmesbury was written at a similar time, as also was Henry of Huntingdon's *Historia Anglorum* (History of the English, see pl. 7). Both of these authors were born after the Conquest and were of mixed English and Norman parentage, so their accounts may reflect a softening of views on both sides of the Anglo-Norman divide, and perhaps an acceptance of the reality of the permanence of the Conquest.

The Tapestry's account

Like these written sources, the Bayeux Tapestry presents its own narrative of events leading up to the Conquest, but it is much less forthright both in what it includes and in revealing its preferences. Sometimes the Tapestry seems to follow the storyline that the Norman chroniclers offer, yet elsewhere it appears to reflect something more akin to the so-called English version of events. Perhaps this is not so surprising, given that the embroidery is a product of the Anglo-Norman period. It would be interesting to know whether the person or people who produced the narrative for the Tapestry might have had access to the early documentary sources and used them as templates, or perhaps vice versa, but that requires precise dating for when each was composed, which unfortunately is not available.

With regards to the vital matter of who should succeed King Edward, the Tapestry is fairly opaque. It does not make any reference to the English King offering the crown to William at any point. It does show Harold going to Normandy and being detained in Ponthieu. It also places Harold in William's company in northern France, in a scene in which Harold is clearly swearing oaths, but the context and the exact nature of the oaths are not revealed. Neither does the Tapestry include anything about an exchange of messengers as discussed by the 'Norman' chroniclers, nor does it ever specifically call Harold a perjurer. So while it does contain elements of the accounts given by the documentary sources, it is all very ambiguous and open to interpretation.

Contrary to the chroniclers discussed above, it is also much harder to label the Tapestry in terms of being a pro-Norman or a pro-English source, or even pro-William or anti-Harold. In fact, one theme that has come out of recent research into the Bayeux Tapestry is just how oddly unbiased it is towards either the victors or the vanquished in the Conquest story, and how unwilling (coy almost) the Tapestry's designer seems to be about being completely candid when representing exactly what is happening in the story, and how the viewer should read or understand events. A picture may well be worth a thousand words, but many, many thousands of words have been expended on trying to interpret what particular images in the Tapestry are telling us – a task not made any easier by the fact that the actual words in the embroidery's inscriptions retain a generally detached air towards proceedings. It has been suggested, though sadly there is no evidence for this, that there might have been a longer written text elaborating the story depicted in the Tapestry, which could perhaps have been closer in approach to the documentary sources. Unfortunately, no such text survives, but could the Tapestry itself contain some clues to its reticence?

Why is the Bayeux Tapestry so economical with its story? Why not lay out the facts more explicitly, as the written sources seem to do? One simple reason could be that the medium itself does not allow for greater elaboration – the embroiderers would have struggled to squeeze in much more text without compromising the pictures (assuming that was a concern). That said, there would surely have been space for the occasional pejorative adjective to have been woven in here and there, to drive home Harold's mendacious backsliding, if that was the desired line that whoever commissioned the work wanted to pursue.

It has been suggested that the Tapestry contains such ambiguity in key scenes that it could have been read or 'decoded' by an English audience who would interpret it in one way, while a Norman audience would be able to discover an alternative meaning. It is an interesting view, though it is hard to believe that it would have been possible to weave in this sort of secretive coding without alerting the 'other' side supposedly being kept in the dark.

If, as will be discussed in the next chapter, the evidence strongly points to the Bayeux Tapestry having been made in England, by English artisans and embroiderers, though perhaps under the overall design hand of a Norman (almost certainly a Norman patron), perhaps there were practical reasons for allowing some leniency to be displayed to the vanquished. The threat of an uprising in England was very present throughout William's reign, and it surely would not have helped matters by igniting passions with an embroidery that showed the English in a derogatory way. The Tapestry might therefore be attempting reconciliation (or at least coexistence), with neither side coming off particularly badly and with the aim of allowing fractured bonds to be reforged in the aftermath of a crunching change in the social order. It certainly provides material for those who want to laud Duke William's martial prowess, but the English do not have to be forcefully reminded of their humiliating defeat in the process. Could there even be a moralizing sub-message by clerical scribes and designers involved in the making of the Tapestry, decrying the sins of the worldly and power-hungry?

All these ideas might just seem too theoretical, the result of modern researchers reading too much into the Bayeux Tapestry. Perhaps it was just a simple work of art that viewers were not expected to scrutinize in great detail. It is dangerous to try to read the minds of people living almost a millennium ago from our twenty-first-century perspective. A contemporary audience familiar with the events and personalities involved may not have needed to have everything spelled out – it could all have been perfectly obvious to them. Alternatively, the real message of the Tapestry may only have been revealed to a live audience, when someone was on hand to retell the details of the story.

One thing that does seem to be true is that it is a work of art about not so much the deeds of Duke William as the actions of King Harold. Though it is constructed so as to glorify the results of the Conquest, it is not done in the overt way that the early Norman chronicles set out to do. The story it tells is one that puts Harold in the role of tragic hero. Harold is shown more frequently than William – by one count Harold appears twenty-seven times, William on a slightly less impressive twenty occasions, although even then it is not always certain who is being depicted. Harold also features at the very start of the Tapestry, while William only enters several scenes later. It feels like the designer wants Harold to be seen as a noble lord of high status and a worthy adversary to Duke William.

This view of Harold as the flawed hero comes through in some of the documentary sources too. He is a man whom fortune does not favour, but whose downfall is also clearly precipitated by his own actions. This slant on the story makes Harold an ideal figure to juxtapose against the Norman Duke, and helps justify William's invasion. Despite the Tapestry's general opacity, the whole narrative thrust is set up as a binary clash between two men, both of whom lay claim to the same throne. For William to come out well, it helps if it is a clear choice between usurper and rightful ruler. Such a simple head-to-head story between these two contenders, though, invites consideration of elements that are missing.

So what is omitted? Notably, as mentioned above, Harold is not shown fighting and defeating the allied forces of his own brother, Tostig, and the invading Norwegian king, Harald Hardrada, at Stamford Bridge on 25 September 1066. Hardrada (meaning 'hard ruler') was a formidable military figure. Born in 1015, the son of a Norwegian sub-king, he had spent much of his early life in exile from his homeland after being on the losing side in a battle in 1030. While he was away, he served as a leader of mercenary soldiers in what is now Russia and then in the Imperial Guard in Constantinople, modern-day Istanbul. He returned with riches and a reputation for military prowess, and became king of Norway on the death of Magnus the Good in

1047, who had earlier made an agreement with King Harthacnut that one should succeed the other as king of England if either died without an heir.

Two decades later, after having spent the intervening years waging a long and ultimately futile war with the king of Denmark, Hardrada rekindled that agreement as his basis for making a bid for the English throne on the death of King Edward. Would it have diminished William's glorious God-given victory at Hastings if it were revealed that his adversary, Harold, only a few weeks before, had been forced to march the length of the country and back to fight a bloody battle against such a threat? William needs to come out of the struggle as a fair winner in a fair fight, and that perhaps is why Harold is not given too hard a time.

Then of course there is the matter of a young relative of the ageing King Edward with an impeccable pedigree, who had also potentially been offered the throne by his great-uncle, or at least been groomed for the job – Edgar Ætheling, grandson of Edward's deceased half-brother and former king, Edmund Ironside. It would not work to William's advantage to include this aspect of the story of the Conquest because his invasion is justified by his mission to challenge a perjuring usurper. Harold's oath-making and oath-breaking are irrelevant if there was a legitimate candidate who had not sworn any oaths to William. Perhaps some at least of the ambiguity of the Bayeux Tapestry, therefore, is to avoid awkward or difficult elements in the story that do not easily fit into the main flow of the narrative, which generally drives the action relentlessly forward through its sequence of episodes.

CHAPTER 2

A UNIQUE EMBROIDERY

Aside from the debates about interpretation and history, the physical properties of the Bayeux Tapestry can also be examined, though again, the results are not always conclusive. In terms of organization, the embroidered work is composed of three horizontal bands extending the entire length of the Tapestry. The larger, central frieze tells the story of the Conquest, broadly running in a chronological progression from left to right, in a series of scenes that show certain events taking place in particular locations. Above and below this central frieze are narrower borders, containing a multitude of different details – decorative motifs, animals familiar and strange, and occasional mini-scenes. The relationship between what is shown in the borders and what is going on in the main frieze has been much discussed by scholars.

Along with all the imagery, there are regular, though generally supremely laconic, text 'captions' written in Latin, normally enclosed within the main frieze above the relevant action, but sometimes encroaching on the upper border. Analysis of the back of the Tapestry has indicated that the embroidery of the main panel, the borders and the text was all done at the same time, rather than the text being stitched on later.

Material and manufacture

The embroidery is sewn on a base cloth of linen, a textile made from the fibres of the flax plant. Once the stalks have been harvested and processed (soaked, dried and crushed), the fibres are spun into thread and then woven on a loom. Technical studies carried out on this base cloth have concluded that it was made of a single, long piece of linen, roughly 1 m (just over 3 ft) wide, which was then cut in half lengthwise to obtain its current half-metre (1½-ft) or so height. Producing such a large piece of cloth would have been quite a task for whoever wove the linen. It was then cut up horizontally into nine separate sheets of linen, of varying lengths but of broadly equal height. It is not known where the flax was grown, where it was spun, or where the cloth was woven, but linen was cultivated and processed in England before and after the Conquest, so it is entirely possible that it all happened there, and future scientific study may reveal more.

The nine panels were then embroidered separately. After this work was finished they were sewn back together again to form the complete Tapestry in one continuous length, with the seams joining the panels stitched over and now mostly almost invisible. Individual panels vary in length from almost 14 m (46 ft) to less than 2.5 m (8¼ ft), becoming shorter as the embroidery progresses. Today the Tapestry is just over 68 m (about 223 ft) long, but it may once have been longer – the beginning and end sections are in poor condition and material could well have been lost, almost certainly so at the end. It has recently been proposed that the panel lengths may have been based on a medieval unit of cloth measurement, the ell. Working from this unit, the original, complete length of the Tapestry could then be calculated as 71.5 m (235 ft). The suggestion is that the present nine panels were cut from three original ell-sized lengths: so pieces I and II came from one length of linen, pieces IV, V, VI and VII from another of about the same size, and III, VIII and IX from a third, smaller one, to which might be added an extra 3 m (10 ft) so that it matched the size of the other two. This thesis relies on the assumption that the ell was in use as a measurement in the later eleventh century, and also that there is nothing substantive missing from the start of the Tapestry.

At some point after the panels were embroidered and stitched back together, another linen strip consisting of 32 pieces sewn together was attached to the back of the original. When exactly this was done is not known, but it was before the early eighteenth century and using late medieval fabric. Sometime later, numbers from 1 to 58 were added to this backing cloth; these numbers are still used to identify scenes in the Tapestry, as they are in this book. The added backing increased the height of the Tapestry to enable it to be hung for display. Later, yet another linen sheet was attached to the rear of the Tapestry, which was removed and replaced with a different backing sheet (of 64 panels of linen) in the nineteenth century. Following the redisplay of the Bayeux Tapestry in 1983, another linen and felt lining was attached to the rear of this later backing, so that the Tapestry could be hung in its (then) new case; these various backings add complexity to the long-term preservation of the eleventh-century embroidery.

To prepare each section of cloth for embroidering, it would most likely have been stretched over a wooden frame, with a mechanism to pull it taut and create an even-tensioned surface on which to sew. It would not have been necessary to stretch out each panel length in its entirety at once, but it is likely that a reasonably long section would have been tensioned at any one time to allow several people to work on it simultaneously. Correct and even tension had to be maintained throughout the embroidery process to avoid panels becoming out of register and skewed, which could allow errors to creep in, as indeed was the case.

So the production and manipulation of the backing cloth was in itself quite a feat, even before the embroidery that makes the Bayeux Tapestry so special could begin. The thread used to create its designs is made of wool, of varying thicknesses and originally in ten colours: two shades of red, three blues, three greens, a mustard yellow and a beige. All the colours were produced by soaking the wool in plant-based dyes. To date, scientific analysis of the dyes has been limited, but chemicals found in madder, weld and woad have been identified. Bone, antler and metal (copper-alloy) needles have all been found in eleventh-century contexts, and these would have been used to stitch the wool on to the linen.

Embroidery was a relatively skilled job, but not beyond anyone with some practical experience. Most women at the time would have been well practised in needlework and it is safe to assume that the Bayeux Tapestry was worked by women. William of Poitiers specifically cites English women as being skilled embroiderers. The case was once made that the Tapestry could have been sewn by aristocratic ladies, perhaps working for William the Conqueror's wife, Matilda. No record survives of her actually embroidering herself, but it is known from her will that she did commission works. High-born women certainly had the time and training for needlework. There are some references to the existence of 'professional' embroiderers at this time, though most of these are said to work with gold thread, which is not used in the Tapestry.

Before they could begin their work, the embroiderers would have needed a guide for the design they were to sew. It is probable that an outline sketch for the embroiderers to follow was drawn directly on the base cloth, perhaps in charcoal. No trace has been found of such an initial cartoon on the linen, although some outlines, probably made during restoration work in the nineteenth century, are visible today. The Bayeux Tapestry has certainly been cleaned, a process which might have been more intensive in the past and which could have removed traces of any original designs.

Detailed studies have been carried out on the nature and quality of the Tapestry's embroidery work, some by academics who are themselves embroiderers. Two main types of stitch were used: normally the outlines of the figures and other details were sewn in a stem stitch, while areas of colour were infilled with laid work, with threads stitched across to fill the required area and held in place using smaller stitches, a technique known as the 'Bayeux Stitch'. Conservation of the Bayeux Tapestry in 1982–83 gave researchers the opportunity to study the stitching from the reverse. Photographs taken of the back of the Tapestry have been particularly illuminating, as they revealed how the different threads overlay each other and thus gave a sense of the order of the stitching operation. It seems the embroiderers on each panel generally worked from left to right and top to bottom, stitching the outlines first before infilling blocks of colour.

Clearly, this sort of work requires some expertise, great concentration, a steady hand and, importantly, good light. The embroiderers must have been aware that expectations of the standard required of them were high, and analysis of the threads on the back shows that they were mostly economical and tidy in their stitching. The quality is not uniformly exceptional, however, and some modern researchers have gone so far as to suggest that from variations in the calibre of the stitching, different hands can be identified, though others doubt whether that is possible.

Later restoration efforts, mostly in the nineteenth century and probably in two main campaigns of 'conservation', are far less accomplished than the original work. Most of the restoration was concentrated at the beginning and end of the Tapestry as it survives today, where it had suffered most damage in the past, and these threads now appear significantly lighter in colour than the original ones. Even so, care is needed when looking at the Tapestry to pick out the later work from the original; an ultraviolet photographic survey undertaken in early 2017 revealed many of these later restorations quite clearly. Not all the restoration work was particularly sensitively done, and not all of it succeeded in maintaining the integrity of the original. In fact, a comparison of the Tapestry today with drawings (and photographs) made of it before much of the restoration work took place reveals that in numerous places the imagery or text appears to have been corrupted by the efforts of the restorers, which were based on their understanding of what they thought it showed.

Furthermore, at least 680 holes or tears have been identified in the backing fabric, along with 518 cloth fragments used to repair it. The research that came up with these figures was carried out some thirty-five years ago, so future analysis may well provide more accurate numbers. There are also various stains caused by rust and the candle wax of past visitors, probably during the antiquarian period. Nevertheless, the Bayeux Tapestry is in surprisingly good condition for a textile of its considerable age.

Given the size of the project, a fair number of embroiderers must have been involved, possibly working in teams and presumably under the overall direction of supervisors of some sort. One theory is that different panels were worked on in separate locations and were only brought together for the joining process. If so, the isolated embroiderers would have been unable to examine the work of their counterparts and so could not check that their own stitching was correct and consistent. It seems more probable that the work was all done in one location, perhaps in several (well-lit) large rooms or buildings, where progress on the embroidery could be monitored. Another question is whether the different panels were worked on simultaneously, but there are hints that this is unlikely; the design seems to become less complex as it progresses, so perhaps just one or two sections were embroidered at any one time. Working on more than one panel at once would in any case have had practical implications in terms of the space and numbers of embroiderers needed.

When the embroidery of the nine separate panels was completed the pieces then had to be joined. Close analysis of the joining seams has shown that the embroiderers stopped work at some distance from the edges of each panel and completed the scenes only once the pieces had been sewn together. This was to ensure that the embroidery continued across the panels without interruption, though it was not always successful. In one notable place (between the first and second panels), the upper borders of the Tapestry are clearly misaligned, which is thought to be the result of an error in the tensioning of the frame on which the backing cloth was stretched. It is odd, nonetheless, that it was never corrected, though it may have been difficult to do so.

The length of time it would have taken the embroiderers to complete the Bayeux Tapestry is also debated. One estimate reckons the actual stitching could have taken between two and four years, but with so many variables it is hard to determine with any certainty. Factors to be taken into account are the skill and speed of the embroiderers (it can be assumed they were fairly well experienced), the number involved (we have no idea), how long they were able to dedicate to the task (this would depend as much on each embroiderer's ability to concentrate for extended periods as on any requirement for them to perform other tasks during the day, or indeed simply on the availability of sufficient natural light), and what their working conditions were like. Some relatively recent parallels might be helpful. When a group of forty Victorian ladies from Leek, in Staffordshire, completed a replica of the Bayeux Tapestry in 1885–86 (now in Reading Museum), it took them eighteen months from start to finish, but that was just for the embroidery work itself, and did not include any design time.

However long it took, and however many people were involved, and of whatever gender or social background, the making of the Bayeux Tapestry was undoubtedly a substantial undertaking. An organizational force would have been required to orchestrate the physical resources for the project, and select, train, accommodate and (possibly) recompense the embroiderers. And of course, there must have been a design mind to create and transmit the story to the cloth. The Tapestry seems to have been an unusual commission in that, as far as is known from what else survives, it was rare to translate such a long secular narrative into embroidery. Stories from the Bible were frequently represented in art, and non-biblical designs were also produced, but extensive narrative sequences were not common and appear mostly to have been religious in nature. Whether it was one person or several, someone had to research the story to be told, work out the broad outline of the narrative, sketch out the design (presumably at a smaller scale, but not necessarily), and transfer that design on to the Tapestry's linen in a cartoon format. To reflect the single artistic vision that is apparent in the Tapestry, the term 'the designer' will be used in this book.

When was it made?

Most historians today would accept that the Tapestry was produced within the first couple of decades after the Battle of Hastings in 1066. Part of the reasoning for this is that stylistically it matches illuminated manuscripts of the late Anglo-Saxon period. By this time, the English were famous for their skills in manuscript drawing, known as 'illumination' because of the coloured pigments used, which was produced in monasteries across the land. Obviously, comparing embroidery with drawings made on vellum presents challenges, but the style and form of the Bayeux Tapestry fits well with important surviving manuscript illustrations and it was made in an English artistic tradition that immediately preceded the Norman Conquest.

It has also been suggested that the content of the embroidery places it close to the Conquest – certain things are shown that would only have had resonance in the immediate aftermath of the event. One line of thought is that the Bayeux Tapestry must have been made within just a couple of years of the Conquest because of the way the story is constructed and leading characters are presented. This speaks of a particular moment in Anglo-Norman politics, when reconciliation between victorious Normans and vanquished Anglo-Saxons was the order of the day. And that state of affairs, so this thesis proposes, only held until the middle part of 1068. After that, rebellion against William the Conqueror among disaffected Anglo-Saxons made any Norman policy of rapprochement with the English difficult to maintain.

For the Bayeux Tapestry to have been made by 1068 would have required remarkably fast work. Considering the necessary rate of production, it seems questionable. That said, the fact that the length of the individual panels gets progressively shorter and the design seems to become less sophisticated towards the later stages could indicate an increase in pace by the embroiderers as the project advanced. Even if it wasn't completed by 1068, with the speed that such an early date would demand, most historians would agree that it was certainly produced by the end of the eleventh century. In around 1100 the churchman Baudri of Bourgueil wrote a poem in which he describes a tapestry (in the true sense) that tells the story of the Norman Conquest of England. The details do not match up precisely with the reality of the Bayeux Tapestry, not least because Baudri's textile is much more lavish, being embellished with gold thread and gems. He also says it was displayed around the bedroom of William the Conqueror's daughter Adela, which would have had to be a very large chamber if it was the same textile, unless of course this was simply poetic licence. Nevertheless, some historians contend that for Baudri to have referred to something resembling the Bayeux Tapestry he must at least have been aware of it, even if he had not actually seen it; in which case the embroidery must have been complete by the end of the eleventh century.

Bishop Odo and the Tapestry

Further clues about the date of production of the Tapestry can be discovered by looking at the question of who was responsible for having it made. The leading candidate as patron is Odo, Bishop of Bayeux, the half-brother of William the Conqueror. Odo was a loyal ally of Duke William in the run-up to the Conquest and was present at the Battle of Hastings. Very shortly after 1066 he was made Earl of Kent, which accorded him great wealth and power, and he was charged with keeping affairs in order in England while William was occupied dealing with matters in Normandy.

Odo died in 1097, so if he is the person behind the making of the Tapestry, it is almost certain it was produced, or at least conceived, before then. Furthermore, in 1082 he fell out with his half-brother and was imprisoned for several years. Two more dating theories arise from this: first, that Odo must have commissioned the Tapestry in 1082 before his disgrace, or second, that his closest followers had the Tapestry made after 1082, to restore the Bishop in William's favour. If the latter was the aim of the Tapestry's creators, it clearly failed. Odo was imprisoned until the King was on his deathbed in 1087, and was only released as a result of pressure from ecclesiastics who were worried about the impact Odo's treatment would have on William's soul.

One other, and more likely, contention is that Odo would have wanted the Tapestry made in time for the consecration of the new cathedral he was having built in Bayeux. That ceremony took place on 14 July 1077, which would give a very clear end date for the embroidery's completion. There is no document that records the gifting of the Tapestry at this time, but since it is known that it was displayed in the cathedral in the late fifteenth century, and it was also rediscovered there in the early eighteenth century, this seems a plausible theory.

Several other circumstances support the belief that Odo was the Tapestry's patron. It has been pointed out by many scholars that the embroidery shows him playing a far more instrumental role in the Norman invasion than other documentary sources give him credit for. He is prominent in several leading scenes: he urges William to build a fleet; he is at the centre of the banquet once the Normans have landed in England; he seems to advise William on tactics before the Battle of Hastings; he also rallies young troops at a crucial moment in the battle itself. How else might his vital, perhaps exaggerated, position in the story be explained?

Furthermore, three enigmatic figures who appear in the embroidery – Turold, Wadard and Vital – might have been retainers of Bishop Odo. It has long seemed odd that these individuals are featured as they are peripheral to the immediate story of the Conquest, whereas most other named characters are clearly influential players – dukes, kings, bishops and the like. These lesser mortals were depicted at Odo's behest, it is proposed, because he wanted to give them recognition. Another factor in support of Odo as originator of the Tapestry is that Bayeux, the centre of his bishopric, is featured as the location of one of the key moments in the entire story – the swearing by Harold of an oath, on holy relics, to Duke William. No other contemporary documentary source places this event at Bayeux. So again, Odo could perhaps have manipulated the narrative of the embroidery to enhance his role.

Odo is often portrayed by historians as a vain, self-seeking individual, and he could well have wanted such an embroidered monument simply for his own self-aggrandizement. Others, however, have challenged the view that Odo was any more self-promoting than his contemporaries of similar social standing. He might simply have commissioned the Bayeux Tapestry in order to please and honour his half-brother, King William. That seems perfectly reasonable, and is not necessarily at odds with the idea that Odo could also have wanted to remind both William and others of his own importance. If the Tapestry was made for the consecration of Bayeux Cathedral in 1077, then perhaps Odo's aim was also to ensure that God was aware of his role in the Conquest – William had sought papal support for his annexation of England, and Odo was the Pope's man in Bayeux. This would not preclude a desire also to show himself in a good light to the rest of William's court, and incidentally to praise the Conqueror's achievements and munificence.

For all the above reasons, Odo is the most likely figure to have instigated the creation of the Bayeux Tapestry. This 'Odonian view' was first put forward almost two hundred years ago, in 1824, and it has been finessed and nuanced, as well as argued against, by numerous historians ever since.

Where was it made?

There is one other substantial link that puts Odo in prime position as the Tapestry's patron, and that is the likely site of where it was made – Canterbury, in Kent. If the view of most scholars on this is followed, then Odo's position as Earl of Kent is even more relevant. The fact that Odo had such strong links with Canterbury is one of the reasons cited in support of it as the location where the Bayeux Tapestry was produced, though the argument does, admittedly, become circular. But Odo aside, it is the style and nature of the Tapestry's artwork that provide the most convincing clues to a Canterbury provenance.

Much work has been done on comparing the Bayeux Tapestry with illustrated manuscripts that are known to have been in Canterbury's monastic libraries in the eleventh century. Canterbury had been an important religious centre ever since Pope Gregory the Great had sent Augustine (later St Augustine) on a mission to England to restore the Christian faith among the pagan locals. Augustine arrived in 597 and went on to become the first Archbishop of Canterbury. Consequently, several important religious houses were founded in the city. Two of these, St Augustine's Abbey and the cathedral church of Christ Church, had scriptoria, where manuscripts were written, copied and illuminated. Their libraries are known to have contained the very high-quality works produced in them, as well as other equally beautiful illuminated manuscripts made elsewhere. It was typical across Western Europe at that time for monastic libraries to acquire and lend books in order to promote learning and knowledge, in that way also fostering the transfer of ideas and culture. The general similarity in style between the Bayeux Tapestry and later eleventh-century Anglo-Saxon illuminated manuscripts connected to Canterbury is an indication that the Tapestry was almost certainly inspired by them. Since it is probable that the design of the Tapestry was sketched out on the linen as a guide for the embroiderers, the stylistic parallels are not surprising.

One book that was certainly in Canterbury by the eleventh century is the Utrecht Psalter, so called because it is now in Utrecht University Library in the Netherlands. This intricately decorated manuscript is a collection of biblical psalms made in Carolingian France in the early ninth century. It somehow found its way to Canterbury by the end of the first millennium and remained there in the cathedral library for several centuries, becoming the inspiration for several copies, one of which is the famous Harley Psalter, now in the British Library (Harley 603). There is a strong argument that the latter manuscript, which was probably produced at Christ Church, Canterbury, influenced the design of the Bayeux Tapestry, particularly in the way the human form is portrayed.

Likewise, the Old English Hexateuch, which was probably compiled at St Augustine's Abbey, Canterbury (now also in the British Library; Cotton Claudius B IV), appears to have influenced the Bayeux Tapestry in numerous ways. In terms of style, similarities have been noted between trees in the Hexateuch, which are drawn in characteristic fashion with tangles of branches on top of trunks made up of multiple, braided strands, and those in the Tapestry. They bear no resemblance to real trees either today or in the eleventh century, and seem ultimately to have been inspired by Viking Age interlace designs. Art historians believe that parallels between this manuscript and the Bayeux Tapestry go deeper than just stylistic similarities, however. The Old English Hexateuch is the oldest surviving copy in Old English of the Old Testament. Surprisingly, given that the Tapestry tells the story of an eleventh-century invasion in northern Europe whereas the Old Testament is concerned with God's creation of the world and subsequent events in the ancient Middle East, scholars have pointed out that specific scenes in the Hexateuch seem to have been used as the model for episodes in the Bayeux Tapestry. A detail in the embroidery's border showing a man with a sling hurling stones at birds, for instance, seems to be based on an illustration of Abraham scaring birds in the Hexateuch. Another example is the similarity between the Hexateuch's depiction of Israelite spies using a rope to descend from the walls of Jericho and the escape from the castle of Dol by Conan, Duke of Brittany, by sliding down a rope in the Tapestry.

Another important Anglo-Saxon illustrated book is the Junius II manuscript, in Oxford's Bodleian Library. Also an extensive narrative sequence of biblical events, this was made in about the year 1000, perhaps at Christ Church, Canterbury. While it contains parallels for some of the images in the Bayeux Tapestry – it shows ships, including Noah's Ark, very like those in the Tapestry – nothing is clearly directly borrowed, as appears to be the case with the Hexateuch. In addition to these major surviving illuminated Anglo-Saxon manuscripts, many other English manuscripts, with fewer illustrations, also have details that are reflected in the art of the Tapestry. All these works have helped to establish the idea, almost a consensus, that the designer of the Tapestry had access to, and drew upon, the illuminated manuscripts held in Canterbury's monastic libraries.

The argument in favour of Canterbury is perhaps weighted by the fact that a large proportion of the surviving Anglo-Saxon illuminated manuscripts happen to have come from there. Other medieval libraries fared less well, their contents being destroyed or lost, particularly during the Reformation in the mid-sixteenth century. Some books are attributed to Canterbury on the basis of similarities in script and imagery with known Canterbury manuscripts, and it may be that several are incorrectly identified. If other libraries' manuscripts had survived better, they might also have revealed links to the design of the Bayeux Tapestry, in which case the current fairly clear-cut connection with Canterbury would be weakened. And even if the

Tapestry was influenced by Canterbury illuminations, this does not necessarily mean it was made there. Books could travel and so could the designer, who might have used a model or sketch book to record designs. On balance, however, the number of similarities between Canterbury illuminations and the Bayeux Tapestry makes a strong case for it as the place of inspiration.

The Tapestry's likely English origin at least, even if not specifically Canterbury, is supported by evidence gleaned from its inscriptions, including the use of Old English letter forms, as in the name of Harold's brother Gyrth, which appears in the Tapestry as GYRÐ. Some personal names, though written in Latin, seem to be spelled in an English way. As often with the Tapestry, there is also evidence to the contrary, with other words spelled using 'continental' forms. The alternation of colours in the lettering of inscriptions in the Tapestry (typically seen in the later part) also appears to have been a practice favoured more abroad than in England. It is worth remembering that in the late eleventh century most of society was illiterate – the skills of reading and writing would not have been widespread beyond the realm of the Church and some of the elite, so the impact of the inscriptions would have been limited without someone to explain them.

One (unsubstantiated) suggestion is that the text was composed and dictated by a Norman, but written down by an English scribe, which could explain some of the contradictions. A fusion of Anglo-Saxon and Norman styles is what might be expected after the Norman Conquest, and English manuscripts certainly influenced those produced in Normandy after 1066.

The strength of the evidence for an English origin for the Tapestry has not prevented suggestions of continental locations for its manufacture. Bayeux has been proposed, for instance, and even the Loire Valley, but such ideas have not received much support among wider scholarship. There are other English contenders too, such as Winchester in Hampshire, which was an important centre of culture and power in Anglo-Saxon England, or Wilton in Wiltshire, which had links with Edith, Edward the Confessor's queen, or perhaps even Waltham Abbey in Essex, where King Harold was a patron of the church and may have been buried. But based on currently available evidence, none of these places can mount a claim that seriously challenges Canterbury.

Possible patrons

Tying together the theories of Canterbury as the origin and Odo as patron of the Tapestry is the fact that the Bishop granted lands to the Abbey of St Augustine's in Canterbury and would have been well placed to have instigated such a major project as the Tapestry's production there. But there is another figure in the picture – Abbot Scolland. Probably a Breton by birth, he was a monk, treasurer and head scribe at the monastery of Mont-Saint-Michel (see pl. 9) on the Normandy coast before King William placed him in charge of St Augustine's Abbey after the Conquest in around 1072. It has been suggested that it was Abbot Scolland, rather than, or possibly under the instruction or guidance of, Bishop Odo, who was the promoter and perhaps even the designer of the Tapestry. This is in part because the Tapestry takes a surprisingly close interest in Duke William's war in Brittany before the Conquest, a campaign that seems rather ancillary to the broader narrative of the invasion of England. Certain places in western Normandy and Brittany, including Mont-Saint-Michel, are also shown with an attention to detail that seems based on intimate knowledge of the topography of the area – the sort of knowledge that a man like Scolland would have had.

Scolland's potential role in the creation of the Bayeux Tapestry does not exclude the involvement also of Odo, but it does demand a bit more thought on what is meant by 'patron'. Scolland might have taken a more active part in the project at the Canterbury scriptoria while Odo was a background figure – either making editorial decisions or influencing the direction of such decisions by dint of the fact that it was known that he would see the end product or had even commissioned and paid for it. Scolland perhaps facilitated access for the Bayeux designer to the Abbey's library and its rare books.

A slightly different take on the Odo story is that the Tapestry was not made by him, or even on his orders at one remove, but rather for him. A recent theory proposes that the Bayeux Tapestry was in fact commissioned for Odo by Stigand, the Anglo-Saxon Archbishop of Canterbury. As archbishop at the time of the Conquest in 1066, he had authority over Canterbury's churches, which would still allow for the embroidery to have been made there and for Abbot Scolland to have had some role in its creation. Stigand was not represented in a favourable light by later Norman chroniclers, both for his possible role in crowning Harold king and because he held two church positions at the same time (a practice known as pluralism), as well indulging in simony, the buying and selling of church offices. However, he retained his position as Archbishop after Hastings, and it was only in 1070 that he was replaced by William's new choice, Lanfranc. Stigand was one of a group of Anglo-Saxon survivors taken by William on a tour of Normandy after the Conquest – an act that has been interpreted as simultaneously a means of keeping his likely enemies close, a victory progress and an effort at reconciliation with what remained of the English hierarchy.

Stigand had been an important figure in court throughout the reign of King Edward. He was an astute political player who may even have suggested Harold Godwinson to the ailing Confessor as his successor in late 1065. In addition, Stigand may also have been someone who could have got on well with Bishop Odo – they were both cultured, learned men who enjoyed the exercise of power. It would have been in Stigand's interests not only to ingratiate himself with Odo after the Conquest through such a gift, but also to ensure that the memory of his now deceased ally, Harold, was not unduly tarnished. As the churchman who possibly crowned Harold and certainly supported him, it would have been of particular importance to Stigand that the idea of Harold as a treacherous usurper was not given too much prominence, because that also sullied his reputation. The Stigand theory has not gained much support, but the ambivalence of the Bayeux Tapestry in terms of an obvious pro-William or anti-Harold stance would fit with the ambiguity that Stigand might have wished to promote.

It seems broadly beyond doubt that Odo was behind the creation of the Bayeux Tapestry, probably directly as the patron. But there are yet other candidates. Previous tradition had it that Queen Matilda, the wife of William the Conqueror, might have commissioned it – so much so that it was named after her for several centuries, and even until quite recently visitors to Bayeux were guided by street signs to the 'Tapisserie de la Reine Mathilde'. Bernard de Montfaucon, describing the Tapestry in 1730, recorded the tradition that it was Matilda and the ladies of her court who made the embroidery in order to honour her conquering husband, and there is a nineteenth-century painting of this in the Baron Gérard Museum of Art and History in Bayeux. In the later eighteenth century, another Matilda, the daughter of William the Conqueror's fourth son, Henry I, was also proposed as patron, but neither of these royal women has for a long time been seriously considered as the sponsor behind the making of the Tapestry.

Next there is King William himself. The Bayeux Tapestry depicts one of his finest hours, his great victory at Hastings and conquest of the Anglo-Saxons, so it is not too much of a stretch to think he might have wanted his achievements commemorated in embroidery. It has been proposed that he commissioned it from a specific abbey in France, St Florent at Saumur, in the Loire Valley, which may have had a textile workshop. William knew the abbot there, and might have paid for the Tapestry with endowments of land in England and Normandy.

Another possibility as patron is Queen Edith, the widow of King Edward and sister of King Harold. She seems to have been able to bridge the divide between belonging to the Anglo-Saxon ruling hierarchy on the one hand, and being a beloved kinswoman (through her marriage to Edward) of the new Norman king on the other. And she had both the means, as an aristocratic woman with links to nunneries where textile work was carried out, and the motive, as someone who needed to gain the favour of the conquering regime. Edith is also known as the benefactor of a biography of her late husband, the *Life of King Edward*, which has some similarities to the account shown in the Bayeux Tapestry. Finally, she is one of the very few women who actually feature in the Tapestry. Edith died in 1075, so if she were the patron, the work must surely have been completed by then.

And what about Eustace, Count of Boulogne? He was not a Norman but a northern French lord who allied himself with Duke William in the invasion of England and fought alongside him at the Battle of Hastings. As the former brother-in-law of King Edward – he had been married to Edward's sister, Godgifu, who died in about 1047 – he had connections with England. It is also possible that he is one of only three Frenchmen named in the battle scenes in the Tapestry (alongside William and Odo), and so it would seem was regarded as worthy of special mention for his role in the victory. Just a year later, though, in 1067, Eustace led an unsuccessful raid to try to seize Dover Castle from its new owner, Bishop Odo, presumably because he felt he had not been suitably rewarded for his deeds in the campaign. Eustace fell from grace as a result, but was reconciled with King William in the 1070s, and it is in this context, it is suggested, that he is celebrated in the Tapestry, whether or not he actually commissioned it. As will be seen, however, a major question mark hanging over Eustace is whether the text that appears to name him is in fact part of the original inscription or the result of much later restoration work. Instead, William's other half-brother, Robert of Mortain, has been proposed as the person originally named – so might Robert be a candidate for having the Tapestry made?

One interesting recent theory argues that there was not actually a patron at all, and that the Bayeux Tapestry was instead made by, and for, the monks of St Augustine's Abbey in Canterbury without the need for an external agency driving the process. According to this idea, the monks, drawing on the illuminated manuscripts in their library for inspiration, created the Tapestry for display in the Abbey for the monastic community to view, use and study. Evidence in support of this interpretation includes the fact that many of the figures who feature in the Tapestry are recorded as donors to the Abbey, and so the

1 TOP The earliest known drawing of the first scene of the Bayeux Tapestry (dating to before 1721) from the collection of papers of Nicolas-Joseph Foucault. It was this drawing that motivated Bernard de Montfaucon to seek out the Bayeux Tapestry, though he was unsure exactly what he was looking for.

2 ABOVE The same scene of the Bayeux Tapestry as published by Bernard de Montfaucon in 1729. Montfaucon was primarily interested in the embroidery because it related to the history of the French monarchy.

THE COMPLETE BAYEUX TAPESTRY

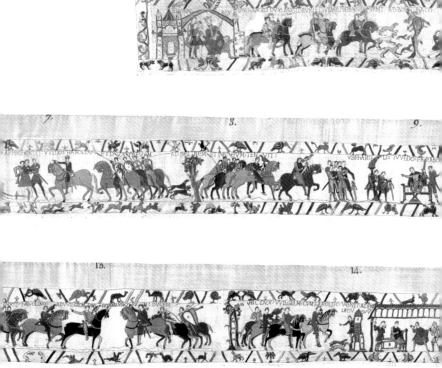

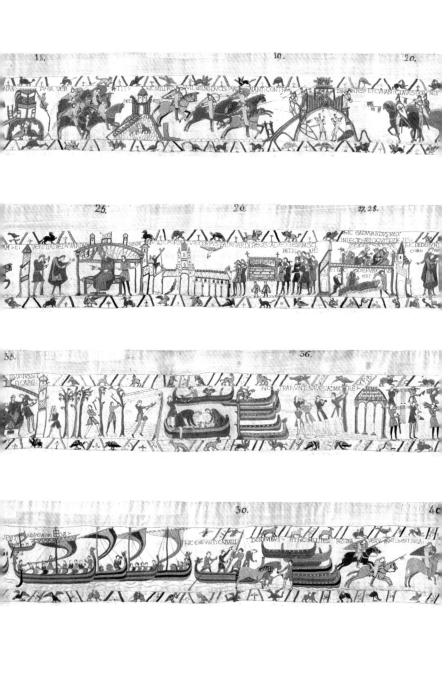

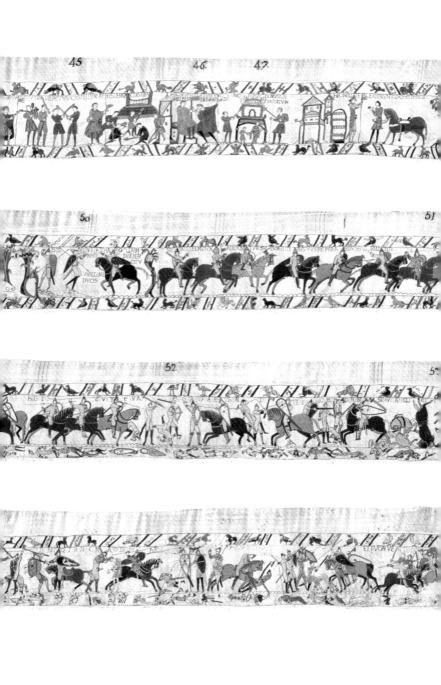

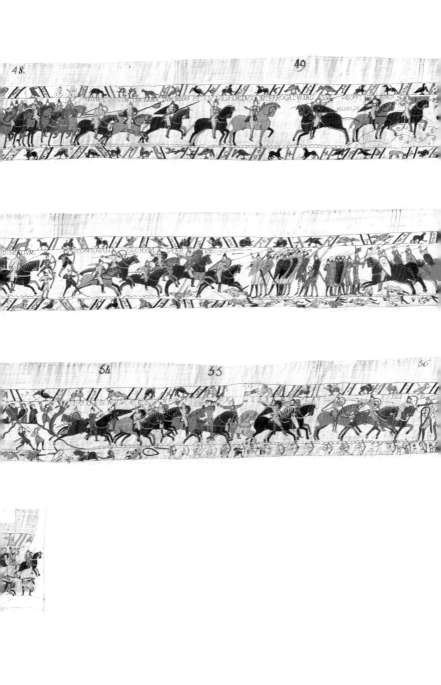

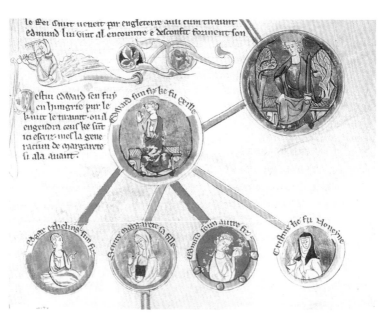

3 TOP Genealogical tree of Edmund Ironside, showing his son, Prince Edward the Exile (centre), and Edgar Ætheling (bottom left) who had a legitimate claim to the throne of England, in a roll chronicle of the kings of England, late thirteenth century (BL Royal Ms. 14 B V).

4 ABOVE King Harold II shown crowning himself in the *Life of King Edward*, an illuminated manuscript dating to c.1250–60. This document suggests that Harold claimed the crown in haste, although his swift coronation might have made practical sense.

monks were obligated to preserve their memory and remember them by name in their prayers. The Canterbury monks would have been sufficiently well educated both to recognize the people and places in the embroidery and also to appreciate any of the double-meanings that have been proposed as underpinning some of the scenes. This fascinating reading of the Bayeux Tapestry sees it as essentially having a religious rather than a secular perspective on the Norman Conquest, one in which the motives of those who valued temporal power and glory over spiritual riches were not necessarily lauded. But it does not explain how or why the Tapestry then ended up in Bayeux.

The claims of all these candidates have their merits and their weaknesses, and are, of course, ultimately conjectural as there is no conclusive proof as to who commissioned the Bayeux Tapestry. Weighing up all the evidence, however, it seems probable that the Tapestry was made in the late eleventh century, in Canterbury, by Anglo-Saxon artisans and on the orders of Bishop Odo. It is most likely that the Tapestry was produced between 1072, when Scolland was installed as Abbot in Canterbury, and 1077, when Bishop Odo's cathedral in Bayeux was consecrated.

Function and purpose

Whoever it was who had the Bayeux Tapestry made presumably wanted it to be put on display, and in a place where it could be seen and admired (though even that might be an unsubstantiated assumption). If so, where might this have been, and who was the intended audience? If it was produced by the monks of St Augustine's in Canterbury or was made for Odo's cathedral in Bayeux, the setting would have been ecclesiastical, but an alternative hypothesis is that the Tapestry was not designed to be shown in a church or abbey. Indeed, some scholars have questioned whether the rather bawdy content of the Tapestry would have made it inappropriate for religious buildings (it has been calculated, for instance, that 93 penises are depicted in it, albeit 88 of them belonging to horses). This theory is somewhat undermined by the fact that the Tapestry was certainly displayed in Bayeux Cathedral on a regular basis from the fifteenth century onwards, and quite possibly earlier. It also relies on a greater separation between the divine and the secular realms than perhaps existed in the eleventh century, when the Church was much more central to everyday life than it is for many people today. But if not in a church, could it have been displayed in one of the great halls that Norman architects were so fond of building? It is conceivable that the Tapestry could have been hung in such a location, perhaps during a feast or some other celebration.

One question perhaps of relevance here is why the panels of the embroidery were sewn together to form the very long strip it is today. If left as individual pieces, it would have been much more easily portable and the technical difficulties of joining up the sections would have been avoided. On the other hand, a series of separate panels would not have been as monumentally impressive, and a potential consideration is that the Tapestry was simply a large, imposing object in itself. The Normans are noted for going out of their way to do things on a grand scale, particularly in the cathedrals and castles they built in England after the Conquest.

Having the Tapestry in one piece may also have been important because of the way it was designed to be hung. An intriguing idea is that it was intended to be displayed on the walls of a large, square room, so that each of the four sections thus formed told a particular part of the narrative, with certain scenes or elements finding echoes on opposite or diagonally facing walls. In this way, for example, the two feasting scenes in the Tapestry might directly face each other. Such a geometrical approach would allow parallels to be drawn between key, paired, events – a narrative technique that it is thought would have been familiar to the audience because it was a method used in both Anglo-Saxon written sources and medieval art and architecture.

This theory has been taken one step further to identify a particular hall – the square keep at Dover Castle in Kent (or at least the predecessor of the one that currently stands today), on the basis that Bishop Odo had close links to the castle in the years between 1066 and his fall from grace in 1082. It is a thought-provoking thesis, though one problem is that it is not known how much might be missing from either the beginning or end of the Tapestry, despite attempts by scholars to estimate this. Any interpretation based on geometrical configurations and specific architecture has to be qualified by that potentially significant, and undeterminable, gap in our knowledge.

Nevertheless, if the Tapestry was designed to be shown in a secular great hall, it could perhaps have been toured around various locations rather than remaining in one place. In that way it would have been seen, and its message absorbed, by the largest number of viewers possible. A jongleur or minstrel could have accompanied it, telling the story of events using the embroidery as a backdrop, which might explain why the written inscriptions are so terse – they were simply an aide-memoire for the narrator. A further suggestion is that deliberate pauses are built into the Tapestry, leaving the audience in suspense to reflect on what they were looking at or being told, as well as interjections similar to those found in epic stories of the time, such as *Beowulf*.

Anglo-Saxon embroidery is particularly famed for its use of expensive and heavy gold thread (as in the tapestry made for Adela's bedchamber described in Baudri's poem), but is notably absent from the Bayeux Tapestry. The embroidery would have been lighter and easier to transport as a result, but it is possible that such thread was also too expensive for such a large piece of work, highlighting the fact that the Tapestry is not particularly opulent for its time, although it is a great treasure today.

Finally, more recently, the idea that the Tapestry was designed for geometric display in a specific location places it in Bayeux Cathedral itself (see pl. 6), with the Tapestry running around three sides of the now lost original eleventh-century nave. Hanging it in this way would have given it a three-act structure to fit the flow around three sides of the rectangular nave, with a layout that reflected the symmetry of the arcade arches. Again, this is a fascinating proposal, but very hard to prove given the difficulties of estimating the original true extent of the Tapestry and the exact dimensions of Bayeux Cathedral and its nave in the eleventh century.

Whatever the original intention of the designer or patron, it seems probable that the Bayeux Tapestry was not on permanent display anywhere for any length of time; otherwise it is unlikely to have survived in such good condition. Tradition has it that it was stored for safekeeping in a wooden chest which still exists in Bayeux Cathedral's treasury, though superficially it looks too small to be able to contain the whole embroidery. The fact that the Tapestry was certainly in Bayeux from the fifteenth century onwards brings us back to the theory that Odo commissioned it for the consecration of his cathedral there on 14 July 1077 in order to justify himself in the eyes of God, stress his role in the successful enterprise of the Conquest to his peers and celebrate Duke William's achievement. One way of accommodating the different possibilities is that the Tapestry was originally designed to be sent on an itinerary around secular halls in England before going on to be installed in Bayeux Cathedral.

If Odo did commission the Tapestry for the consecration, would he have hoped for a serious analysis of its contents by those in attendance, or would he simply have wanted a dramatic and impressive work to form an artistic centrepiece to the celebrations? One interpretation is that the Tapestry was presented and received as an act of conspicuous gift-giving, and its manufacture, offering and initial display were more important than what happened to it afterwards. Once that had been achieved, the Bayeux Tapestry could have been consigned to the chest and left largely undisturbed, to be unpacked and rehung once a year or so, much as it was from 1476 onwards, again explaining its remarkable survival. Indeed, if it had been hung in the nave of the new abbey, it is doubtful whether many people would have been able to appreciate it in great detail, simply because good light and a good location are needed to see it well – a challenge that remains to this day. That said, great artworks in church settings are often not easily visible; later medieval stained glass, for example, can be so high up that only the colours can really be seen. But the idea that the Tapestry was offered to the cathedral, packed up and forgotten is an intriguing one.

Now, though, it is time jump into the story and examine the details.

CHAPTER 3

THE STORY BEGINS

I n the year 1064, one of England's most powerful men, Earl Harold Godwinson, embarks on a journey from England to France. His true purpose is no longer clear, but he may have been sent as a messenger by King Edward the Confessor of England to designate Duke William of Normandy as his successor – an idea that formed part of the Norman justification for the Conquest of England. An alternative, and more likely, view is that Harold was travelling by his own choice, with the aim of securing the release of some family members who were hostages at William's court. Whatever the case, Harold's journey takes him off course, because he does not initially arrive in Normandy but in the lands of Ponthieu, a territory to the northeast, where the welcome he receives is not a warm one.

The Bayeux Tapestry begins with King Edward in discussion with two men (Scene 1). We know that the crowned figure is Edward because the Latin text above him – EDVVARD REX (King Edward) – says so. Edward is shown facing out of the Tapestry, seated on a throne which looks to be richly carved with some sort of beast's head on the arm and a leg ending in an animal's paw. Clothed in a long gown, he is bearded and wears a crown, and is holding a sceptre in one hand. Is he smiling, nodding or tilting his head to one side to listen attentively to his two companions? It is hard to say because the embroidery, though effective, is too stylized to allow for much of an assessment of his expression and what it might mean.

There is no preamble or further annotation to guide the viewer as to what is going on or to set the scene in any less ambiguous way. It has been suggested that up to seven scenes have been lost from the Bayeux Tapestry at the beginning, but that seems unlikely. Most experts believe there is a missing panel or panels at the end, but there is not much consensus that anything significant is lacking at the start. So, despite some major restorations, mostly carried out in the nineteenth century, there is no compelling reason to think that we are looking at anything other than the original opening scene of the Tapestry. The intention of the designer appears to have been to drop us straight into the story in this abrupt fashion, leaving us to make our own inferences about what is happening.

Certainly, it is clear that Edward is engaged in conversation with the two men standing to his right. He is pointing at one of them, who points back, so that their index fingers almost touch. The man's other hand is raised in something like an explanatory wave, while the second man, behind him, adopts the same pose. Both these standing figures have similar bowl-shaped haircuts that taper to their necks, and both model thin but prominent moustaches that dominate their upper lips. Like many characters in the early scenes of the Bayeux Tapestry they are wearing tunics and tight-fitting trousers, as well as cloaks fixed with shoulder brooches. One notable aspect of this tableau is that the hands of all the protagonists are somewhat larger than their body proportions would dictate, a style that is typical of late Anglo-Saxon art, and which gives the Tapestry its lively animation.

This conversation is taking place within a palace of some sort. On either side of Edward and his companions are the outlines of an impressive building, with a tower, turrets, numerous windows and handsome decoration. Arching over the figures appears to be a canopy, so the action is taking place inside this grand building.

In the borders above and below the Tapestry's central band is a parade of a variety of beasts, birds and plants, separated by oblique lines. At this point in the narrative particular images do not appear to have any direct relation to what is happening in the main frieze, though the fact that the animals are facing each other could be an attempt to set a tone of confrontation for the rest of the story. Historians disagree over whether the borders are anything more than purely decorative, but some marginal scenes later on in the story are more complicated and worthy of closer examination.

So what can we unpack from this opening frame of the Bayeux Tapestry? King Edward the Confessor rightly looks quite venerable because these events relate to the year 1064 or thereabouts; no date is given but working back from what happens later in the Tapestry, that must be the year when this is taking place. By then, Edward would have been around sixty years old and had been on the throne of England for more than two decades. He is described in the contemporary account of his reign, the *Life of King Edward*, as 'a very proper figure of a man – of outstanding height, and distinguished by his milky white hair and beard, full face and rosy cheeks, and long translucent fingers'. This description may well be more generic than accurate, and the rosy cheeks or long fingers are not apparent in his opening Tapestry portrait, but he does seem to be in good health for a man of his age at that time.

And who is the moustachioed man in close conversation with the King and pointing towards him? He is almost certainly none other than Harold Godwinson (son of Earl Godwin), the tragic hero of this story. Unlike Edward, he is not named in the inscription in this first frame, but it must be Harold since the following scene specifically labels him and depicts him riding away. Perhaps it was not felt necessary to name him in the first scene because it would have been obvious to the audience who he was.

Why is Harold there with King Edward, and what are they talking about? The Bayeux Tapestry is mute on these matters, but contemporary written sources can cast some light. The discussion perhaps took place either in Winchester, a long-held bastion of Anglo-Saxon royal authority, or, more likely, Westminster, where Edward had recently built a palace, adjacent to the great abbey that he was also having constructed. By 1064, the fortunes of the Godwin house were very much in the ascendant. Edward seems to have presided over a reasonably stable period after the death of Earl Godwin in 1053, made possible by the support and backing of the Godwin sons. If anything, the Godwin power base increased at this point, as a series of deaths, revolts and disputes led to almost every earldom in England falling into their hands. Harold, as the leading figure of the family, held considerable sway across the land, so it is no surprise that the two men should be meeting.

What they are discussing is more contentious. The following scenes show Harold heading off on a journey abroad, and the contemporary Norman sources report that this voyage was made on the orders of Edward. So the Bayeux Tapestry could be showing the King delivering his royal command to Harold, with the touching of the two men's hands signifying the import of the message being conveyed and the king's blessing. This was an accepted visual device that would have been familiar to the eleventh-century audience, while the prominent hands are designed to draw further attention to it. Harold, it seems, is being sent to Normandy, and, if we believe the Norman sources, is taking with him royal instructions to confirm that Duke William is to be the English King's appointed successor, since Edward had no heirs. Whether by design or accident, Edward's marriage to Queen Edith had been childless. It was widely believed at the time that the couple were so devout that they abstained from sexual relations, though they may simply have had difficulty conceiving.

King Edward's relative weakness compared to the strength of the Godwin family in 1064 is the main reason why the idea that he is sending Harold to William's court armed with the confirmation of the Duke's right to succeed him strongly hints at Norman propaganda. It is unlikely that the King would have had sufficient authority over Harold to force him to carry out this mission, and it is equally unlikely that Harold would have undertaken it voluntarily, because it was not in his interests to have the Norman Duke on the throne of England. If he was backing any candidate (other than himself) as Edward's successor, it would more likely have been Edgar Ætheling, grandson of

Edward's long-dead half-brother Edmund Ironside. Edgar was both of Anglo-Saxon royal stock and, being but a boy, more easily controlled than a battle-hardened Norman duke.

While contemporary English sources do not specify the motive for Harold's voyage across the Channel, later chroniclers and commentators provide alternative reasons – a fishing trip being one improbable explanation, or perhaps to set up a marriage alliance, or to secure the release of family hostages. Another suggestion is that Harold made the journey entirely of his own volition as a fact-finding and support-gathering initiative across northern France to obtain continental backers for his own ambitions to succeed King Edward. Henry of Huntingdon, an English churchman writing in the 1130s, states that Harold was going to Flanders, but does not elucidate why.

Of these explanations for the journey, the hostage story is particularly compelling because it is known that in the aftermath of the confrontation between Earl Godwin and King Edward in 1051, Godwin's son Wulfnoth, and grandson Hakon, were handed over to Duke William. Being a hostage was not necessarily a traumatic ordeal at that time, and the young men are likely to have been treated well, perhaps enjoying many of the luxuries experienced by other aristocrats in the ducal court. Furthermore, it was quite common for aristocrats to be brought up at the courts of others, even if relations between the rulers were not particularly cordial. Wulfnoth and Hakon were perhaps handed over as part of a treaty between Edward and William to ensure both parties kept their side of an agreement. This may have had nothing to do with the succession to the English throne, but rather was aimed at maintaining a balance of power in the complex geopolitics of the Channel zone in the mid-eleventh century. In all likelihood, William would have offered hostages to Edward in return, though these are not named. However, by 1064 it would have been a source of dissatisfaction for Harold that his relatives were still hostages, especially now that the political outlook in England had changed. He may have wanted to put things in order before Prince Edgar came of age and the situation evolved once more.

Making for Bosham

So, there are various options to explain what King Edward and Earl Harold are discussing so animatedly in the opening scene of the Bayeux Tapestry. But whatever it was, the action moves swiftly on, with Harold taking leave of the King and heading off on a journey to the south coast. The Tapestry (Scene 2) depicts a group of six men riding horses, led by a pack of five trim and fast-looking animals. Three are clearly dogs and are wearing collars with bells, so presumably they would also have been leashed (and therefore domesticated); the two animals in front are harder to identify, but are probably also dogs.

There is literally no space between the palace and the riding scene: the tails and hooves of the rear horses touch the edge of the open door of the hall, which they appear to ride straight out of. Is this to move the action on apace, and to stress to the viewer that the riders include the same people as shown in conversation with the King? Or is it simply that the embroiderers did not quite get the spacing right? The upper border of the Tapestry takes a noticeable jolt upwards at this point, above the hall's second turret, but this is probably the result of later restoration of the embroidery. There has been a lot of work on the original base-cloth here to patch up around the horses, and the numbered backing-cloth attached to the Tapestry much later is clearly visible in places. These early scenes, along with ones at the end, seem to have suffered the worst wear and tear and consequently needed most repair work, which may be directly related to the way the Bayeux Tapestry was wound and unwound for viewing before it found a permanent home for display in 1842.

What is happening in this scene is spelled out above the riding figures – VBI hAROLd DVX ANGLORVM ET SUI MILITES EQVITANT AD BOShAm (Where Harold, Duke of the English, and his knights, ride to Bosham). Quite a lot is packed into that short sentence. It is interesting that Harold is described as a duke, rather than the Old English for earl. England at this time was divided into large geographical areas known as earldoms; following the Norman Conquest these were significantly reduced in size, perhaps so that

William could better distribute England's landholdings. Harold was Earl of Wessex, a large region that encompassed all of southern England below the Thames. Clearly, Harold was a man of significant status, and this is expressed in the Bayeux Tapestry. By giving him the title *Dux*, the designer is emphasizing Harold's importance, and that he is someone who occupies the same level of aristocratic seniority as Duke William in Normandy.

The caption tells us that the party is on its way to Bosham, but there is not much indication of what the journey was like because the Tapestry only shows the horses and riders, with nothing by way of background scenery. In fact, there is rarely any scenic context in the Tapestry, or in late Anglo-Saxon art in general. The riders' destination, Bosham, is today a pleasant coastal village, not far from Chichester and on the edge of Chichester Harbour. It has a venerable church, several pubs and a long history. In the eleventh century Bosham was an important place – the major port in Harold's ancestral lands and probably the chief seat of his father, Earl Godwin. It had also been the setting for two notorious episodes in recent Godwin family history. It was here, or at least on a ship in the harbour, in 1049, that Harold's nefarious brother Swein murdered his cousin Beorn, and it was from Bosham that Earl Godwin is said to have fled into exile in 1051 after his confrontation with King Edward. There is also a tradition that it was on the beach at Bosham that King Cnut demonstrated that he could not hold back the advancing tide, though several other places also lay claim to that accolade, and Cnut's daughter is said to have been buried in the church. These stories relate to Bosham's position by the sea, and it was its proximity to the generally calm tidal waters of Chichester Harbour that made it well sited as an embarkation point for sea journeys, as was Harold's intention now.

Harold is named as one of the riders en route for Bosham, and though he is not explicitly identified, there is an obvious distinguishing accoutrement that only one rider boasts, and that is the hawk perched on the fist of the leading figure. So this must surely be Earl Harold. Hunting with hawks was an activity associated with the higher echelons of Anglo-Saxon (and later medieval) society, and it seems the Tapestry designer was using the hawk to single out Harold. It is known that Harold owned a book on hawking (which sadly does not survive), so he, like many high-status people of his day, was keen on hunting.

The horses of Harold's party are mostly depicted as clearly in motion, with bowed heads and forelegs raised. More problematic is understanding their exact gait and speed, as the position and order of their legs varies considerably between a walk, trot and gallop. Superficially at least, it might seem that the designer had a good grasp of the way horses move, but it is more likely that these depictions were based on representations found in Anglo-Saxon illuminations; similar horses, for instance, are seen in the Old English Hexateuch.

Given that some attempt appears to have been made to show the anatomy of the animals in naturalistic detail, it may seem odd that the colours used by the embroiderers are so unnatural, both here and throughout. By way of explanation it has been suggested that the choice of particular colours was a way of trying to represent perspective. Alternatively, and more likely perhaps, the embroiderers were simply free to work with the colours they preferred, without aiming to achieve a naturalistic representation, or just made use of whatever coloured wool they happened to have to hand.

It is generally thought that horses were not much ridden in war in the eleventh century, at least by the English, but they were commonly used for travel, agriculture and industry. Elements of horse equipment are some of the most frequent types of artifact dating from the late Anglo-Saxon period found by metal-detectorists in England (and recorded with the Portable Antiquities Scheme), including stirrup-strap mounts, stirrup terminals and other horse-riding gear. Some of these are visible in the Tapestry, but not in great detail.

In terms of the narrative thread of the overall story, the journey to Bosham does not seem particularly important and so we might wonder why the Tapestry designer felt it necessary to give it quite such prominence, and also to stress the hunting element so strongly. Besides introducing Harold as a key player, and highlighting him as an aristocratic figure who travels with a retinue and indulges in a high-status pastime, the Tapestry also seems to focus on the hunting dogs and hawk. Harold could be taking these creatures as diplomatic gifts for whoever he was intending to visit, and perhaps 'the hunt' provided a metaphor for Harold's quest abroad. Possibilities multiply the more a scene is examined – something that will be encountered throughout the Tapestry.

This episode concludes with a somewhat fantastical-looking tree. A number of these occur throughout the Tapestry, and their inter-woven, tentacle-like branches are characteristic of the embroidery's style. The tree in this case could plausibly be part of the action, indicating that the hounds are pursuing their prey into a wood. However, trees like this (as well as particular buildings) appear at the end of defined moments in the story, like punctuation marks. So its purpose here may be to indicate that the ride is completed and events have now moved on to Bosham itself.

Piety before a feast

Following the tree, in the next frame (Scene 3) two figures with similar moustaches and hairstyles as the horsemen, so no doubt the same people, are entering a church. It is certain it is a church because two crosses crown the roof and the text above it reads ECCLESIA (church). Presumably this is Bosham church, though the version shown in the Bayeux Tapestry does not much resemble the exterior of the current building that stands in the village. Bosham, like many English churches, has seen a lot of rebuilding since Anglo-Saxon times, so this is not so surprising. However, inside the church today is a chancel arch that is thought to date to the eleventh century – probably before the Tapestry was produced – and this could be the feature that is depicted in the centre of the lower part of the building in the embroidery. This may represent the interior of the church, while its exterior, with the roof and crosses, is shown above.

The two men entering the church are surely Harold and a compan-ion, and it is almost certain that the figure wearing a cloak is the English

Earl. They appear to be pressed up against the wall of the building, indicating that they are going inside. Nothing further is said or shown to explain what is happening, but their most likely intention is to worship, particularly as they seem to be bending their knees in an attitude of veneration as they step inside. If that is the case, one interpretation is that the designer is using the scene to represent Harold as a pious man – someone who takes time out of a journey to pause and pray, perhaps to ask for safe passage. Since Harold's sea journey was not successful, however, the message could instead be that God is not on Harold's side.

Taking this one step further (though this may be a modern, overly complicated interpretation), it has been speculated that Harold is portrayed as godly precisely because the designer thought the opposite. According to this argument, we are supposed to recognize his deceitfulness by seeing him outwardly going to pray when we know that his intentions are perfidious. Moreover, the fact that we are told that this is all taking place in Bosham – one of only eleven places specifically identified in the Tapestry – has been seen as a direct reference to the Godwin acts of treachery and rebellion, murder and banishment known to have taken place there, and so it is a reminder that Harold came from untrustworthy Godwin stock. The twelfth-century royal clerk and raconteur Walter Map says that Earl Godwin first took ownership of Bosham through trickery in the early eleventh century, a story that could have been widely familiar at the time the Tapestry was made. So the specific naming of Bosham in this context would have prompted comparisons between the duplicitous behaviour of Harold here and the way he will later take the crown of England.

The act of apparent devotion is anyway swiftly followed by one of worldly indulgence. The next frame of the Bayeux Tapestry takes place in another building, a grand hall of some sort, with an arched ground floor above which a group of men are drinking and eating from richly decorated long horns and round bowls. This gathering must consist of Harold and his companions, who are gesticulating dramatically and appear to be engaged in what look like lively discussions. In the embroidered border below the hall a pair of wolves lick their paws, possibly to indicate that this is a scene of gluttony and greed. In contrast to a later feast in the embroidery, the revellers here seem to eat little and drink copiously as they wait for favourable winds to take them across the Channel.

The ornate drinking horns two of the men are holding may also be significant, as some historians think that by this point in the eleventh century such items were associated with sinful behaviour – perhaps another hint by the designer that Harold's party is not an honourable one. On the other hand, the scene could be read as a further reflection of Harold's status as a great lord and a man who looks after his people and feeds them well, one of the main responsibilities of elite leaders. Feasting played a particularly important part in early medieval culture, so it is not surprising to see it portrayed in the Bayeux Tapestry, nor does it necessarily show us anything other than Harold's munificence to his followers.

As for the building they are feasting in, this could be Harold's manor or lodge at Bosham, with the lower floor open to the elements and possibly raised up above the level of the tide, and the upper floor enclosed for banqueting. Five of the figures, whose legs are not visible, are presumably seated, while a sixth man is standing outside and seems not directly involved in the revelry. He is poised at the top of a flight of steps which leads down from the building to the water, and is pointing away from his companions with one hand while in the other he holds a small, unidentified stick-like object, perhaps a piece of equipment used by sailors for navigation. There is a certain urgency in his pose, as if he feels the drinking has been going on a little too long and he is encouraging the travellers to finish their feasting and hurry up – they need to press on.

Embarking at Bosham

And that is what happens next (Scene 4). Reaching right up to the foot of the banqueting hall's steps is the sea, indicated by a few wavy lines of stitches, but quite obviously water. The men walk down the steps into the waves and wade through them to an awaiting boat. This is a dynamic scene, full of colour, life and energy. The wavy lines in red and green speak of nothing more than a gentle tide, and the real pleasure is in the way the figures are moving through the water. Two of the men have hitched up their tunics and walk barefoot into the sea, just as someone might stroll along a sandy beach today. One man carries a collared hunting hound in his arms, while the other, perhaps Harold since he is at the head of the party, manages the unlikely feat of holding a dog under one arm while his hawk sits serenely on the other. This is perhaps the Bayeux Tapestry showing Harold as a man of mythical strength, something certainly suggested later in the story. The fact that the designer has included the dogs and hawk again may be evidence that they are intended as diplomatic gifts. Gems and jewels, or a fine horse or magnificent ship, might have been more befitting if Harold was planning to meet Duke William, as such items are more typical of diplomatic gift-giving mentioned in written sources.

The storytelling and attention to detail here make for a vivid, and slightly comedic picture, though Harold and company are not shown actually struggling to clamber on board their craft. We do, however, see the drama of the ship casting off and making away from the shore, with two men leaning hard on their long poles while another attends to the mast, presumably to set the sail. Oarsmen sit in readiness with their blades, and a final figure seems to be raising the anchor and staring out to sea, perhaps hailing or shouting to compatriots in other boats.

Everything is depicted with great clarity and there is no doubt about what is going on, but the words above the action also spell it out: HIC hAROLD MARE NAVIGAVIT (Here Harold sailed the sea). The ships are not setting out from a port with a dock or jetty, but simply move off from the shore. Most craft at this time were designed to be beached rather than needing a purpose-built dock, which gave them great versatility and allowed them to land and depart from almost anywhere. It could however, make embarkation slightly awkward, with a degree of unpredictability captured magnificently in the Bayeux Tapestry.

So this is the sea voyage undertaken by Harold (Scene 5), the much-debated one that might have been a fishing trip (though in that case hunting dogs seem an unnecessary burden), or a diplomatic mission on the command of the King, or perhaps a personal voyage to bring about the release of relatives being held hostage, which seems the most likely explanation. Aside from the dogs and the hawk, nothing else is shown being loaded on to the ships, such as food and drink for a long voyage, or military equipment for war, though curiously, once they are in the open sea, the ships are shown battle-ready. Rows of shields are ranged along their sides, as is the case with other vessels depicted later on in the Tapestry.

Talking beasts

At this point in the Bayeux Tapestry, the images in the lower border change character somewhat. Rather than the paired birds and animals interspersed between small plants and diagonal lines that have appeared so far, there are vignettes of animals more clearly interacting with each other. Some of these images have been interpreted as illustrations from Aesop's Fables, which attribute human characteristics to animals in order to draw moral messages from their actions. These fables have come down to us from ancient Greece and were told across Europe in later times, so it seems reasonable to assume that the Tapestry's audience would have been familiar with them and possibly able to spot any intended allusions to them in the main frieze.

Scholars are not unanimous about the material in the borders, and in particular on this question of the fables. Numerous potential references to them have been identified throughout the Bayeux Tapestry, but there is no absolute agreement on how to interpret them. Where the link to the stories is reasonably clear, historians then disagree about whether the moral messages being conveyed are in some way a commentary on what is happening in the central narrative, or completely independent of it. And if it is accepted that the fables are being referenced in the borders, and that they do relate to the main story, there is still the problem of interpreting exactly what it is they are saying about the action in question, especially as the tales involve animals with various traits and characteristics.

In the border directly beneath the steps by which Harold's party descend from their banqueting hall to wade into the sea is a clear example of one such fable. A bird perches in a tree above a dog-like creature on the ground with its mouth open, while an object of some sort is depicted in the air between them. This looks like the story of the Fox and the Crow, in which a fox tricks a crow into giving up a piece of cheese it is eating by using flattery. The same story reappears later in the borders, and the viewer would presumably have understood that the fox successfully relieves the crow of its cheese by deceitful means. Is the cheese a metaphor, perhaps for the English crown? And if so, is Harold the fox and William the crow, or vice versa? Who is deceiving whom? It might be that they are they both deceiving Edgar Ætheling, arguably the rightful heir to the English crown.

Further fables are alluded to shortly after this one, including that of the Wolf and the Crane. In this story a crane is persuaded to use its long neck and beak to remove a bone lodged uncomfortably in the throat of a wolf, in expectation of a reward. But the crane's reward is simply that it escapes being eaten, the moral being that no benefit should be hoped for when dealing with the wicked. Is this perhaps a hint that Harold should not expect to do well in his dealings with William, or is it a warning to William to be wary of Harold? Of course, the reading depends on which party is seen as the crane and which the wolf.

Crossing the Channel

In the main frieze, following the embarkation of Harold and his company, the next scene shows a ship in motion in full sail, with a Latin inscription reading ET VELIS VENTO PLENIS VENIT IN TERRA VVIdONIS COMITIS (and with the wind full in his sails, he [Harold] came to the land of Count Guy). This is one of the few places in the Bayeux Tapestry where the text becomes at all lyrical, with the alliteration giving it a pleasingly poetic touch.

Several ships are shown in this section of the Tapestry, one of which is a very small and seemingly empty boat, possibly a tender for a larger craft, though it would not be typical for this period. The boat Harold boards at Bosham is on the face of it smaller, simpler and less impressive than the sea-going one, which holds a lot more men, has a row of shields lined up along the gunwale and also has elaborate decorative figureheads at the prow and stern. The first craft at Bosham does not have the figureheads, though it is possible they could be removed from the stem posts they sat on, and the mast (and sail) could have been set up on the move. The small empty boat may have been tethered to the main ship so that Harold's crew could embark on a separate voyage, perhaps to scout foreign shores before landing.

The large ship's sail has also received attention because it appears to be square rather than triangular, as seen carried by ships elsewhere in the Tapestry. However, close inspection reveals that it is actually triangular, like the others, but the embroiderers failed to fill in its triangular tip, making it look like a square sail. It is an error – a reminder that not everything in the Tapestry is as it first seems.

A figure at the stern of this ship on the high seas holds the steering oar as a rudder and is also pointing. This, it is generally assumed, is Harold, which might seem odd as piloting the ship would have been a job for a mariner of lower status, practised in seafaring, rather than a lord. But it could be a symbolic rather than an accurate depiction, with the Tapestry designer considering it important to show Harold in control of the voyage (in some late Anglo-Saxon manuscripts such as Junius II, Noah takes a similar position in the Ark), or even responsible for the calamity that follows. Most of the rest of the crew are seated and quite motionless, though two are more active, standing and working on the mast and sail ropes. Ships at this time were open and exposed to the elements and there would have been little for the men on board to do, apart from tend the sails. One man standing at the prow thrusts a pole forwards into the water, presumably to sound the depth, and the line of his pole crosses over the rear steering oar of another vessel.

This next ship could be the same craft, perhaps in an attempt by the designer to indicate its progress across the Channel, or an entirely different vessel. Certainly, the two ships' stern and prow figureheads are not very similar, but reading the Tapestry too literally can be a mistake, as elsewhere scenes do seem to be duplicated. Either way, this ship is clearly shown in readiness for landfall. The figure steering at the stern is still pointing, with the tail end of the ships' sail running under his pointing finger. He seems to clasp a horn, or something similar, tucked under his other arm, the mouth end of which arches over the top of his head. The crew are now much more animated – standing and heaving on ropes, or pulling in the unfurled sail, most likely to stow it away. Two sailors hold long poles dipped in the water, probably to help manoeuvre the craft as it approaches the coast, or to test the depth. One man has climbed the mast and is on the lookout for land, while at the ship's prow another figure leans forward in readiness to drop the anchor. Something about this man's expression and posture makes him look slightly shifty, but he may just be concentrating on the important task of anchoring the vessel.

Finally, one more ship is portrayed in this section of the Bayeux Tapestry (Scene 6), below and ahead of the vessel about to land. Confusion in the rendering of perspective makes it look as if the one behind is actually sitting on top of its stern. The leading vessel has no mast, no shields and only the figurehead at the prow is visible since the stern is hidden. A single man is shown on this ship, standing at the front, pointing with one hand and holding a spear in the other. Directly above his head is the inscription HARoLD, so it seems to be him. The ship is approaching the shore and lies lower in the water than those behind, perhaps to represent it coming into the shallows. Its anchor, attached by a rope, is already on land.

We are now in the 'land of Count Guy'. It is clear from what follows that the ships have beached in the county of Ponthieu, a little to the north of Normandy, so some distance from Bosham and definitely not the shortest route from there to the continent. Channel crossings were undertaken fairly frequently at this time and the ships used were well capable of the journey, which it is estimated would have taken a full day. But it is likely that Harold's ship was blown off course and ended up somewhere he had not intended. If the voyage had been challenging and the landing point was not one of their choosing, then Harold and his sailors might have felt somewhat the worse for wear. They undoubtedly would have hoped for a much warmer welcome than the one they were about to receive when they stepped ashore.

CHAPTER 4

CAPTIVE IN FRANCE

Harold's arrival in Ponthieu is soon noticed. The local lord, Count Guy, seems to have quickly seized the opportunity to take Harold and his men into custody, presumably with the intention of demanding a ransom for their release. Even though the two men are known to each other, the Norman sources tell us that Harold is poorly treated by Count Guy, but this is not seen in the Bayeux Tapestry. The English Earl is held at Guy's court in Beaurain until Duke William hears of his predicament and negotiates for his release. Harold is then transferred into William's hands, and thus the two key protagonists in the Conquest story are thrust together for the first time.

The next few scenes of the Bayeux Tapestry relate the story of Harold's adventure on the other side of the English Channel. This is a curious and slightly impenetrable interlude – it is somewhat secondary to the broader narrative of the Conquest story yet a considerable amount of embroidery is devoted to it. It is clear from the outset that the landing place where the little English fleet has arrived is not a safe haven because there is immediately a tussle on the beach. Indeed, hIC APPREhENDIT VVIDO HAROLD[VM] (Here Guy seizes Harold) is the commentary above the dramatic action that occurs the moment Harold steps down from his ship in northern France (Scene 7).

The last time we saw Harold in the Tapestry he appeared to be in control of his destiny, a potent man standing armed and ready at the prow of his ship. Now he is in the water, barelegged and barefooted, flanked by two men, both of whom are armed, one with a sword and the other with what may be a knife slightly concealed behind his back. Harold no longer has the spear he was holding in the ship, but he does have another weapon, perhaps a *seax* (an Anglo-Saxon knife), which he seems to have quickly drawn. He has also lost the voluminous cloak that was wrapped around him in his last portrayal and has acquired instead a skirt-like tunic, highlighted with alternating coloured stripes. The anchor of his ship is lying in front of his legs, and he has not had time to pull his leggings back on. This looks like a sudden assault.

Harold understandably does not want to be captured and seems to be struggling against his apparent assailants. The Latin word *apprehendit* (seizes) is positioned directly above the incident. However, as with many things in the Tapestry, all is not necessarily as it seems. It is not entirely certain whether there are one or two assailants, or even none at all. Harold is being engaged by two figures. One, on land (he has his shoes on) and with a sword in his belt, is more obviously taking hold of the Earl, with a hand at his chest. The other, behind Harold, is barefoot, so is either a companion who is trying to assist Harold as they disembark or a second would-be captor who has sensibly, though rather improbably, taken off his shoes before wading into the action.

It has also been suggested that both men are companions of Harold who are actually trying to restrain him from getting into a fight that they think would end badly for their lord. In support of this interpretation is the fact that all three men are attired in the belted short tunics that Harold's party were wearing back in Bosham, and one also has the tight-fitting trousers seen there. This style of dress appears to designate the Anglo-Saxons in this section of the embroidery (though not throughout), whereas the Normans wear cropped trousers, sometimes referred to as culottes.

If Harold is being held back by two of his own men, the reason for their caution is soon apparent, as a troop of armed soldiers on horseback is approaching. A fight between them and the lightly armed sailors would have been an unequal match. The leading horseman is shown pointing at Harold from his mount, and the man touching the Earl points back, while Harold brandishes the object he is holding in the horseman's direction. The whole tenor of the scene takes on something of the feel of a modern-day bar room brawl if Harold is being restrained rather than seized, with an angry gesticulating man being held back by his friends to prevent him from launching a furious assault on a calmer figure of authority.

In this scene, as elsewhere, details of shoes, clothing and arms and armour can help in establishing identities and dating, and are a fascinating aspect of the Tapestry. Broadly speaking, footwear looks fairly simple and could easily be slipped off if needed, for instance when running into the sea to grab someone, but that might be because the embroiderers have not included any details of stitching or lacing. Shoes are mostly narrow, often quite pointed, with rounded heels, and are generally fairly similar, regardless of whose feet they are on. The one exception is King Edward, whose footwear gets special treatment – some of his shoes have 'vamp stripes' decorating the top, presumably as a sign of his status. Archaeological evidence indicates that shoe fashion changed from blunt toes in the early tenth century to narrower, pointed toes in the late eleventh century (though ankle boots also become fashionable at this time), so the Bayeux Tapestry is apparently showing more-or-less contemporary footwear.

Up to this point, all the figures in the Bayeux Tapestry have been dressed in civilian clothes, and this is the first occasion when armed men ready for combat have appeared. Arms and armour feature heavily further on in the story, but it is worth briefly considering the shields seen here. A total of 241 shields are shown in the Tapestry, most of which are the kite-shaped type that these soldiers are brandishing. The distinctive designs they are adorned with resemble medieval heraldic devices, but are more likely to be purely decorative. Elsewhere in the Tapestry, shield devices do seem to be used to differentiate between English and Normans, or to draw attention to particular individuals. The shield of the first of the riders here bears a striking design looking like a dragon or wyvern – a mythical flying beast – which appears to be biting one of its own wings. At the rear of the party, the fourth rider also has an animal motif on his shield, perhaps a lion. The two riders in between have less elaborate shield designs, one a geometric pattern and the other a cross. Three of the shields that Guy's men carry have unique designs that are not encountered anywhere else in the Tapestry, and shield motifs generally seem to become less complex in later scenes, another hint that work on the embroidery speeded up under pressure to get it finished. The designer's original plan may have been to show all the shields in the Tapestry with elaborate motifs, but such ambitions had to be scaled down in the face of more practical considerations.

Immediately behind the shield-bearing horsemen, a pair of hunting hounds bound off in the opposite direction. They are dashing towards a tree, probably another punctuation mark in the narrative, which would mean that they form the final act of the beach scene. It seems reasonable to identify these dogs as the same ones that Harold and his companions carried on to the boats back in Bosham, so they are either making a bid for freedom in the melee of the landing or more probably simply prompting us to progress from one scene to the next.

In the lower border, things are becoming decidedly odd. Beneath Harold two club-wielding men, clearly running, are chasing after a pack of animals. The man at the rear is looking back over his shoulder at two goats, and behind them is a wolf, which one of the goats is confronting. Startlingly, the leading man appears to have a bulging black penis hanging below his tunic, with his testicles obviously exposed, a condition which demands some explanation. One idea is that this represents a version of the fable of the Kid and the Wolf, in which a young goat is separated from the rest of the flock and meets a wolf. The wolf, uncharacteristically, does not immediately eat the kid, but instead allows it to sing Mass before its death. The kid's singing attracts the dogs that should have been guarding it, and the wolf is chased off. In the Tapestry's version the running men bear aloft their weapons and demonstrate their obvious masculinity as they drive away the wolf. The contrast between them and Harold in the main frieze being apprehended, and therefore in a sense emasculated, would perhaps have been obvious to those who were able to grasp such complexities.

Harold and Count Guy

Whatever the precise meaning of the border details, in the main narrative Harold is being seized on the orders of Guy, Count of Ponthieu. The situation Harold now finds himself in was an unhappy one, judging by the account of the general behaviour of the men in this part of France given by the Norman chronicler William of Poitiers. He describes them as having 'cunning born of greed', who adopt 'an appalling practice, barbarous and far removed from all Christian justice', whereby 'they seize the powerful and rich, throw them into prison and inflict violence and torture upon them. Then, weakened by every sort of ill-treatment and close to death, they are released, most often for a large ransom'. Poitiers's words are somewhat ironic, since Guy himself had suffered this fate when he was imprisoned by Duke William in what appear to have been dire conditions. It seems, then, that Harold is a victim of this practice and has been taken captive by the local lord.

What do we know of Count Guy of Ponthieu? He ruled a small but not insignificant territory which he had inherited in 1053 after the death of his brother Enguerrand II, who had battled to keep the more powerful Norman dukes at bay. Guy sided with the French king Henry I in his ongoing clash with Duke William, and in 1054 was on the losing side against the Normans at the Battle of Mortemer. This is when he found himself imprisoned by the Duke for two years. He swore an oath of fealty to William, but subsequent relations between the two men were probably somewhat frosty.

Some of the documentary sources suggest that Harold received harsh treatment at Guy's hands. William of Malmesbury, for example, tells us that he was bound hand and foot and held in fetters. It is hard to know for sure how brutal Guy might have been to his fellow nobleman, but it is worth mentioning that the two men were not complete strangers. They had met in November 1056 at Saint-Omer in Flanders, and perhaps had even discussed the English succession.

This whole episode is one of the more difficult ones in the Bayeux Tapestry to unravel. The story of Harold's ill-treatment by Guy rests on the idea that he arrived in Ponthieu accidentally and unexpectedly.

If, as seems most likely, Harold was on his way to visit Duke William to discuss the hostage situation, he has strayed a long way off his track. The quickest and most direct route from Bosham to reach William would have been to head for the port near Caen. But this could have been very dangerous, and a preferable route might have been to sail up the English coast first and across to France, and then travel south. If Harold was blown off-course and shipwrecked, then those lyrical words in the text accompanying the sea voyage, *velis vento plenis*, which suggest strong winds, are apt. However, the men on the ship closest to that caption do not look unduly concerned as they sit calmly on board. They are more occupied as the craft approaches land, but that is to be expected when the sails need to be furled away and the depth checked to prevent grounding. It is not completely obvious that the Tapestry designer has aimed to show a storm or shipwreck.

So, if it was not a storm that brought Harold here, perhaps human agency was involved, and something rather more conspiratorial. A curious line in William of Malmesbury has inspired a whole range of creative theories. He tells us that Harold made up the story about being sent with a message for Duke William in order to get himself out of the sticky situation he found himself in with Guy, and that he held 'more secret intentions' (which are not revealed). On the basis of this, it has been postulated that it was actually Harold's intention to visit Ponthieu, perhaps even on the orders of King Edward or at least with his agreement, as part of a fact-finding mission, or to gather support among non-Norman French lords, including Count Guy, in the event of the Normans attempting to become involved in the question of the succession to Edward's throne. This is not so far-fetched, especially as Guy had previously rebelled against William, and if, as was almost certainly the case, Edward considered Edgar Ætheling as his heir. It might then have served Harold's story to appear to be captured and held against his will, in order not to arouse the suspicions of Duke William about any political subterfuge going on. Alternatively, or additionally, the idea has also been floated that Harold simply wanted to find out from Guy about his experiences as a captive of Duke William in advance of any discussions to gain the release of the English hostages at his court. Yet another suggestion is that there was treachery among Harold's crew, and he was taken to Guy against his will. The possibilities are numerous, and further obscure the fact that even at the time few people really knew why Harold had travelled across the Channel.

After the initial seizure, Harold does not seem to be particularly badly treated in the Tapestry's version of events. In fact, the next time we see him (Scene 8) he appears to have recovered his dignity and authority, because he is riding his horse again and has his hunting bird on his wrist. We can tell this is Harold because of his characteristic moustache, haircut and cloak. However, despite being shown as a man of status once more, and even at the head of the riding party, he is nevertheless clearly being escorted under some duress. The text above reads ET DVXIT EVM AD BELREM ET IBI EVM TENVIT (and he led him [Harold] to Beaurain and kept him there), so there is definitely a hint of coercion.

Behind Harold in this frame rides another man holding a hunting bird, followed by a group of mounted knights. Presumably the three knights on horseback are the same ones as in the scene of Harold's capture, though their hairstyles are slightly different because now the napes of their necks are shaved, whereas their predecessors had hair completely covering the back of their heads. It seems that the embroiderers of the two scenes were either inconsistent or possibly not aware of what was shown in both, which supports the theory that different hands worked on different parts of the Tapestry.

As the Bayeux Tapestry progresses, the device of the shaved nape is generally used to typify a Norman protagonist, so perhaps there was some confusion as to whether these soldiers should be identified as Norman (the soldiers of Ponthieu might have seen themselves as enemies of Normandy, and therefore cut their hair differently). Another explanation is that the embroiderers at this early stage of the Tapestry had not yet established a system of differentiating between Normans and other French versus Anglo-Saxons by their respective hairstyles. The first section of the Bayeux Tapestry might have been designed and embroidered as a prototype, with such schemas and conventions being devised as work progressed and only formalized in the later sections. This is all speculation, but inconsistencies do occur in one or two places, giving a sense that not all the embroiderers were working to the same brief.

Popping up between and behind these sharply shaved French soldiers are a couple of longer-haired, moustachioed Anglo-Saxon heads. They are entirely incorporeal from the neck down and nothing can be seen of the horses they are riding, so the sense is that they are being taken (rather than taking themselves) to their destination.

There is also the question of whether the rider behind Harold, also holding a hawk, is Guy of Ponthieu or not. Like the rider ahead of him he is clearly using stirrups to control his mount, which was essential when one hand is occupied with the hawk. It probably is Guy, because a hunting bird is generally used as a device to signify a man of status. If so, then the man pointing at Harold in the scene at the beach was also Guy, as the two figures are wearing similar clothes, and we are therefore supposed to assume that Guy was present when Harold was seized; or at least it was thought important to show him as being there within the Tapestry's tale, even if he was not in reality.

But if it is Guy, it seems somewhat odd that he occupies second place behind the captured Harold, who is leading the party. Surely it ought to be the other way round in a situation like this? It is possibly to indicate that, despite his imperilled position, Harold is more important than Guy. Or it could be a way of subtly undermining Guy's character and role in the story. Guy's hunting bird is facing towards him, whereas Harold's faces away from him, looking confidently forwards. Is that also a way of taunting Guy, suggesting he is not quite in control of his hawk, and by implication not in control generally?

Conversations and subtle insults

In Scene 9, the riding party eventually reaches its destination. The previous caption had informed us that they were on their way to *Belrem* (Beaurain). Of all of Guy's strongholds, this is furthest from Norman territory, so it appears that he was keen to keep William out of the picture for as long as possible. Guy and Harold are then shown in discussion beneath an arched structure, which in two places interrupts the caption UBI hAROLD 7 VVIDO PARABOLANT (where Harold and Guy talk).

Two ornate pillars with vegetal elements halfway up their height support some sort of coloured arch, seemingly tiled, which curves upwards from the capitals. A wavy black line at the base of the central frieze, which first appeared at the point where Harold was seized on the beach and then flowed on beneath the horses' hooves, now continues into the building. This wavy line motif seems to be used to indicate that the action shown is taking place outdoors, and it occurs regularly later on in the Bayeux Tapestry in this way, though oddly not in scenes before this. Count Guy is seen enthroned in the centre of the structure, now with a very clearly shaven nape. To the right of him stands one of his countrymen (with the hairstyle and culottes of a Frenchman), who is heavily armed; he touches his lord's elbow with one hand and points away beyond the building with the other. The Count himself is gesturing at two standing figures on the left, one of whom must be Harold, while his companion is somewhat in the background, lurking behind a pillar. Outside the building, behind Harold, a group of men, both French and English (as we can now tell from their haircuts, facial hair and attire), are watching the action intently.

The whole arrangement of this scene is not dissimilar to the one that the Tapestry opens with, in which King Edward was also seated on a throne, holding a sceptre in one hand and gesturing to a standing Harold and companion with the other. In contrast to Edward's regal and almost avuncular bearing in that first scene, however, Guy seems altogether more threatening: his pointing hand is accusatory and instead of a sceptre he holds a large sword in the other. Interestingly, he appears to be grasping the weapon by its unsheathed blade, rather than by its hilt. This, it has been suggested, is another example of Guy being depicted in a less than positive light, and perhaps is even a reflection on his masculinity, because either his weapon is blunt, or, worse, even though he possesses a large sword he does not know how to use it. Whether or not the Tapestry designer is trying to undermine Guy with these subtle hints, it is clear that the Count is in control of the situation. Earl Harold, though pointing back at Guy with both hands, looks rather hunched, perhaps on the defensive, and although he is holding his sword by its hilt, it is unbuckled and so he is not in a position to wield it.

The Tapestry's inscription simply says they 'talk', and although we are not given any details of what is being said it does feel like the conversation is an uncomfortable, potentially adversarial one. If the version of the story that the English party ended up in Ponthieu because of a storm is accepted, then the discussion may well be about why Harold has suddenly appeared in Guy's lands, and how much money he is prepared to proffer to buy back his freedom. If, however, the more involved explanation that Harold is in France on a personal mission is preferred, or some combination of both, then the possible talking points would be more conspiratorial. Given that Guy was almost certainly aware of William's aspirations to become king of England, and that Harold was England's most powerful earl, the arrival of this accidental guest is a stroke of good fortune for him.

Whatever the subject of their discussion, it does not remain confined to the two of them. Not only are all their henchmen listening outside, but also, to the right of the scene, is another figure, also partly obscured behind a pillar of the building like Harold's companion, but in this case quite clearly hiding. This man, who is oddly attired, perhaps even dressed in rags, is listening closely to the conversation. It is fairly certain that he should not be there, and indeed Guy's standing companion may be drawing attention to him, alerting his lord to his presence by tugging at his elbow and pointing to the interloper, though he might also simply be gesturing on towards the next phase of action. The secretive stranger does not look like a man of power or influence, so is possibly a spy. Presumably this is how the messengers of Duke William, who make an appearance in the next scene, discover that Harold has been captured.

In the lower border, below the furtive figure, is the beginning of several scenes of agriculture. In one, a man steers a plough pulled by a donkey and trap being driven by another man. The donkey-handler might be pointing upwards, perhaps significantly, towards Count Guy in the main frieze. In front of them, a third man, with notably large hands, is scattering seeds from a shoulder bag. He in turn is walking behind another man who guides what looks like a slightly leonine horse as it pulls along some sort of agricultural machinery, and in the furrows are what appear to be unrealistically large seeds. Finally in this sequence a man is casting stones using a slingshot to scare off troublesome birds.

These little vignettes are interesting in several ways. First, the artwork is a good example of the Tapestry's similarity in style to early Anglo-Saxon illuminated manuscripts, as well as its derivation of certain imagery from them. As noted in Chapter 2, large hands are a particular feature of the illustrations found in such manuscripts, and more specifically the bird-scaring scene has been compared to a drawing in the Old English Hexateuch showing Abraham throwing stones at birds with a sling. The ploughing scenes are also reminiscent of depictions of farming life found in contemporary Anglo-Saxon calendar illustrations. It has been suggested that they might even hint at the time of year, either late spring or early summer, that Harold travelled to France in 1064. However, while seeds are sown in spring, and need protecting from birds, ploughing is typical of autumn. In addition, these images also provide information about agricultural techniques. They appear to show ploughs being pulled by horses, which conflicts with a long-held view that the Anglo-Saxons used oxen for this rather than horses because the necessary horse collars were not known in England at the time. But if these illustrations do derive from art, and the Anglo-Saxon artistic prototypes were borrowed from continental models, then the question of the extent to which the Bayeux Tapestry accurately reflects eleventh-century life remains open.

Messengers from the Duke

After another elaborately twisting, scene-ending tree, an inscription announces VBI NVNTII VVILLELMI DVCIS VENERVNT AD VVIDONE[M] (where Duke William's messengers came to Guy). This is the start of a fascinating section of the Tapestry (Scene 10), in which a lot is going on. Beneath this latest caption we see Guy again, with a companion. Count Guy has had a costume change and is now wearing a voluminous cloak over an eye-catching garment patterned with what look like scales (probably armour of some sort). He is also standing in one of the most striking and memorable poses taken up by any of the characters in the embroidery. His right hand rests on his hip, while in his left he is gripping an even larger weapon than before, this time a very long-handled and fearsome-looking axe, presumably a battle-axe. This is an odd choice of weapon for Guy, as otherwise in the Bayeux Tapestry only Anglo-Saxons are shown with such weapons.

Guy is in discussion with two emissaries from Duke William; they look well-built, burly and more than a little intimidating. Both are armed with sword and spear, and the lead envoy is pointing firmly at the Count, clearly delivering his message in a forthright fashion. Guy, though, seems unruffled, perhaps because of the axe he is holding, though again he is gripping it at the top of the haft, and so would not be able to swing it into action instantly. This impressive weapon is probably not without meaning, though exactly what is unclear, and it certainly marks Guy out.

Guy's pose, rather than being one of manly defiance, has been interpreted by one Tapestry researcher as a somewhat effete stance, and is possibly therefore another jibe at his masculinity. A little way further along in the upper border are two centaur-like figures, half-man, half-horse, which brings to mind William of Malmesbury's reference to Guy as a *semivir* (half a man), so perhaps there is a theme questioning the character and potency of the Count of Ponthieu. It was undoubtedly not in the interests of either the Anglo-Saxons or the Normans to go out of their way to flatter Guy, so this ambivalence towards his character is appropriate for the Tapestry, which is an Anglo-Norman work of art, after all.

Whatever the Tapestry's intention regarding Guy, it seems likely that his conversation with the Duke's messengers is no friendlier than his exchange with Harold was. But this time it is Guy who is on the defensive. According to the documentary sources, William sent his men to demand Harold's release; so that, presumably, is the message they are delivering. But are they rescuing Harold, or merely entrapping him further?

The messengers have just arrived on horseback and behind them in the Tapestry their two mounts are still in full saddle and tack and appear to be snorting and tossing their heads as if fresh from a hard gallop. One of the horses is unmistakably a stallion. Along with the human male genitalia shown in the border below the scene of Harold's capture and elsewhere, there is something of a 'priapic predilection' in the Tapestry, as one historian who has studied this aspect has phrased it. Among several observations arising from this research is the conclusion that the focus on the phallus is deliberate, and indicates that the designer of the Bayeux Tapestry felt the audience would be amused by it. Though this interpretation may again depend on seeing things from a modern viewpoint.

It does seem that there was some sort of joke going on in this scene that viewers were expected to share in. A figure between the Duke's messengers and their restless horses, holding the reins, is very atypical. He appears to be a dwarf, with a distinct goatee beard and a French-style haircut, and he looks as if he is suspended in mid-air, several feet off the ground, perhaps in an effort to achieve a comic effect. Alternatively, he may simply be a person of average height shown in diminutive style to reflect his lowly social status. Directly above him is written the name TVROLD. Whether Turold is the name of the small figure or refers to the messenger next to him has been much discussed. Text in the Tapestry does usually sit above the image it relates to, but not always.

Who was Turold and why is he named here? One problem in answering this is that the name is not particularly rare; scholars have identified at least twenty-nine people called Turold in written sources for pre-Conquest Normandy. A theory already mentioned is that Turold was one of several vassals of Odo of Bayeux who appear in the embroidery. A possible candidate then is Turold of Rochester, who had fought for Odo in Kent and also at Hastings. He was perhaps custodian of Rochester Castle, and had been rewarded with lands; he also has a reputation for 'appropriating' land, and became quite wealthy. But he is never referred to as being of short stature. A more speculative view is that Turold, the bearded dwarf, is also the designer of the Tapestry.

Speedy negotiations

Whoever Turold is, the action in the story is too hectic to allow any time to pause and delve deeper into the mystery. In one of the most vivid evocations of movement in the whole Tapestry, two warriors on horseback are shown galloping at full pelt from right to left (Scene II). We know these riders are William's messengers because the text above them – NVNTII VVILLELMI (William's messengers) – says exactly that. Directly below, in the lower border, a man armed with sword and shield is baiting a tethered bear. The presence of this bear has been variously interpreted as a simple depiction of contemporary sporting pleasures or a metaphor for Harold's coming treachery. A more complicated theory is that it is a coded pro-English message telling us that Harold is under duress when he later makes his oath to William. Above the bear in the upper border a pair of cockerels perhaps highlight the fact that the riders are here to impart important information, much as cockerels crow to announce the essential news of the dawn of the day. The men are clearly flying along at speed – their urgency whips their hair back and their mounts' tails stream out behind them. In front of them is a pagoda-like structure, with four thin columns supporting a domed roof, very much like ones found in the Harley Psalter and its exemplar, the Utrecht Psalter. It is nothing like any building that would have existed in eleventh-century France, or England, and clearly has Classical roots, which is why it is thought it was copied from art.

Nonetheless, this invented architectural structure is, we are supposed to believe, Beaurain.

Something strange is going on here, because we have already met these messengers in the preceding scene, and assuming that the Bayeux Tapestry is supposed to be read from left to right, as has been the case so far, events seem to have got out of kilter. Three options present themselves. The first is that the designer and embroiderers realized that they had made a mistake and had omitted to show the messengers riding from William to Guy, and so just put them in afterwards. This might sound unlikely, but there is a theory that the Tapestry design was initially sketched out on individual pieces of parchment or tracing linen before being transferred to the main linen backing sheet by pricking and pouncing to provide a guide for the stitch-work. In this method, after the lines of the drawing had first been pricked with tiny holes, the sheet would have been placed on the linen and a powder forced through the holes by pouncing, leaving little dots on the fabric. If this was the method used, it is not impossible that the sketches could have got out of order, though given the price of parchment relative to linen this sort of production process on such a scale would seem very costly.

A second, and more likely, option is that this is a specific narrative device to produce an effect that today would be referred to as a flashback. As will be seen later, this is not the only place in the Bayeux Tapestry where the designer apparently telescopes and reverses the order of events, so it is perfectly possible that this is what is happening here. Or thirdly, it could be a representation of something mentioned in one of the chronicle sources. According to Eadmer's *Historia Novorum in Anglia*, two sets of messengers were sent by William. The first conveyed the request that Guy must release Harold as quickly as possible and send him to the Duke, in order to retain 'his friendship for the future as he [Guy] had had in the past'. Then, when that initial request was rebuffed, the second two were despatched, advising Guy that he had better send Harold immediately or he could 'rest assured that William, Duke of Normandy, would come to Ponthieu to release him'.

One more element of the picture here is worth mentioning. To the right of the galloping horsemen is a figure halfway up a tree, with one hand gripping the trunk and the other shielding his eyes as he watches the riders disappear, or perhaps he is shouting out to them. The tree is again a stylized tangle of limbs, the like of which could never be found in any forest, its branches seemingly shaped by the wind and bending over as if to direct the viewer onwards along the Tapestry.

Duke William makes his appearance

Finally, in the next scene (12), Duke William of Normandy enters the story. It has taken a long time for him to appear – we are already about one-sixth of the way along the embroidery – considering he is such a key player in the dramatic events of 1066.

The Latin text for this scene reads HIC VENIT NVNTIVS AD WILGELMVM DVCEM (here a messenger comes to Duke William). The action takes place in the shadow of an unnamed, but clearly grand, turretted structure manned by two soldiers. A popular view is that this is a depiction of the earlier castle of Rouen, in the heart of William's duchy. Rouen had been a stronghold of the first duke of Normandy, Rollo, from 911, and thereafter became the administrative capital. In 1060, William established his castle at Caen, so another possibility is that this is the location shown, but perhaps less likely given that Rouen is closer to Beaurain. To what extent it might be a literal representation of the castle, or just artistic licence, is debated, but it would not be surprising to find William receiving messengers and holding court in either Rouen or Caen.

On the left of this scene are two messengers, both standing and holding spears. One of them also rests a hand on a handsome shield, decorated perhaps with a wyvern or dragon design. Duke William is seated on a throne, holding a large sword, which he is pointing upwards over his shoulder in a statement of authority. His sword slices through the words 'Duke' and 'William' in the inscription, so removing any possible doubt as to who is the main focus of the image. He wears a cloak, like other individuals of the highest status in the Tapestry, but his is fastened with a square brooch rather than the usual circular type, and he has long tassels below his knees, further marking him out as someone of importance. His throne, like those of Edward and Guy before, is typically ornate, with arms ending in animal heads and feet in the form of paws.

Between the messengers and the Duke is another figure, a crouching supplicant of a man, with bent legs. He is standing on a small patch of wavy ground line, perhaps to illustrate the fact that he has just entered from outside. This figure has the hairstyle, dress and moustache of an Anglo-Saxon. With his palms open and no discernible weaponry, he seems to be pleading or explaining something to William. The Duke's long finger hovers dangerously close to the Englishman's face, while one messenger behind him also points directly over the man's head. It appears he is being very sternly talked to, even interrogated.

The cowering man has been interpreted as an Anglo-Saxon who has somehow made his way to William's court and is telling the Duke about Harold's predicament. This would fit with the account of Eadmer, who says that 'Harold managed to bribe one of the common people with a reward and sent him secretly to the Duke of Normandy to report what had happened to him'. It is odd, however, that a commoner on the French side of the Channel would be an Anglo-Saxon, so perhaps he was with Harold on the beach but managed to escape Guy's clutches. Or alternatively the spy in the earlier scene could have passed on a message to an Englishman, possibly a merchant, who was not one of Harold's party. But on this, the Tapestry is silent.

In the lower border is a lively hunting scene, with a dog-handler struggling to control two leashed hounds while also blowing a horn. Ahead of them two more dogs are shown running free, and another two are attacking a deer. A further pair of dogs, racing in the other direction, are followed by a man on a horse waving a baton or club. The hunter Harold may thus have become the hunted, and his predicament is becoming even more precarious.

Harold and William meet

The inscription for the next scene (13), stretching above another montage of horsemen, states that HIC WIDO ADDVXIT hAR-OLDVm AD VVILGELMVM NORMANNORVM DVCEM (here Guy brought Harold to William, Duke of the Normans). Four French knights with spears and shields ride behind Earl Harold, who is identifiable by his characteristic haircut and moustache. Count Guy rides out in front of them and is pointing back at Harold. The two men again carry hawks on their fists, both of which are looking forwards this time. Guy's horse, however, has very obviously been given long, pointed ears, more suggestive of those of a donkey than the usual, shorter equine ones of all the other horses. This could just be accidental, or perhaps not.

Meeting them from the right is a second party of men on horseback, led by Duke William himself, who is pointing upwards in the direction of the words 'William, Duke of the Normans'. He wears a cloak now embellished with an embroidered hem and tassels or ribbons fluttering from the neck, and is clearly being distinguished as the most important person in this scene. One of his retinue gestures backwards, and above in the upper border is a pair of strange, round-bodied, apparently headless birds, which have tucked their heads into their plumage in sleep or to avert their eyes from what is going on below. Immediately above William, somewhat improbably, are two camels (with modest humps). Camels were obviously not a regular feature of the wildlife of northern France or southern England, so their presence is slightly surprising and could be evidence that the ultimate source of some of these border motifs is imagery found in Byzantine textiles. Although it is fun to speculate, it is hard to think of any explanation for camels being shown here other than purely decorative.

If the building with the towers where William received his messengers was Rouen, the scene of the action must have moved on to somewhere else in northern France – not Beaurain, but also not Rouen. William of Poitiers states that Count Guy willingly brought Harold to the Duke and that the meeting took place at the castle of Eu, roughly midway between Beaurain and Rouen. In return for handing over Harold, Guy received great wealth, land and riches, but any payment, ransom or reward is not shown or referred to in the embroidery.

This is the last we see of Guy of Ponthieu. He has had quite a large walk-on part in the Bayeux Tapestry but seems not to have been held in high regard by whoever had it made. The fact that his horse has donkey's ears in his last appearance is surely the final slight, telling us that he is either stupid or stubborn, perhaps alluding to the fact that he had to be asked more than once to give up Harold to the Duke. So why the generally low opinion of Guy? From William's point of view it was good propaganda to be seen as the saviour of Harold by freeing him from the greedy clutches of the grasping Count of Ponthieu, as this bolsters the theme that plays out later of his generosity to his English counterpart. Following this line of argument, it helps William if Guy is not seen as a worthy individual. As for Harold's side of the story, it was useful to have Guy as the villain because that would explain how he came to be in William's debt, and thus why he was forced to make oaths under duress. It is possible that this is reading too much into the Bayeux Tapestry's depictions of Guy, but what is not in doubt is that its designer regarded the Count of Ponthieu as relevant to his version of the tale of Harold's visit to France in 1064, and the events that subsequently followed.

The scenes in the lower border here are even more surprising than those in the one above. Beneath Guy's troops escorting Harold is the rider on a horse wielding a club or baton. After him, directly below Harold, is a naked couple; a man, with a notably tumescent penis, stretches his arms out towards a woman who partially hides her modesty with one hand and is shielding her eyes with the other, or perhaps is simply hiding her face. The two figures are delineated by a single outline stitch with no colour infill, so they stand out in contrast to the more colourful images around them. It is hard for the eye not to be drawn to them, particularly with the arresting nature of the content, though the precise meaning is, once more, obscure. One theory is that this striking vignette relates to a fable in which a father rapes his own daughter, a truly heinous crime. Does that cast a negative light on the person closest to these characters in the main frieze, Earl Harold, directly above? Perhaps, in the sense of it being an act of predation and thus possibly an allusion to Harold's (or even William's) presumed usurpation of the throne. That perhaps stretches the interpretation a bit too far, but there must surely be some link between this disturbing scene and the action in the main frieze. It may also relate to the mystery of the lady Ælfgyva, discussed in the next chapter.

Birds feature regularly in the upper and lower borders of the Tapestry and sometimes also in the central frieze, an obvious example being the hunting hawks. As with practically every element in the embroidery, they have been counted and categorized and subjected to detailed study. Often they seem to be there solely for decorative purposes, but they also tend to ape or mirror the action in the main narrative. For example, when Harold bends his legs on entering the church at Bosham before he crossed the Channel, the birds in the border bow down in imitation of his movement. At other times, they appear to be taking an interest in the events in the story through the way they fold their wings, crane their necks or open their beaks. One interpretation is that the birds in the upper border here tuck their heads under their wings in fear of the hunting hawks, perhaps referring to the fact that birds of prey inevitably bring about the death of their victims, which is of course where the Tapestry's narrative is inexorably heading – towards a dramatic, bloody conclusion.

That brings us to the end of this section. Two braided trees provide a breathing space before the story moves on again. It was also a natural pause for the designer of the Bayeux Tapestry because this is the end of the first (and one of the longest) of the nine linen panels that make up the original base fabric. There is a clear mistake in the embroidery at the point where the two panels join, with a noticeable jump in the baseline defining the upper border at the beginning of the second panel. This has been explained as an error in the tensioning of the linen cloth on the frame when the two sections were being joined. It is a slip that has survived for over nine centuries, despite much restoration work elsewhere, and is the only time the join is so noticeable. And it is also a break in the action so far, before the pivotal scenes in which the two main protagonists of the Tapestry, Earl Harold and Duke William, begin to interact directly with each other.

CHAPTER 5

AT THE COURT
OF DUKE WILLIAM

T hough freed from the clutches of Count Guy, Harold, journey-
ing with William deep into Normandy, is certainly not out of
danger. As they travel together, it is likely that the question of the
succession to the English throne would have cropped up, but whether
William and Harold collude on how to deal with Edgar Ætheling's
claim to the crown is not known; perhaps they keep those thoughts
to themselves. The Bayeux Tapestry shows the Duke and the Earl
discussing matters of import in one of the ducal palaces in Normandy,
at Rouen, or perhaps Caen, but again the actual topic of conversation
is not elucidated.

Now, at last, Earl Harold and Duke William are brought together
in the Bayeux Tapestry as they ride away from the encounter with
Count Guy (Scene 14). The text above the riding party reads HIC DVX
VVILGELM CVM hARoLDO VENIT AD PALATIV[M] SVV[M]
(Here Duke William comes with Harold to his palace). Oddly, Harold
once more seems to be leading the riding party, as he did when he was
travelling under escort to Beaurain, though there is nothing to suggest
that Duke William (almost certainly the figure riding directly behind
Harold, under the inscription Wilgelm) is in any way inferior. Harold
no longer has his hawk, and the only man distinguished by having
a prestigious hunting bird on his fist is William. The Duke has not
previously been shown with one, so this may be a way of signifying

that the higher status, along with the bird that symbolizes it, has been transferred from Harold to William.

There are just two Norman warriors in escort, each with a spear or lance and both pointing (if rather ambivalently) to the words Hic Dux. Another indication of the relative seniority and rank of the two main players is that Harold is not wearing a cloak, whereas William is swathed in one, pinned with a brooch on his shoulder. Harold holds his left hand in a curious position next to his face, with his index finger pointing upwards, probably towards his name in the text (hARoLDo). That this figure is Harold is also clear from his characteristic English haircut, though his moustache is not as prominent as earlier; in fact, it is not really visible at all. The riding party is accompanied by hunting dogs wearing collars with bells, which charge off in front, encouraging the eye of the viewer to move onwards.

Two lions (one black, one red) in the upper border directly above William and Harold are positioned facing each other in what appears to be a confrontational manner. Perhaps they represent the two men, or are just heightening the tension and general atmosphere of looming conflict. Below Harold, in the lower border, two long-necked birds are either feeding on the ground or burying their heads – possibly averting their gazes from Harold's perilous situation.

As the party approaches the Duke's palace, the riders come to a tall, narrow gatehouse-tower with an elaborately patterned exterior. As is often the case in the Tapestry, it is not drawn to a realistic scale, otherwise the man standing beside or behind it would be a giant. There is no indication of who he is, but he points back very deliberately at Harold, or at the group as a whole. He is probably a watchman, looking out for the return of William and his party, though he could also be someone known to Harold.

Earl Harold and Duke William converse

And with that, we enter the Duke's court and encounter another very evocative scene. It unfolds inside a large hall-like structure, with two thin pillars at the sides supporting a long arcade of round arches of the type associated with later Norman architecture. The roof almost touches the upper border, so that the cross-shaped plant elements above, centred between oblique lines, almost look like they decorate its ridge. Inside the hall a heated discussion is taking place, though there is no caption to tell us what is being said. William is prominently seated on the edge of a large throne. His face is stitched in three-quarter view rather than profile, making his features visible. Looking straight out of the Tapestry in this way seems to indicate status and significance in certain places in the embroidery, though the designer is not completely systematic. It is notable in comparison that Guy of Ponthieu was not shown in portrait format in his court scene. William is again wrapped in a large cloak, now black, and his leggings are bound with garters from which ribbons hang. He looks as if he is resting on a cushion on his throne, the base of which is a large chest of some sort, with a small window or opening in it. Behind William, the back of the throne has an upright post ending in a carving of an open-mouthed animal, similar in style to the stern posts of the Tapestry's ships.

William is gesticulating with one hand, not surprisingly, at Harold, while in the other he holds a long sword. The English Earl is portrayed in a striking and animated pose, with his legs splayed and upper body turned almost in the opposite direction from the one in which he is facing, and with his arms stretched out to both sides. He is wearing an ample red cloak pinned with a small round brooch at one shoulder, and his moustache is now clearly visible. He looks slightly agitated, as if he is struggling to get his argument across. His right hand, held open and palm out, is raised towards William, and he seems to be attempting to explain something to the Duke, while with his left hand he points away, perhaps to the figure standing next to him.

The person to whom Harold appears to be gesturing has a more individual and less stylized face than those around him, with a neat beard covering his chin and hair swept back over his scalp. Armed with sword and shield, he bends his body slightly in the direction of Harold, whose hand he almost touches with his own. His neck is craned forwards and his legs are also somewhat splayed. Does his pose simply mirror Harold's, or suggest that he has something to add to what Harold is saying? One suggestion is that he is one of the English hostages whom Harold has come to release, though the fact that he has weapons and a shield like those of his companions somewhat undermines that. His hair does mark him out from the others in the scene, though, so it seems there is something worth knowing about him. Behind him are three clearly Norman soldiers who look on fairly impassively. To complete the scene, to the left of Duke William is another standing Norman, again with a spear, who is pointing towards Harold and the men behind him. All the figures in this scene, except the Earl and the man with the unique hairstyle, have hair in the Norman fashion. In the upper border, two peacocks seem to model themselves on the poses of the two main protagonists in the action below, and the colour of their plumage (like the lions and winged creatures in the border just before them) matches the clothing of William and Harold respectively.

Although the Tapestry gives us no clues about the substance of the conversation taking place, the historical sources are more helpful. William of Poitiers tells us that 'the courtesy of [Duke William's] generous hospitality and celebration made good the hardship of the journey' undertaken by Harold. He also says that the Duke 'hoped that Harold would be a faithful mediator between himself and the English amongst whom he stood second only to the king'. Writing later, Eadmer of Canterbury also notes that Harold was 'received with all honour' by William, and adds that the Duke was told about Harold's mission to release his brother and nephew. So they could be discussing the hostages, or perhaps talking about William's aspirations to succeed to the throne of England. Alternatively, is Harold gesticulating at the bearded man to his left in an accusatory fashion, hinting at some unknown slight or indiscretion, or is this somehow connected with what happens next in the Tapestry?

As is generally the case, relatively little can be learnt from the facial features of the characters in this scene. Faces in the Tapestry are on the whole portrayed in a stylized way and are not enormously expressive, though with a little faith and some retrospective knowledge, a sense of a particular person's motivation or emotions can be gleaned occasionally. As one researcher has put it: 'No one ever looks *happy* in the Bayeux Tapestry, but emotion is not absent.' How a person is feeling is generally only discernible by looking closely at the mouth – perhaps the lips are slightly down-turned or there is just the hint of a smile. Such apparent expressions might be unintended or completely accidental, though, resulting from the way features are rendered by the embroiderers' stitches at this small scale.

Little effort is made in the Tapestry to show even the leading characters in the story in the same way consistently throughout, aside from Edward the Confessor, who does receive more attention. Instead, particular defining characteristics (Harold's moustache, for instance) or names provided in the captions are used to establish identities. That said, not all facial types and features are exactly the same; various chins are on show when faces are in profile, and noses come in different shapes and sizes. Hairstyles, of course, also differ and are often used to denote nationality. Different colours are used to define the outlines of faces and fill in hair, but mostly it seems for the sake of variety or sometimes for emphasis, rather than in an attempt to achieve any true likeness. In many ways this was common to all visual representations of the time, including manuscript illuminations and Anglo-Saxon coinage.

More meaning can be discerned in the eyes of the Bayeux Tapestry's faces than might be imagined. Some are just simple dots, while others are rendered in more detail, with eyebrows, upper and lower lids, and pupils delineated. From this it is possible to tell which direction a character is looking in, and perhaps even to get some sense of the meaning an individual's glance is intended to convey. Along with various gestures and postures, this gives some scope for the designer and embroiderers to guide viewers' attention and thus make them aware of what they should be concentrating on in the story.

That brings us back to the court scene, because here the eyes are definitely meaningful. William's gaze appears fixed on Harold, with his eyes wide open. In fact, everyone in the hall seemingly has their gaze firmly locked on Harold, aside from William's adviser, who is concentrating on delivering his counsel to his lord. Given the almost total focus on Harold, whatever it is he is saying must be very interesting and makes him the central figure in the scene. William, in a way, is overshadowed by his guest, which is not so surprising because up to this point the story has really been all about the Englishman.

Face to face with Duke William

What can we say of Duke William now that we have finally come face to face with him? From his portrait in the Tapestry it is not possible to work out how old he is, but we know from written sources that he was born in 1027 or 1028, so would be in his late thirties in 1064. His life up to now has certainly been eventful, even for a young aristocrat of the eleventh century. Born outside Christian wedlock, he was the son of Duke Robert I, the Magnificent, and his mistress Herleva. Their love story was the subject of much discussion at the time and remains so to this day. Whether Herleva was the lowly daughter of a tanner or undertaker in the town of Falaise (according to the traditional tales) or the child of a member of the Duke's household (perhaps more likely), the fact that she was not married to William's father in the eyes of the Church seems to have troubled William in later life, and some of his contemporaries. However, it was not unusual for Norman dukes to have relationships with women they were not married to, or to father children outside wedlock (in this they followed their Norse ancestors). It was a similar situation elsewhere in Europe; Earl Harold also had a long-term relationship with a woman outside Christian marriage.

Duke Robert's death in 1035, when William was only around eight years old, was a blow to the boy's life chances, though he was acknowledged as his father's heir. William's appearances in charters show that by the 1030s he was being pushed into prominence, but as he was still a minor, matters were not in his control. For a while Normandy experienced a degree of turmoil as rival families sought to extend their influence at the expense of one another. At times the young man's life was in danger, and from now on William was always to have enemies. It was not until 1042 or thereabouts – the same time that Edward the Confessor became king of England – that William was able to assert himself and truly begin to contest for his legacy. The young Duke's first military campaign, probably in 1043, saw off a local lord, Thurstan Goz, who had sought support from the French king, Henry I. The dispute is complex, as Henry's efforts seem to have been designed to counteract external aggression that threatened Normandy, but William's flexing of his muscles shows that he believed that he, and no one else, was ultimately responsible for the security of the Duchy.

William's credentials as a warlord were established by his victory at Val-ès-Dunes in 1047. Here, this time in alliance with Henry I, he defeated an army led by his cousin, Guy, Count of Brionne, who was looking to wrest Normandy from the young Duke. Although it is likely that King Henry was in overall charge of the victorious army, the battle was notorious for William's savagery to the defeated; there is no record of any prisoners being taken. Even by the norms of the society in which he lived, William was markedly brutal. Following this, William joined Henry against Geoffrey Martel, the powerful Count of Anjou, though success this time was much more limited.

By 1053, William had made a prestigious match by marrying Matilda, the daughter of Count Baldwin V of Flanders. An important alliance politically, it also seems to have been one based on love. It was productive, too, and ensured William had sons who could succeed him. This is not to say William's rule in Normandy was now secure, however. In 1054 he fended off an invasion on two fronts by the king of France in support of a rebellion led by William's uncle, William, Count of Arques. An army that included Count Guy of Ponthieu attacked northeast Normandy, while Duke William faced the French king in the east. The defeat of the French army in the north at the Battle of Mortemer (where Count Guy was captured and imprisoned) saw King Henry withdraw in the east. Three years later, in 1057, William was again victorious against Henry, who this time was joined by Geoffrey Martel of Anjou. The invading forces became divided by the rising tide of the River Dives near Varaville, and William took the opportunity to attack the stranded troops. Later chroniclers record the battle as a massacre. Never again was Normandy invaded in William's lifetime.

With these victories, by the time Duke William was in his early thirties he was finally in complete command of Normandy and was well tested in battle (see pl. 8). More than that, he had become a threat to his neighbours. He was also now well placed to consider the matter of England and his potential to become king there. None of this back story is shown in the Tapestry, and certainly none of the calculated cruelty with which William treated his opponents. Indeed, it could be argued that William's tyrannical disposition is downplayed in the Bayeux Tapestry.

One curious feature of the scene showing William and Harold's conversation is found in the border below. Here is yet another naked man, this time bending over and holding an adze, a type of long-bladed axe often associated with shipbuilding. It has been interpreted as another reference to a fable, one in which a man persuades trees to provide him with wood so he can make a handle for an axe, which he then uses to cut down the very trees that had helped him. The moral of this story is that it is unwise to give your enemy the means to destroy you. If that is what is intended, then the inference is that Harold has done just this by finding himself at William's mercy in his court. Why the man has an adze rather than axe, and why he should be naked, is hard to determine. However, perhaps his nudity is in some way linked to another naked man who appears shortly after in the lower border. This man is squatting frontally, with one hand on his hip and the other outstretched, and with his genitals very clearly and prominently on display. His pose is striking, and also intriguing since it mirrors in some ways that of a figure in the main frieze above him.

The enigma of Ælfgyva

This second nude man sits underneath a new and different picture (Scene 15). It is one of the most debated and most perplexing scenes in the entire Tapestry. Although it occurs immediately after the episode in William's court, it might be understood as separate from it because it takes place beyond the wall of the courtly hall. However, a second tower which follows this new episode is similar to the one that preceded the arrival at the ducal hall, and seems to form a closing bracket to the whole scene. This suggests that although this element of the story is distinct from what went on just before, it is not completely divorced from the action there. One line of thought is that Harold is not pointing to the man next to him in William's court, but is gesturing generally or metaphorically past him in the direction of this next scene. Similarly, William's eyes might not be fixed on Harold at all, but gazing ahead. That leads to a further theory about the nature of William and Harold's conversation, which is that they are in fact talking about this next vignette.

What we see is a woman standing between two columns joined by an upper lintel. The columns are ornamented with a spiral pattern and topped by two impressive capitals in the form of outward-facing heads of beasts with protruding tongues. It is an extremely ornate and fabulous structure, and almost complete fantasy. The woman is wearing a full-length gown and a headdress that covers all but her face and a small part of her neck. Some researchers have also identified a veil over her eyes, of the sort associated with a bride, though that requires a certain dexterity of observation and interpretation. Oddly, she seems to be hovering a little way off the ground, though whether this is deliberate or simply accidental, or even a mistake in the embroidery, is not certain. Her arms are bent and her hands are slightly raised towards a man with the tonsure of a monk, who she is looking directly at. He is standing outside the strange structure and his right arm is shown passing behind one of its columns, presumably over some sort of threshold, with his hand, palm outwards, touching, or slapping, the woman's face. His other hand rests on his hip, and he appears to lean slightly inwards towards the woman. This is the figure whose posture seems to be mimicked by the naked figure in the border below. The man in the central frieze, however, is not naked – he wears a tunic, along with a fine, long, blue-green cloak, which is fastened at the throat, unusually, with a square brooch, perhaps a mark of his status.

The text above the scene reads VBI VNVS CLERICVS ET ÆLFGYVA (Where a cleric and Ælfgyva). The statement not only lacks a verb, differentiating it from most of the other inscriptions in the Bayeux Tapestry, but also, rather than clarifying what is going on, simply adds to the enigma, in an embroidery for which the word enigmatic might have been invented. Ælfgyva is the name of the woman, and the cleric is the man with the monk's tonsure, though he is not wearing religious vestments. That much is clear, but what are they doing? The cleric may be gently caressing the woman with love and care, or pressing unwanted attentions on her, or even slapping her in anger or disgust. And why is the woman seemingly levitating, and what is the significance of the architecture?

To answer the last question first, one – rather fanciful – idea is that some form of temporal or spatial displacement is intended. According to this theory, the twisting columns and animal-head finials are there to signal that the setting has shifted, from the classically inspired, gently rounded Norman structures of previous scenes to something that would be more at home in a pagan, northern European hall; the architecture is certainly more akin to Viking art. This would then be a kind of dream scene, a mental digression that transports the viewer to somewhere completely different, in both space and perhaps time, before returning to the here and now of the Tapestry. The floating feet of the woman, and, less obviously, those of the monk (his are superimposed over the pedestals of two buildings), might be a further device to suggest that this is all happening somewhere else and in another time.

Who is Ælfgyva? This is a question that has been asked many times and answered in numerous ways, none of them conclusive. She is probably English, or at least her name is. Ælfgyva was a common name for Anglo-Saxon women of the period, and was popular among the high-born and English royalty. Edmund I (r. 939–46), for example, had a wife called Ælfgyva (of Shaftesbury), who was later venerated as a saint, and also a sister (of Wessex) of the same name. The first wife of King Æthelred II (r. 978–1016) was called Ælfgyva (of York), as was that of King Cnut (Ælfgyva of Northampton), and a daughter of Æthelred and Ælfgyva of York was also called Ælfgyva. The name was further extended to incoming royal women: Emma of Normandy (the mother of Edward the Confessor) took the name Ælfgyva when she married Æthelred II, though she is also referred to as Emma. So there is a multitude of Ælfgyvas, which has led to a great deal of theorizing about whether any of them might be the Ælfgyva of the Bayeux Tapestry. She could, of course, be someone else completely.

The presence of a veil, if correct, could hint that the scene involves a story of marriage or betrothal, and one idea is that Ælfgyva was a daughter of Duke William. William of Poitiers and Orderic Vitalis both suggest that Harold was betrothed to one of William's daughters. It is unlikely, however, that a daughter of William of Normandy would have been given an Anglo-Saxon name at birth, and Vitalis names the daughter as Agatha. Some historians have then equated Agatha with Ælfgyva based on the similarity between the two words and the fact that it was possible in Normandy at this time for a person to have two synonymous but different names (Rollo and Robert, for example). Alternatively, a Norman woman might have taken an Anglo-Saxon name after marriage, in the same way that Emma of Normandy did when she married into the English royal line.

The Tapestry's Ælfgyva has also been identified as one of Harold's sisters who was the Abbess of Wilton Abbey. She had been blinded in an accident with a lamp, but her sight was miraculously restored by Saint Edith (Eadgyth), and thus the cleric in the Tapestry would be sweeping his hand across her eyes to draw attention to this act of divine intervention. In this interpretation she is not in Rouen but at Wilton, perhaps explaining the architecture, and Harold is talking about her, emphasizing her saintliness, to show himself in a good light. Even if that is all true, the theory does not explain other elements of the image.

Another candidate is the aforementioned Ælfgyva of Northampton, the wife of King Cnut from about 1013 until 1035 (before he married

Emma of Normandy) and mother of Harold I (Harefoot) of England and Swein of Denmark. John of Worcester reported a story that this Ælfgyva, unable to have a son by Cnut, took the newborn baby of a priest and told the king it was theirs. This would account for the presence of the monk and the woman in the Tapestry. In a second story she also convinced Cnut that she had borne him another son, which was actually the child of a cobbler, who then would be the naked man with the adze or axe; though why a shoemaker would have an axe and no clothes is not clear. If this is the Ælfgyva who is represented, the theory then goes further, explaining her presence in the Tapestry as a way of casting doubt on the legitimacy of Cnut's descendants to reign as kings, and by extension the claim of Harald Hardrada to bid for Edward the Confessor's throne. But it is a convoluted journey to reach this conclusion, and not everything seems to add up.

It has also been proposed that Ælfgyva is none other than Ælfgyva-Emma, the double-named, double-married wife of both Æthelred and Cnut, who, it was reported, was also sexually involved with several men, including Ælfwine, Bishop of Winchester. According to the early fourteenth-century *Polychronicon Ranulphi Higden monachi Cestrensis* (Multi-chronicle of Ranulph Higden, monk of Chester), her son, King Edward, had goods taken away from her and sent her to the monastery of Wherwell 'for suspicion with the Bishop of Winchester', whom he imprisoned. If this is correct, the cleric with Ælfgyva in the Bayeux Tapestry and the naked man below are both Ælfwine. Ælfgyva-Emma was then able to prove her innocence through the ordeal of walking over hot irons or ploughshares, which might explain the depiction of the earlier naked man with the 'axe' – if this line of thought is followed, he is putting in place the hot irons with tongs. Emma was certainly an influential person in the politics of northwestern Europe in the eleventh century, not least because she was Edward the Confessor's mother and also Norman by birth. So, might this mysterious scene in the Bayeux Tapestry be a reference to her rumoured scandalous past, perhaps implying that not all was well with the Norman court, especially as it is suggested the scandal took place in Rouen? But if this is the case, what has it got to do with William, or with Harold for that matter?

All these ideas (and there are more) are interesting and worthy of some consideration as they each bring something to our understanding of the Bayeux Tapestry – but none of them can be definitively proved. Therefore, some historians have instead tried to understand the scene in a different way, one that goes beyond the question of individual identity. One such approach sees the episode as relating to a societal development at the time – the subjection of female sexuality to male dominance, particularly through the aggressive advances of young, educated men who had taken clerical orders but held positions as scribes and clerks in secular settings. This interpretation would make this an interlude of social commentary, which would presumably have been linked to the story told in the Tapestry in some way and have been understood by the contemporary observer. One of the justifications that Duke William makes for his invasion of England is the need for a reform of religious standards, so perhaps this is what is alluded to here, though unlikely.

Another, perhaps more logical, approach focuses on the position of the scene within the overall structure of the Bayeux Tapestry. Women are few and far between in the embroidery – they are only depicted in the main frieze three times – but when they are shown it is at pivotal points, presaging key events that occur soon after. On that basis, the very fact that a woman appears in the embroidery makes viewers sit up, take note and prepare themselves for what is coming next.

A final question about this strange scene is why the verb is missing from the caption. Surely it is not just a simple mistake? Perhaps the story being referred to, whatever it truly was all about, was so well known that it did not need any more overt explanation. A verb would have been superfluous when it was so obvious to everyone what was happening (or what was so scandalous), so it feels like the phrase is intentionally left hanging, as something perhaps best not stated.

Despite the multitude of possible explanations, the real meaning of the Ælfgyva episode and the story behind it are still obscure. If it is accepted that it must in some way be linked to Harold and William's meeting, possibly even a subject of their conversation, perhaps we can look ahead to what happens next for clues? The action moves on rapidly, but in quite a different direction, and it is hard to see exactly how Ælfgyva fits into what follows. From William and Harold's perspective, however, their conversation must have been reasonably fruitful, because they are next seen setting out on campaign together.

CHAPTER 6

THE BRITTANY
CAMPAIGN

Following their meeting in Normandy, William and Harold head off together on military campaign into Brittany. William attacks his neighbour and rival, Duke Conan II of Brittany, in support of a lesser lord, Rivallon of Dol. It is not clear when exactly this took place, but it is likely to have been in late 1064. Few other documentary sources devote so much attention to this conflict as the Bayeux Tapestry, which presents the campaign as a comprehensive triumph for William, and one in which Harold demonstrates his bravery and martial prowess.

After the interlude of the enigma of Ælfgyva, the thrust of the Bayeux Tapestry becomes more straightforward and dynamic for the next few scenes, as we follow William's Brittany campaign. The text takes us immediately to the heart of the action (Scene 16): hIC VVILLEM DVX ET EXERCITVS EIVS VENERVNT AD MONTE[M] MIChAELIS (Here Duke William and his army came to Mont-Saint-Michel). Mont-Saint-Michel, at the western edge of Normandy, is a small tidal island set in a large bay off the north coast of France, where the River Couesnon flows into the sea. Today it is a UNESCO World Heritage site because of the famous medieval abbey that dominates the summit. Tourists crowd the steep and narrow streets of the village below, buying trinkets and stopping for refreshment as they climb upwards to the abbey precinct. A modern causeway means the island is no longer cut off from the mainland by the tide twice a day as it was in the past.

It was certainly not as busy in the eleventh century, but even by then it had a long history of religious activity. It was a pilgrimage site from the eighth century and an important abbey from the tenth century. Crucially, Mont-Saint-Michel sits on the border between Normandy and Brittany, which explains why William and his men are here. This is the start of the Breton campaign, a Norman incursion into Brittany to deal with a tricky rebellion.

This is quite a leap from where we were just before in the Tapestry, so some background is needed. Duke William had spent much of the 1050s fending off aggressive military moves from his near neighbours in northern France, and by the time of the events in the Bayeux Tapestry he had done much to consolidate his position. Brittany, to the west of his duchy, remained a cause of insecurity, especially since it bordered the powerful County of Anjou. It was within this context that William embarked on a campaign against Conan II of Brittany. Understanding the causes of this event, and how it unfolded, is complicated by the fact that it is only recorded in any depth by William of Poitiers and the Bayeux Tapestry, and even more so because these accounts do not entirely match.

Poitiers says that William invaded Brittany to come to the assistance of the regional lord, Rivallon of Dol, who was considered by Conan to have acted rebelliously. The author also implies that Conan had declared war on William by welcoming the protection of Anjou in the east, and suggests that the Norman Duke was responding to aggression by Conan. The Tapestry does not give this justification, nor indeed any justification or further commentary at all on what led up to William and his army entering Brittany. After the meeting between William and Harold in Rouen, we are suddenly transported some 240 kilometres (150 miles) or so to the west, as a troop of armoured knights on horseback rides up to and beneath the island abbey of Mont-Saint-Michel. Without showing or explaining anything about how or why William's army has arrived here, the Tapestry plunges us into a new and eventful chapter of the story.

Eight horsemen are depicted, two of whom are wearing full body-length mail armour and helmets, while the others are dressed in the looser tunics seen previously. This is the first time in the Tapestry that fully armoured knights are shown, emphasizing the fact that we are witnessing a military adventure. One of the knights holds a spear topped by a fluttering pennant bearing the sign of the cross, perhaps indicating that William has God on his side.

Which figure is Duke William is not absolutely certain, but presumably he must be one of the riders shown, given that he is named in the text. One figure, riding just in front of the armoured knights, wears a chequered tunic and carries a staff of some sort, perhaps a commander's baton or mace, though otherwise he is not dressed for war. He is a little larger than the riders around him, probably to emphasize his seniority, so this could be William.

An alternative view is that this distinctively dressed man is not in fact William, but Odo of Bayeux. Bishop Odo is not named in the caption, but if he was instrumental in having the Bayeux Tapestry made, there would be some logic for him to appear in the picture at this point as the next place mentioned after the Breton campaign is Bayeux, where he was bishop. Odo is shown later in action at the Battle of Hastings riding a horse, wearing a similar costume and carrying a baton, so it is not too implausible to link the two portrayals. On balance, however, it seems more likely that William is the chequered commander.

In front of William is another rider, whose mount is just wading into some water, and ahead of him is a further horseman, who holds his legs in an odd position, almost as if he is riding side-saddle or lifting them to keep them out of the water, or perhaps is in the act of dismounting. Above this foremost rider, who holds his shield up behind his head, is Mont-Saint-Michel (Scene 17). The abbey itself sits within the upper border (highlighting its prominence in the narrative) and is portrayed as if standing on a platform on top of a rounded hill. At each end of its ornate roof is a cross, like Bosham church before. The building and its setting are clearly stylized, but even so it has been suggested that the Tapestry designer must have had personal knowledge of what the island and abbey looked like at the time. Others disagree, since the structures do not reflect what is known of either the later Romanesque abbey or the earlier Carolingian church. Next to the abbey in the upper border is a figure seated in a chair, with one arm extended towards it, whose significance will be discussed in due course.

Harold's heroics

Mont-Saint-Michel was a significant place for several reasons. Not only was it a notable religious foundation and at the boundary between Normandy and Brittany, but it also stood at a dangerous, even lethal, liminal place, where the sands were treacherous and the tides strong enough to catch out the unwary. The Bayeux Tapestry shows William's party crossing the river mouth (rather than approaching the Mount), which in the 1060s was a perilous undertaking.

The risks involved are made abundantly clear in the scene following, where three men are wading through waist-deep water carrying shields above their heads. Ahead of them, a horse has tripped and fallen headlong into the river, pitching its unfortunate rider into the water. It is not clear whether this man is also one of two figures who are then seen being hauled from the water by a rescuer, who carries one on his back and pulls the other up by the hand. This is a moment of high drama and heroism, of danger averted, and the hero is none other than Earl Harold himself.

The text above this scene is surprisingly prolix, comprising two separate statements: ET hIC TRANSIERVNT FLVMEN COSNONIS (And here they crossed the River Couesnon) and below that hIC hAROLD DVX TRAhEBAT EOS DE ARENA (Here Duke Harold pulled them out of the sand). Aside from the fact that the rescuer has Harold's trademark moustache, it is also spelled out that he was the saviour. Swimming below the action, in the lower border, are two fish, as if to demonstrate the depth of the water and potential peril of the situation; they have been the subject of much scholarly discussion.

Several eels also swim along the lower border, perhaps for the same reason as the fish, though they also seem to be linked to a strange vignette involving a prone man stretching out towards them with one hand and carrying a large knife in the other. He might be trying to catch the eels, while also being pursued himself by a small menagerie of beasts. What is going on is hard to decipher, but this detail has also received a fair amount of analytical attention.

One suggestion is that the purpose of the eels is to highlight the slippery and devious nature of Harold. Eels were associated with such attributes in later medieval bestiaries, so the imputation would likely have been obvious to the contemporary audience. The prone man has been identified as Harold himself, as he has an Anglo-Saxon-style haircut and moustache – though that is not completely evident – and his weapon appears to be an English type. But if it is Harold, why would he be pursuing or attacking the eels? Perhaps it is a hint that he is actively intending to be duplicitous, like an eel, and that although he is seemingly brave and admirable, there is something about his actions that is much less laudable. This is entirely supposition, and as with all such explanations is influenced by how the overall message of the Tapestry is interpreted in its entirety.

The scene of the rescue of the two Norman soldiers, with one being carried and the other pulled along, has also been linked to Virgil's *Aeneid*, with Harold identified with its hero, the Trojan Aeneas, the founder of Rome. William of Poitiers does not record this episode, so any reference seems specific to the Tapestry and is another example of its depiction of Harold as a heroic figure – a man to be admired for his bravery and also a worthy adversary for Duke William to take on and defeat in the future. If the eels are intended to have a bearing on Harold's character, there may also be an implication that all is not as it seems from outward appearances. The border illustrations could, of course, have been chosen at random by the embroiderers for purely decorative reasons, or because they had some other relevance to the scene. Parallels can be found in contemporary illuminations, especially for the fish and some of the beasts.

After the drama at the Couesnon, William's men move on to the small town of Dol (Scene 18), as related by the text: ET VENERVNT AD DOL ET CONAN FVGA VERTIT (and they came to Dol and Conan fled). Dol is a few miles from Mont-Saint-Michel and is today a pleasant provincial town with a fine cathedral and a handsome high street dotted with medieval and later half-timbered houses. Nothing now survives of the substantial castle atop a large round mound that we see in the Bayeux Tapestry.

The lack of any visible remains means it is hard to judge the accuracy of the Tapestry's portrayal of the eleventh-century castle. It looks odd, as it appears to be triangular in plan, which would make it highly unusual, but this may just be an unsuccessful attempt by the embroiderers to show perspective. The chequer-board pattern on its upper section has been interpreted as a covering of protective plates made of metal, wood or hide, the like of which is documented for castles of this period. To the left of the building is a vertical line of rounded motifs, thought by some to be flames, but more likely a row of overlapping kite-shaped shields, as seen on the Tapestry's ships. The lower part of the building is not decorated or patterned and looks open, so this could be a type of stilted structure, for which there is archaeological evidence from post-Conquest castles in England. A stepped bridge protected by a gateway at the top leads from ground level up to the castle, and the base of the mound is defended by a ditch. The mound is shown as a pronounced feature, with curious wavy lines and two posturing birds within shown at enormous scale. Given that there is no evidence for a fortified mound today in Dol, this is perhaps a conventional rendition of what the Tapestry designer thought this style of defensive structure should look like, or even a formulaic depiction of the entire town.

Castles of this type – the famous motte and bailey – are synonymous with the Normans, and are generally thought to have been introduced into England after the Conquest. The motte was a large mound, either natural or often manmade, which overlooked a defended outer enclosure or courtyard, the bailey. The speed and relative ease with which an earthen mound topped by a wooden palisade could be constructed was an important element in Norman success in taking control of their new territory.

Such structures would have been vividly etched in the memories of the occupied people in England after the Conquest, who might even have witnessed them being erected before their eyes. If, as is likely, the Bayeux Tapestry was designed and embroidered in Canterbury by English hands, perhaps we are seeing a reflection of that experience depicted here. The Anglo-Saxon Chronicle mournfully notes this process taking place in the aftermath of the Battle of Hastings, recording that after King William returned to Normandy, 'Bishop Odo and William [fitz Osbern, Earl of Hereford] were left behind here, and they built castles widely throughout this nation, and oppressed the wretched people.'

In the Tapestry, Dol is being attacked by four horsemen who are charging headlong towards it, spears and shields raised, though they are lightly armed compared with later clashes. It is another of the Tapestry's well-composed action scenes, with the sense of movement vividly conveyed. However, as a military tactic, charging on horseback straight at a wooden wall on a mound of earth is unlikely to have been very effective, so there is an element of artistic licence. Alternatively, the mounted soldiers may be riding up the stepped bridge, or galloping around the castle, or chasing its occupants as they flee. Above the riders, in the upper border, two boars confront each other. Since these beasts are rare in the Tapestry, their depiction may have had some special purpose, or perhaps they are just there to add extra visual vitality to the theme of conflict.

A further oddity of this castle is that it is apparently entirely unmanned. No one is shown defending it, and the only figure we see is rather obviously and dramatically escaping from it by sliding down a taut rope on the far side of the building. This is almost certainly Conan, given that he is named in the text above and is said to be fleeing. In reality it seems unlikely he would have made his escape in this way, especially since a close parallel has been identified in an illustration in the Old English Hexateuch which shows Israelite spies fleeing from Jericho using a rope. The Tapestry designer is probably borrowing an artistic device he has seen elsewhere to inject more drama into the narrative. In the Bible, the Israelite spies are saved from capture by God's grace, so whether this gives the Tapestry's version any extra meaning is debatable, though unlikely since Conan was an enemy of the Normans.

This is one of the places where the Bayeux Tapestry diverges from William of Poitiers. In his account, Poitiers describes Conan laying siege to Dol, which presumably means the castle was being defended by its owner, Rivallon of Dol, but abandoning his siege in advance of the arrival of Duke William's forces. If so, it would make no sense for any occupants of the castle to be escaping, since they would surely have welcomed the arrival of the Normans who were coming to their relief.

But there is no time to rest and consider such questions because the action runs rapidly on to the next encounter. This does not have a unique handwritten scene number and so was seemingly regarded as inconsequential to whoever in the antiquarian period added them. The text here reverts to its more usual curt form, with the single word REDNES (Rennes) ranged on either side of another castle (or town) on a mound. Rennes was an important centre in Brittany, the ancestral base for the county of the same name. The counts of Rennes were also generally the dukes of Brittany during this period, as was the case with Conan, who was Count of Rennes and Duke of Brittany. So here the Norman troops are striking right at the heart of Conan's domain, a powerful visual symbol, and surely one that would have resonated with a contemporary audience.

The structure shown at Rennes is different from the one at Dol. A palisade, presumably made of wood and with alternately coloured planks, protects a dome-shaped tiled tower. In the centre of the palisade a doorway opens out on to a stepped bridge descending to the bottom of the mound, which appears to be sheathed with scales. Given that two sheep are grazing on the mound, the scales could represent grass. There is also a large wall at the mound's base, implying it had a curtain wall or other defences.

Four mounted knights are approaching Rennes. This time they are wearing full armour, presumably in anticipation of encountering more resistance than at Dol, but as before, no one appears to be defending the castle. Again it is debatable whether the knights are actually engaged in an assault or are just riding past, though they are shown in what looks like an attacking posture. William of Poitiers says nothing of Rennes in his account; he does, however, talk of Conan's forces being in continual retreat during the campaign, so perhaps the Bayeux Tapestry depicts William's knights chasing the Breton army through Conan's comital lands.

The Normans join in battle, Conan is defeated

Battle is finally joined at Dinan (Scene 19), as the text informs us: hIC MILITES VVILLELMI DVCIS PVGNANT CONTRA DINANTES (Here Duke William's soldiers fight against the men of Dinan). This first scene of real conflict is dramatically depicted, with the fully armoured horsemen galloping forwards, spears raised in readiness to attack or already launched at the enemy. They are charging at another palisaded structure on top of a mound, again with what looks like an outer wooden wall and a central tower with an elaborate roof. A clearly delineated outer bank and ditch surround the mound and a walkway leads down from the palisade. This time the castle is fully defended by a group of knights on foot who are dressed in very similar fashion to their assailants and are hurling their spears down at the horsemen. There is an air of desperation to their defence because beneath the tower two attackers brandishing flaming torches on poles are setting fire to the wooden walls.

How realistic is this attack? Well, once more, the idea of a cavalry charge against a castle seems rather far-fetched, but an attempt to fire the wooden walls would have been a sensible tactic. No evidence has been found for a structure like this within Dinan today, and William of Poitiers does not mention events in the town in his account. In fact, he says that Conan and William did not engage in battle at all, but that William decided to withdraw to Normandy rather than pursue the rebel leader too far west, thereby avoiding the possibility of Count Geoffrey of Anjou becoming involved in the war.

The Bayeux Tapestry tells a different story, because while all the fighting is taking place on the left-hand side of the castle, on the right-hand side a knight on the battlements is holding out his pennant lance with a bunch of keys at the tip to a horseman who receives them on the end of his weapon (Scene 20). These are presumably the keys to Dinan being handed over by Conan to Duke William, as the text reads ET CVNAN CLAVES PORREXIT (and Conan offered up the keys). Both men are dressed in full armour, so there is no real way of identifying either person with certainty. Nevertheless, according to the Tapestry, the outcome of the assault on the castle is that the Breton defenders surrender to the Norman attackers, which represents a humiliating defeat for Conan. In the version given by William of Poitiers, in contrast, the honours of the whole campaign are more evenly shared between the Bretons and Normans, though William did achieve his primary objective of relieving the siege of Dol. This discrepancy is interesting, since if William's victory was as comprehensive as the Tapestry would have it, then Poitiers would be the more likely source to recount it, as he generally makes great efforts to praise the Norman Duke.

The final vignette of this adventure in Brittany (Scene 21) focuses on the two main protagonists, Harold and William, who are shown beneath the inscription hIC WILLELM DEDIT hAROLDO ARMA (Here William gave arms to Harold). The two men, unaccompanied and both kitted out in full armour, stand face to face, with William touching Harold's arm and head. Harold, head slightly bowed, holds a pennant-banner in his free hand, outstretched behind him. It is a significant moment, and leads on to further crucial incidents in the next scene. The suggestion here is that William is rewarding Harold for his good service. This at once emphasizes the English Earl's brave soldiery, while simultaneously stressing his subservience to the Norman

Duke. Some historians have gone so far as to state that this scene shows Harold becoming the vassal of William, although exactly what that would have meant to both men at the time is not entirely clear.

Understanding the Brittany campaign

By the end of the campaign in Brittany we are a little better informed about the important relationship between the two central characters in the Tapestry's narrative, but in terms of the main story being told matters do not seem to have moved much further on. That raises the question of why this episode is included in the Bayeux Tapestry at all, let alone why it occupies such a considerable proportion (about 10 per cent) of its visual narrative. A lengthy diversion to Brittany does not seem entirely relevant to a story that is describing the invasion of England. Most other contemporary sources seem to regard it as not worthy of inclusion in their accounts, so why does the Tapestry place so much emphasis on it? There are a few theories, as might be expected.

First, and most simply, it is a good story, and presents an opportunity to depict plenty of action and violence. The excitement of the chase across enemy territory, the armed assaults on fortified strongholds, the burning of palisades and dramatic escapes all provide stirring material. It would appeal to any viewers of the Tapestry who were soldiers or military men, which would probably be quite a few if the embroidery was commissioned by the warrior-bishop Odo of Bayeux. The episode also serves to break up some slightly complicated political wrangling and the narrative moves briskly along, so it also keeps the audience engaged. In terms of structure, this digression, along with other moments in the Tapestry that seem not directly related to the main thread of the action, could be in the tradition of Anglo-Saxon narrative poetry, particularly *Beowulf*, where ancillary episodes are integrated into the main text to enrich the story.

It has also been noted by numerous scholars that the designer of the Bayeux Tapestry appears to have a particularly intimate awareness of, and interest in, affairs in this part of northern Brittany, and so must have been personally familiar with the area. This points to

Scolland, Abbot of St Augustine's in Canterbury after the Conquest (from 1072) and previously head monk of the scriptorium of the abbey of Mont-Saint-Michel. Not only might he have had a direct hand in the Tapestry's production, but it has even been proposed that he appears in it, in the form of the figure who sits in the upper border just to the right of the image of the abbey itself, stretching one arm out towards it. That is quite a leap of interpretation, particularly as this character is not named and is depicted in lay dress, but there may be something to it.

Finally, and perhaps most importantly, is the way in which the campaign in Brittany informs the general narrative of the Tapestry. It seems the designer has chosen to focus attention on Duke Conan: he is specifically shown (and named) in somewhat humiliating circumstances twice during the campaign – dangling from a rope at one point and handing over the keys of his castle at another. Is the designer deliberately disparaging this rival to Duke William, while at the same time finding opportunities to celebrate the actions of his other main rival, Earl Harold? Perhaps it was necessary to find a way for Harold to recover his standing after the humiliation of the Ponthieu incident.

It has been pointed out that there are parallels between aspects of what is shown in the Breton campaign and what occurs later in the Norman invasion of England. In both, troops cross water before they come to battle, and Normans on horseback attack enemy foot soldiers; there is also a similarity between the mound of Mont-Saint-Michel and a fortification thrown up by the Normans when they arrive at Hastings. In several ways the depiction of the Brittany campaign in the Tapestry thus foreshadows events that take place later in England. It is a compelling theory, particularly in the light of the treatment meted out to Conan, and it does feel like a point is being made to the viewer: if you declare war on Duke William you will lose, and you will be humiliated. That is what happens to Conan. And it is also what happens to Harold. William of Poitiers notes that 'Brittany at this time was presumptuously at war with Normandy', and Harold essentially declares war on William through his duplicitous actions – if we accept the Norman version of events.

The viewer, then, is being invited to compare the fate of Conan with that of Harold. Harold's downfall is even more conspicuous and compelling because through the course of the Bayeux Tapestry he is built up as a great heroic figure, whereas Conan is introduced and then dismissed as merely a bit-part player. This harks back to the idea of the duality of the clash between William and Harold, which overlooks Edgar Ætheling. Count Conan is not important in the story, but what happens to him is, because it reflects on the role of Harold. And Harold's story is about to become a lot more complicated. Having shown his mettle and received arms from William, he is involved in one more very significant development during his time across the Channel in Normandy, and that takes us to the heart of the Tapestry's tale.

CHAPTER 7

A SACRED OATH

With the adventures in Brittany behind them, William and Harold return to Normandy. It is at this point that a crucial event occurs. The English Earl swears a sacred oath to the Norman Duke, apparently promising to help him become king of England. This scene is the crux of the Norman Conquest, because the oath, and the later breaking of it, provides the justification for Duke William to lead his forces into England. The Bayeux Tapestry seems to have the event taking place in Bayeux, while other sources cite different locations, and it is possible multiple oaths were sworn, in various places, perhaps not all relevant to the English succession.

Following the dangers and violence of the Breton campaign, the Bayeux Tapestry moves the scene of the action back across the border from Brittany to Normandy, as the next inscription tells us: hIE [sic] WILLELM VENIT BAGIAS (Here William came to Bayeux). This caption runs above an image of three fully armed men riding towards yet another building on a mound (Scene 22). None of the riders is obviously discernable as William, but the leading horseman, riding a red stallion, has a decorative band at the bottom of his mailed trousers similar to that seen on William's garments in the preceding scene, so this is probably him. As has been the case for much of the Breton campaign, paired birds and beasts adorn both borders of the Tapestry as the soldiers progress into Bayeux.

Bayeux occupies the full height of the main frieze and projects up into the upper border to the top edge. A round, bare, central mound is formed of several alternately coloured layers that rise in a stepped design, on top of which is an imposing structure with two crenellated turrets spanned by a tiled dome. A walkway descends the mound, protected by an additional structure to one side, possibly a gatehouse, which has an elaborate ornamental animal-head motif on top of one column. The building is probably the ducal castle that existed in Bayeux at the time but which has since been demolished, though it may be an attempt by the Tapestry designer to represent the town as a whole rather than any particular individual structure.

Beyond the town, the main event now takes place (Scene 23). The text offers us an important but characteristically Delphic statement: VBI hAROLD SACRAMENTVM FECIT VVILLELMO DVCI (Where Harold swore a sacred oath to Duke William). The imagery in the main frieze is very significant in terms of the overall Tapestry story and is worth considering in detail. Duke William is again seated on the edge of a throne with legs ending in clawed animals' feet. A commanding figure of status and authority, he is dressed in long robes and holds a sword over his shoulder, and is both looking at and pointing towards Harold. Behind William, two figures, one with a spear and shield, the other unarmed, gesture (somewhat conspiratorially perhaps) towards the inscription. One seems to point up at the word hAROLD, the other at SACRAMENTVM, thus linking the words together.

Swearing an oath

Harold, meanwhile, is at the centre of the scene; his moustache is very obvious, but he is wearing much humbler clothing than William. He stands, almost on tiptoes, between two objects raised up to the height of his shoulders. His arms are outstretched to either side (a little like the cleric in the Ælfgyva scene) so that he touches both objects, to his right and left. As with William, two men stand near Harold, both looking at him and one pointing towards the inscription, though they also relate to the following scene, linking the two. Their hairstyles suggest they are Anglo-Saxons, while the men behind William have Norman coiffures. Norman or English, everyone is taking a considerable interest in what Harold is doing.

The items that Harold is touching are reliquaries, richly decorated caskets designed to hold sacred relics. The one seen to Harold's right appears to be placed on an altar, while the one to his left is on a portable pedestal since it has what look like carrying poles beneath it.

Many questions arise from this. Various documentary sources tell us that Duke William had gathered together a large number of religious relics for this occasion. Several refer to one notable reliquary known as the 'ox eye', because it had a huge and beautiful gem at its centre. It has been suggested that this is the reliquary shown to the right of Harold because it has a detail that could correspond to this description on top of its lid. Whether or not it was this particular reliquary, it is clear that Harold touches one casket with the fingers of his right hand and rests his left hand on the other. He is making an oath, as the inscription says – an oath that by its nature everyone at the time would have recognized as sacred and significant. The question of where, and when, this happened is controversial. A literal reading of the Tapestry would mean that it is taking place after the events in Brittany and must surely be in Bayeux, because that has just been shown and nothing in the text would indicate otherwise.

Except that William of Poitiers, our other main source for the Breton campaign, informs us that 'at a council convened at Bonneville [-sur-Touques] Harold publicly swore fealty to him [William] by the sacred rite of Christians'. This statement comes before the description of the adventure in Brittany, so it would place the event both in a different place (Bonneville is some distance to the east) and at a different time. Orderic Vitalis locates the oath-swearing in Rouen. Guy, Bishop of Amiens, says it happened in secret, and yet here in the Bayeux Tapestry are several witnesses who are pointedly paying great attention to what is going on.

So, did the oath-swearing ceremony occur in Bayeux or not? Harold might have sworn several oaths in several places. He is criticized in the *Life of King Edward* for being 'rather too generous with oaths', and William of Jumièges says Harold 'swore fealty concerning the kingdom with many oaths'. It is possible therefore that the designer simply chose Bayeux as the location for the Tapestry's scene of oath-swearing. Of course, it would have been in Bishop Odo's interests, assuming he was the patron of the Bayeux Tapestry, to have the emphasis placed on an oath in Bayeux, his bishopric, at this important moment in the story, even if other oaths were sworn in Bonneville, Rouen and elsewhere. But if that is the case, it is interesting that Odo is not shown.

Bishop Odo's new cathedral in Bayeux was not consecrated until 1077, so at this point, in the mid-1060s, it would potentially not have been ready as the setting for such a ceremony as shown in the Tapestry. The relics may have been housed elsewhere, perhaps in a monastery nearby, and taken to another place for the purpose. Alternatively, the way in which the scene is composed could suggest that William and Harold are in completely different locations. Immediately following the swearing of the oath, Harold very quickly departs from William's lands and sets out to sea, so Harold may have been somewhere close to the Channel and the Duke in Bayeux (which is about 10 km or 6 miles from the coast). However, placing the events in multiple sites does not seem likely. If the oath shown in the Tapestry is one of several made by Harold, then perhaps the precise details of where and when are not so significant. What is more problematic is that the Tapestry tells us nothing about the nature of the oath itself.

The content of the oath

Fortunately, the documentary sources are far less opaque on the subject. In the twelfth century, Henry of Huntingdon states unequivocally that 'Harold swore to William, on many precious relics, that he would marry his daughter and after Edward's death would preserve England for William's benefit.' William of Poitiers, writing much closer to the events in question, does not refer to a marriage, but he does say that Harold agreed to 'be the agent of Duke William at the court of his lord King Edward as long as the latter lived' and 'that he would strive with all his influence and power to bring about the succession of the English kingdom to William after Edward's death'. Poitiers also talks about Harold handing over Dover Castle to William, a place that was not in the Earl's authority to bestow.

This is arguably the critical moment in the Bayeux Tapestry, the point at which Harold solemnly vows to support William. On this rests the whole issue of whether he perjures himself when he takes the throne of England. So, it is curious indeed that the embroidery does not take a clearer line on exactly what is happening. This brings us back to the debates concerning what the embroidery is all about, and who it is for. The Tapestry probably reflects a crucial time in the Conquest period, when the victorious Normans and the vanquished Anglo-Saxons were trying to coexist – or at least the Normans were hoping for peaceful domination over their former foes. For many at the time, the events of 1064 to 1066 were extraordinarily confused, and the truth by no means clear. It might have been important to present the story in such a way that it allowed different groups to understand it in slightly different ways, or to portray the reality of conquest with some sensitivity.

The underlying question is why would Harold have agreed to swear such an oath? William could have made some sort of promise in return, perhaps to uphold Harold's position and standing in England following his accession. Eadmer of Canterbury suggests that Harold simply didn't have much choice because he was in William's hands and would have been in considerable danger if he had objected. It would be reading a lot into the embroidered stitches to be certain that such a sense of coercion is intended, but perhaps there is a hint in Harold's somewhat contorted and unnatural posture. Could this be to indicate that he is being pulled in two directions, experiencing some internal conflict between what he is promising on the holy relics and his future ambitions? Perhaps, although it may just be the awkward pose of a man trying to reach out to two pedestals that are slightly too far apart for comfort, especially as it is not certain that he had decided by this point that he would attempt to take Edward's crown when the old king died. It has also been noted that Harold's fingers barely touch the reliquaries, a sign perhaps that his oath was not in earnest.

Such interpretations assume that Harold was not comfortable making this oath because it related directly to the English succession, but what if that were not the case? Harold could have been swearing loyalty to William in a general way. After all, the English crown was not in Harold's gift to promise anyway. By 1064 it is almost certain that King Edward (and the nobility of England) regarded Prince Edgar Ætheling as the rightful heir when the time came, not Duke William.

One further indication that perhaps Harold is acting under duress is what happens next. There is a sense that the oath having been made, Harold's departure swiftly follows, with the action very quickly moving on. The two Englishmen who are standing and watching Harold from beyond the reliquaries form a transition. One of them is fully engaged in the ceremony, pointing towards the inscription, with his face shown in three-quarters and perhaps looking somewhat concerned or quizzical about events. The second man, while also looking towards Harold, is doing so over his shoulder, with his body twisted away from the scene. He seems poised, even anxious, to leave. Immediately after him a ship is very actively being made ready to sail.

The Tapestry seems to be showing Harold leaving France as soon as possible after this significant event. William of Poitiers, however, directly contradicts the idea of an abrupt exodus. He says that on the return of William and Harold from Brittany, 'the Duke kept his favoured guest with him a little longer before letting him go, laden with gifts which were worthy both of him [Edward] by whose command he had come and him [William] whose honour he had come to augment'. Eadmer of Canterbury, on the other hand, is more succinct, again suggesting a quicker leave-taking: 'when all this [the oath-swearing] had been done, he took his nephew and returned home'. So the historical sources allow for either timescale of events.

Several do agree that one of the results of Harold's expedition, and perhaps the main objective of his voyage overseas and his reward for swearing the oaths, was that his nephew Hakon was released and allowed to return to England with him; the other hostage, Wulfnoth, remained in Norman captivity for many years. The Anglo-Saxon at the water's edge eager to journey home, or one of the men on the boat, might be Hakon, but there is nothing in the Tapestry to confirm this.

The Bayeux Tapestry progresses quickly from this point to show Harold back in England – a somewhat changed and chastened man, perhaps, compared with the figure who had set out from Bosham several scenes previously. He has gone through many trials, and we, the viewers, have learnt much about him and his personality. Or, at least, much has been communicated by the vibrant imagery and taciturn commentary that accompany his adventures. We are now about to discover what happens to him when he reaches home, and what kind of reception he receives from his countrymen.

CHAPTER 8

HAROLD BECOMES KING

Once Harold has sworn the oath he is able to return home, where he has a reunion with King Edward. In the autumn of 1065, unrest breaks out in Northumbria, with the rebels demanding that Earl Tostig – Harold's brother – be ousted. King Edward delegates Harold to deal with the situation, and he concedes to the rebels' demands. Tostig is furious and sets off overseas to gain support. Shortly afterwards, the king falls ill, and by early January 1066 he is dead. England now faces likely invasion from both north and south, with the nobility choosing Harold over Edgar Ætheling as the candidate who can best protect the kingdom. No sooner is the old king buried than the new one is crowned, and with that a comet – interpreted by some as a harbinger of approaching catastrophe – is seen in the skies.

Harold is soon in England again, as the Bayeux Tapestry text informs us: hIC hARoLD DVX REVERSVS EST AD ANGLICAM TERRAM (Here Duke Harold returned to English soil). This inscription begins above the heads of the men watching him swear on the reliquaries, then pauses as a ship takes up the full depth of the main frieze, and concludes on the other side of the Channel as Harold reaches home. It is a clever way of combining text and image to enhance the narrative.

There are no firm dates for when all this took place because the documentary references to Harold's continental expedition are not precise, and even, as noted, somewhat contradictory as to whether he remained in William's company after the Breton campaign or very quickly decamped from the perilous pleasures of the ducal court. It is most likely that the events shown happened in 1064, and certainly no later than the end of 1065. If the Anglo-Saxon Chronicle's chronology can be relied on, then Harold has to be back in England a lot earlier than the end of 1065, in fact before Lammas, the first harvest festival of the year, celebrated at the start of August. This is because the Chronicle records that he had an estate prepared in Wales at that time in order to host a hunting party for King Edward.

Harold's return to England (Scene 24) is depicted in fairly perfunctory style in comparison to his earlier Channel crossing to France. Only one ship is shown, with all the men on board actively engaged in sailing tasks, in contrast with the generally rather passive attitude of Harold's men on their outward journey. Perhaps this reflects their desire to leave Normandy as quickly as possible. William of Poitiers describes a following wind and calm seas for the return, so they may have enjoyed a speedy and uneventful trip.

The ship is sighted by a lookout on the shore, who is standing (though the embroiderer has omitted to stitch his lower legs and he is left slightly floating) on a platform or balcony supported on pillars with bases lapped by the water. The balcony is attached to an elaborate, domed tower and people are staring out from its every window, observing the arrival of Harold's ship with considerable interest. Their faces are stylistically simple, with no obvious indication of emotion, yet there is something about them, and the way their heads are craned forwards at the windows, which is extremely expressive. Harold's return is clearly eagerly awaited. It is thought the single building represents an urban environment and street frontage, or even a major port with a quay. Dover or Southampton have been proposed as likely places where the ship makes landfall.

Something is going on in the upper border above the tower, with a dog-like creature seemingly gripping the beak of a long-necked bird in its jaws. This may be a repeat of the fable of the Wolf and the Crane shown earlier, with the wolf persuading the crane to remove a bone lodged in its throat, for which assistance the bird receives scant reward.

This is open to interpretation, but perhaps the inference is that Harold should not have helped William in Brittany. It is almost certainly some commentary on the events seen in the main frieze, though perhaps was worked later in the embroidery's production.

Following this, two men ride off away from the coast, and presumably one of them is Harold. He is probably the figure at the rear, protected from the elements by a large cloak and on the dark stallion, but his appearance is very different from before. His riding companion turns in his saddle to look back at him, continuing the theme of everyone's eyes being fixed on Harold and his actions in this section of the narrative. It would seem that what he has done and agreed to in Normandy is already well known. In the upper border are the Fox and the Crow once more (though separated), reminding us of the fable and the deceitful dealings it alludes to. But who is deceiving whom?

A meeting with the King

The two men are most likely riding to Westminster or Winchester, because the next scene (25) brings to mind the very first one in the Tapestry, with Harold and King Edward in conversation. The text above the action reads ET VENIT AD EDVVARDV REGEM (and he [presumably Harold] came to King Edward). Edward is shown seated on an elaborate chair or stool, with carved animal heads on either side and legs ending in clawed feet, like other thrones in the Tapestry. He is robed and wears a crown, and looks, if anything, in more robust health than at the beginning of the Tapestry, with a richly coloured flowing beard and an authoritative bearing that does not suggest a man struggling with old age or even at death's door. That said, he is holding a staff, which has been interpreted as a walking stick and therefore an indication of infirmity, though it could be a symbol of his office.

The building King Edward is seated in has a shallow dome, with what looks like a curtain or some sort of hanging suspended from the ceiling. Behind him is a guardsman with a mighty axe, and both men are emphatically pointing towards Earl Harold, who presents an interesting figure. He and his companion, also holding a large axe, seem to be outside Edward's chamber as they stand on a cobbled surface and are separated from the King by a column. Either they have not been physically admitted into Edward's presence completely, or perhaps metaphorically they have not been fully accepted into his trust or confidence. This sense of an uncomfortable distance between the two men is strengthened by Harold's stance. He appears very much a supplicant, with a deeply bowed head and palms outstretched in what looks like an apologetic, explanatory, almost begging pose. It is similar to the attitude Harold presented when he was in a less than ideal position at the court of Count Guy in Ponthieu. Harold has even lost his moustache, though that may be accidental rather than a deliberate attempt to belittle him.

It is worth recalling at this point the words that Eadmer of Canterbury puts into King Edward's mouth upon Harold's return to England: 'Did not I tell you that I knew William and that your going [to Normandy] might bring untold calamity upon this kingdom?' If that is the context here, then the King is pointing a stern finger of admonition at Harold for placing himself in danger in Normandy, and perhaps swearing an oath to something that he knew he could not, or would not, commit to in future. We would then be seeing an embarrassed Harold being rebuked like a naughty schoolboy. The most likely reason for Harold's trip was to press for the return of his kin who were hostages, which may or may not have been a project that King Edward supported. But whatever the initial purpose, the potential consequences of Harold having reached any sort of deal with William, or been forced into some form of obligation to him, could have displeased the King and have led to a division between him and Harold.

A slightly different take on this scene brings Edgar Ætheling back into the picture. If Edward (and for that matter the English nobility) had Edgar in mind as the man to succeed to the English throne, the King would have been justifiably aggrieved at hearing the report of the Norman adventure. Harold's actions in swearing to be William's man (if he had) would clearly run the risk of a disputed succession after

Edward's death, creating serious trouble for his kingdom. Ironically, William's involvement in the succession crisis benefited Harold in the short term, for it seemed that only he was strong enough to protect England from such a threat. Does the narrative, then, contain a small admission that there is another player in the story – Edgar – who is being overlooked in the simple Harold versus William version of events traditionally told? Underlying this would be the notion that Edward sent Harold to France to try to build alliances with non-Norman magnates, in order to counter any possibility of Duke William making a bid for the English crown and therefore give the Ætheling a chance to succeed to the throne. If so, then we might be seeing Harold apologizing for failing to reach such an agreement and instead falling into William's hands.

Of course, this conflicts with one other alternative interpretation, namely that King Edward actually sent Harold across the Channel to offer his crown to William, or at least give him some form of endorsement for his claim, which is the version of events promoted by the Norman historians. Harold would in that case have succeeded in his mission and there would have been no reason for him to be upbraided by King Edward on his return. Following that line of interpretation, Harold's posture can be seen as simply bowing in the royal presence, in accordance with court protocol. Interestingly, neither of the chronicle-writing Williams, Jumièges or Poitiers, has anything to say about this return meeting between Harold and Edward. So there is no way of knowing how this episode might have fitted into their pro-Norman line – though Harold being reprimanded for going to Normandy would seem incompatible with it.

While this is going on in the main frieze, in the borders the regular confronted pairs of animals have been replaced by beasts mixed up in a different pattern. Above Harold is a lion, coloured like him, facing a golden eagle below Edward. Another lion, coloured like Edward, faces the same way as the King. This irregularity continues for a while, and the reason for the break in the Tapestry's conventions is unclear. It might just be a confusion by the embroiderers, though the colouring of the lions (who face each other on either side of the eagle) seems purposeful.

A church fit for a king

Events move on very quickly indeed after the encounter between Harold and the King. The domed building Edward is seated in appears almost to overlap two towers next to an altogether larger structure, the newly consecrated Westminster Abbey (Scene 26). Running across the top of a long and complicated scene is the text hIC PoRTATVR CORPVS EADWARDI REGIS AD ECCLESIAM S[AN]C[T]I PETRI AP[OSTO]LI (Here King Edward's body is being carried to the church of St Peter the Apostle). So now, suddenly, King Edward is dead.

We have arrived at this crucial moment of Edward's demise very abruptly. So we should step back a little and assess the details before we delve into what has led up to it. Holding on to the shorter of the two towers is a precariously perched figure who is fixing a weathervane to the east end of the church of St Peter the Apostle – Westminster Abbey. Very little of the eleventh-century building commissioned by Edward remains today because it was largely demolished in 1245 to make way for a magnificent replacement under King Henry III (r. 1216–72), who was a devoted admirer of Edward the Confessor. Much scholarly debate has centred on how closely the detailed representation in the Bayeux Tapestry reflects what the building actually looked like in Edward's time. Excavations have revealed that it had a crossing tower and an east end with two bays, which could be implied by the presence of two windows in the Tapestry. The *Life of King Edward* describes a church with a crossing, a central tower and numerous ascending spiral staircases, which could also be consistent with what is represented in the Tapestry. The final structure had towers at the west end, which are not visible in the embroidery, but experts agree these were completed later.

What is not in doubt is that the Bayeux Tapestry depicts something that is sizeable and very new. We know the church has only recently been completed because we see one of the traditional finishing touches in the construction of a church prior to consecration – fixing the weathervane in place. Few other structures in the Tapestry are shown on quite such a scale and with such careful attention to detail. This is a building meant to impress and is not just part of the scenery. Emphasizing this even more forcefully is the fact that above the church, in one of the most beautifully executed pieces of embroidery in the whole Tapestry, is the hand of God, pointing downwards from Heaven directly at the nave in a gesture of blessing. It is a dramatic piece of art, with the hand seemingly ripping through the fabric of the sky (and almost of the Tapestry itself). Given that God is drawing our attention to the church, it is hard to overlook it. Perhaps this divine intervention is also to remind us of Edward's saintliness (though he was not canonized until 1161).

Edward's church would have been a statement building, both in size and appearance. It brought to England a European architectural style that had rarely been seen there at that time. William of Malmesbury emphasizes that the design was a 'new manner of building' for the country, and it was probably inspired by the great Norman abbey at Jumièges in Normandy. It also represents the beginning of a process of constructing ever larger churches in both England and Normandy after the Conquest. It is as if the Tapestry designer wants to remind us that King Edward, the man behind the church, was open to impressive ideas and innovations, and embraced a continental European, rather than a Scandinavian, outlook.

A funeral procession is approaching the church from the right. Eight men bear a bier draped in a heavily embroidered pall and with a cross at either end, on which lies a corpse wrapped in a shroud. Beneath the bier, two small figures, bell-ringers or choristers, accompany the solemn procession. Following behind are seven larger figures, most of whom, perhaps all, are tonsured, and are therefore clerics. Some are holding open books and others appear to sing, while the man in front is carrying what looks like a crozier and so is probably a bishop. It would not be surprising to find an important churchman in attendance here, because this is the funeral party of King Edward, taking his body for burial in Westminster Abbey. Edward died on 4 or 5 January 1066, having been too unwell to attend the dedication of his church on 28 December 1065. He had suffered a series of strokes during November and December, and there may have been a shared understanding among his immediate circle that it was only a matter of time before he would die.

The death of King Edward

In a very short space in the Tapestry, and with no warning at all, a vigorous-looking King Edward in conversation with Harold is now suddenly dead. This cannot have been as immediate a development as it appears here because almost half a year, perhaps more, would have elapsed between the two events if Harold had returned to England by August 1065, since Edward's death occurred at the beginning of 1066. The chronology becomes even more complicated as the Bayeux Tapestry moves on, because directly after the funerary procession, in another reversal in time, we are taken back to a living, though clearly ailing King Edward. The embroidery at this point is also divided into an upper and lower scene within the main frieze.

In the upper section (Scenes 27 and 28), the text tells us that hIC EADVVARDVS REX IN LECTO ALLOQVIT[VR] FIDELES (Here King Edward in bed addresses his faithful friends). The King is looking melancholy and ill, but is still strong enough to wear his crown. He is being supported or comforted by a figure behind him, while one of his hands touches that of another man. Watching them is a tonsured cleric, unusually shown with what looks like stubble on his face, who raises his palm. At the edge of the scene, at the foot of the bed, a woman weeps into her veil. Directly beneath this, accompanied by the words ET hIC DEFVNCTVS EST (and here he is dead), the King is being laid out, presumably having just passed away, while a robed priest administers rites and two servants attend to the corpse. There is so much to convey here that the first caption had to be fitted into the upper border.

In these few scenes the Tapestry designer has telescoped time, first leaping forward very briskly from mid-1065 to the end of that year and then reversing the order of events to show the funeral of King Edward before his death. It is notable that this curious vertical division in the narrative occurs at the second seam in the Tapestry, where the embroiderers had to join the second and third linen panels. The join, almost invisible, is just to the left of the divided hall and runs through the body of the man attending to the corpse on the left of the lower section. This could be another example of the designer following models he has seen in the Old English Hexateuch and other illuminations of a similar date, where events are shown on top of each other, or at least very close together. Perhaps with one panel ending and another about to begin, there was also some pressure to squeeze a lot of material in.

Another way of looking at this composition is that it is simply a depiction of the upper and lower storeys of a building (perhaps Edward's hall adjacent to the new church), with the King shown dying in the upper chamber and being laid to rest below. However, it seems a touch simplistic to view it in such a straightforward fashion. A more imaginative, and more likely, explanation is that the arrangement and reversal in time places emphasis on the link between the living King Edward and the completion of the great church he sponsored, while also highlighting the conjunction of the old king's death and the swift move by Harold to take the crown and secure the kingdom.

As for Harold's role at this dramatic moment, the doubling up of the scene also allows the designer to stress the moment of Edward's death and the events and people that surrounded it. The key matter of what the King did or did not say as he lay close to his end is critical to the understanding of the entire Conquest narrative. The Bayeux Tapestry does not enlighten us about the identities of the figures attending Edward in his final hours, but documentary sources offer guidance. The *Life of King Edward* gives the fullest account of who was in the room just before Edward's death, listing those present as 'the Queen [Edith], who was sitting on the floor warming his feet in her lap, her full brother Harold and Rodbert, the steward of the royal palace and a kinsman of the King, also Archbishop Stigand and a few more' (see pl. 10).

This description seems to fit the imagery in the Bayeux Tapestry so closely that it is hard to imagine that one has not influenced the other; they must at least be based on the same version of events. The *Life* even mentions that the assembled party had been roused from their sleep to wait on the King, so perhaps that accounts for the stubble on the churchman's face. According to the *Life*, Edward woke after being unintelligible for two days and suddenly described a vision from God telling him that all his leading officials were servants of the Devil and that within a year of his death, the kingdom would be in the hands of enemies. That chilling warning troubled some but was taken by others (especially Stigand) as deranged rambling. The King then stretched out his hand towards Harold and said, 'I commend this woman [Edith] and all the kingdom to your protection. Serve and honour her with faithful obedience as your lady and sister, which she is, and do not despoil her, as long as she lives, of any due honour got from me.'

If we take this description at face value, we can indeed see Edith there, sitting at the foot of the bed, Earl Harold touching hands with the King, the tonsured Archbishop Stigand looking on, and perhaps that is the steward Rodbert lending his support to make Edward's last moments comfortable. The phrasing of this momentous statement, seemingly telling Harold to take the crown (or at least to serve as protector of the kingdom), is curiously vague, and perhaps reflects the desire of the author of the *Life* to sit on the fence on this matter. This attitude is also typical of the Tapestry's narrative and some scholars have pointed out similarities in tone and approach between the two sources. Other documents, though not describing the King's final hours in such detail, are less equivocal about the nature of the offer. John of Worcester, for instance, tells us that 'Harold, son of Godwin, whom the King had chosen before his demise as successor to the kingdom, was elected by the primates of all England to the dignity of kingship', while the Anglo-Saxon Chronicle talks of Edward 'entrusting' or 'granting' the kingdom to Harold. Even Duke William's apologist, William of Poitiers, acknowledges that King Edward made a deathbed promise of his kingdom to Harold.

The use of words such as 'commending' and 'entrusting' the kingdom to Harold's protection clearly leaves room for interpretation. Perhaps Edward was in fact asking Harold to protect the land during the minority of his chosen successor, Edgar Ætheling. Such a reading makes it even more striking that Edgar is absent from these scenes, and the Tapestry as a whole.

Queen Edith

As for the cast of characters who were with Edward in his last hours, Harold we know all about now, Archbishop Stigand we will come back to shortly, and Rodbert, the steward, is an obscure figure. And then there is Edith. Though she is not named here, it is generally accepted that this must be a depiction of Queen Edith. This is her first (and only) appearance in the embroidery. She was queen, as the wife of King Edward, and also the sister of Earl Harold, and probably the patron of the *Life of King Edward*; she is even a possible (though unlikely) candidate for the patron of the Tapestry itself. She is also one of only three (clothed) women shown in the Tapestry. We've already met the first, the enigmatic Ælfgyva, and we'll come across one more later.

Edith, then, would appear to be the most significant female character in the entire Tapestry. Her depiction here may straightforwardly reflect the fact that she was present at this important event in the story, but it has also been proposed that she is shown symbolically too – to remind us of Edward's lack of an heir, perhaps, which is of course fundamental to the reason why matters reach such a crisis in 1066.

As already noted, women only feature in the main frieze at key moments in the story. Their appearance in the narrative catches the viewers' attention because of the very rarity of a female presence, and thus accentuates the importance of what is happening at that point. The fact that more women are not shown in the Tapestry is of course a reflection both of the story being told and of society at the time. The main narrative is concerned with military conflict and courtly politics, two areas where female participation would probably have been limited in reality. Despite women taking part in the annual re-enactment of the Battle of Hastings at Battle Abbey today, as part of the Saxon shield-wall and in the Norman cavalry and infantry, there is nothing in the Bayeux Tapestry that looks like a female fighter and none of the written sources refer to women in the battle.

Symbolic or not in terms of the Tapestry, Edith was an important figure in England. As well as being Edward's wife and a consecrated queen, she was a sizeable landowner in her own right. It has been calculated that on Edward's death she was one of the richest individuals in the land. She also provided a link between the Anglo-Danish faction in English politics and the crown, and must have had the ear of King Edward and provided him with counsel. The precise nature of their relationship is hard to judge, but their marriage was a long one, from their wedding on 23 January 1045 until Edward's death in early 1066. That said, Edith was put aside and sent to a nunnery in 1051 (at the height of the clash with Earl Godwin, whose daughter she was), but was then restored to court in the aftermath. She was apparently educated and eloquent, and the fact that she appears as a witness in various royal charters during Edward's reign suggests that she was involved in governance. In short, she mattered – but not enough, it seems, to be named here. Perhaps this is misogyny, or it may be another example of a reticence on the part of the Tapestry designer to bring in too many names of characters that might distract from the straight Harold versus William clash and require a more nuanced account. Edith notably had a role in a series of seismic contemporary events that are not dealt with at all in the Tapestry, events which the designer simply might not have wanted to engage with. But this missing part of the story is of great relevance to what happened in 1066.

Harold and Tostig

In 1063, before Harold's trip to France, he and his younger brother Tostig, the Earl of Northumbria, made a joint expedition to Wales to attack the Welsh king Gruffydd ap Llywelyn. Harold sailed with a fleet from Bristol, while Tostig took cavalry into the north. The mission was a success and ended with Gruffydd's head being detached from his body by a Welsh traitor and delivered to Harold, and thence to King Edward. Tostig and Harold, it might be assumed, would have been on good terms as brothers-in-arms in this victorious venture. Not so, according to Henry of Huntingdon, writing in the twelfth century, who talks of simmering jealousy between the two men over who stood higher in the King's affections. By his account, this leads to a brutal episode, when Tostig went to Hereford and interrupted preparations by Harold's servants for a royal feast by killing and dismembering the servants and gruesomely making their remains part of the banquet. This story is not paralleled in any other source, and is perhaps just an invention by Henry of Huntingdon, so it is hard to know whether the two brothers were quite so ill-disposed towards each other in reality.

What certainly did happen is that in the second half of 1065, discontent at what was felt to be Tostig's heavy-handed rule in Northumbria led to rebellion. It is generally thought that Tostig was attempting to establish southern laws (in other words, King Edward's laws) in the north, highlighting the fact that England was still very much a divided kingdom, as it had been during the partition between Anglo-Saxons and Danes under King Edmund Ironside and King Cnut. The north was to some extent semi-autonomous, with Edward's court rarely venturing there. The revolt may have been prompted, and was at least preceded, by the murder in 1064 of a key northern noble, Gospatric, a crime in which Queen Edith herself was implicated. Details are sketchy, but it does suggest that Edith was acting in Tostig's interests. The rebels marched on York in October 1065 and elected Morcar, brother of Earl Edwin of Mercia, as their new leader in place of Tostig.

The rebellious Northumbrians continued south and it was agreed at a royal council that Harold should go to meet them and try to negotiate. The rebels reiterated that they would no longer accept Tostig. King Edward wanted to challenge and suppress them, but Harold argued against this and his view won through, with the result that Tostig was deposed and then exiled, with Morcar taking his place in Northumbria. Tostig, unsurprisingly, saw this as an unforgiveable betrayal, and both Edith and King Edward were distraught at the turn of events. Ultimately, this has consequences for the Conquest story because Tostig later allied himself with the Norwegian king, Harald Hardrada, and invaded England just before Duke William of Normandy landed. It is not clear why Harold turned against Tostig in this situation. One possibility is that it was simply because of the enduring bad blood and jealousy between them (see pl. 12), or, more likely, Harold was seeking a practical solution to end a rebellion that could have split the country in two when he knew that unity was needed. Another suggestion is that he was already bidding for the crown, and this move would bring the Mercians and important northern nobles to his side.

In a perhaps not unrelated development, at some point around this time Harold married Ealdgyth, sister of Morcar (and widow of the decapitated Gruffydd ap Llywelyn), and may even have had a son or sons by her, further cementing his links to the Mercians. Harold had a long-standing 'Danish marriage' (often interpreted today as concubinage, but more likely a wife outside Christian wedlock) with a woman called Edith Swanneck, which had resulted in several children. The union with Ealdgyth was a more formal arrangement, which would presumably have ruled out any possibility of Harold marrying a daughter of William of Normandy (as suggested by some of the chroniclers), although at this time wives could be 'set aside' or even divorced. What is apparent, whichever way it is interpreted, is that Harold was politically astute, had gravitas and was ultimately ruthless.

This all happened in the autumn and early winter of 1065, and is clearly of significance in the broader picture, but we see nothing of it in the Bayeux Tapestry. It seems to be a deliberate omission. Given that the story includes the drama of a violent rebellion, it is surprising that a way was not found to include it, particularly as it could be interpreted as Harold rather cynically manoeuvring, even at his own brother's expense, to gain support for his intended usurpation of the crown, which would suit the Tapestry's message if it was following a pro-Norman line. Though, put brutally, it is also possible that events in the north may have mattered little to the southerners who were probably responsible for producing the embroidery and whose eyes and interests were directed more towards continental Europe.

Another consideration is the importance the Tapestry seems to attach to telling its story in terms of the straight duality of the clash between Harold and William. Including an account of the rebellion in Northumbria would have involved the narrative of Tostig forming an alliance with Harald Hardrada of Norway to invade England, and that might not have been an angle the Tapestry designer wanted to get involved with.

The last testament

Why would the dying King Edward have decided to make Harold his heir at this point, if he still harboured ambitions that the young Edgar would succeed him? Henry of Huntingdon tells us that after Edward's passing 'some of the English wanted to elevate Edgar the Ætheling as king', so it was not completely out of the question that he could have succeeded Edward. Perhaps the ageing King recognized that circumstances had changed in the last years of his reign, and, given what he knew of Harold's trip, he now thought it inevitable that the Normans would invade England if the crown was not offered to William. If so, it would have become obvious to him that only Harold and the Godwin power base (coupled now with the Mercian connection and support from other northern lords) could guarantee that his kingdom would be in a strong enough position to resist a Norman incursion, or perhaps avert the possibility of it happening in the first place. Harold may even have calculated this outcome and engineered the whole situation when he made his trip to France, ostensibly with the aim of freeing the hostages but ensuring that William would threaten England; then, back on home soil, he would be seen as the only man who could stand up to the Normans.

An alternative view is that Edward appointed Harold protector of the kingdom, and that he had in mind some sort of caretaker government that would support Edgar until he was politically astute and battle-hardened enough to fend off external aggression. Edgar might also have been thought too foreign, not in terms of his English lineage, which was undeniable, but because he had been brought up at the Hungarian royal court since birth, a decade before. In which case he could perhaps not guarantee the support of the English elite, who were distrustful of outsiders – especially after 1051 when King Edward's apparent preferment of foreigners led to the clash with the Godwins.

It is certainly significant that neither Tostig nor Edgar are referred to in this key episode. The Bayeux Tapestry writes them out of the narrative completely, concentrating solely on the actions of Harold. This makes everything simpler to understand of course, particularly as we move on to what happens after Edward's burial.

The old king died on the night of 4/5 January 1066, and his funeral took place on 6 January. Harold was crowned, according to the documentary sources, the day after Edward's passing, so the same day that Edward was buried. Although Harold was not the only possible contender for the crown, he must have had significant backing among the Anglo-Saxon nobility to be able to assume Edward's place so quickly, as the Tapestry next shows (Scene 29). Here the inscription reads hIC DEDERVNT hARoLDo CORONA[M] REGIS (Here they gave Harold the King's crown), and it is placed above three figures who stand outside the palace in which Edward has recently breathed his last. Harold is surely the man on the right (though his moustache is less obvious than usual), holding an axe and looking at two men, one of whom is also holding an axe while the other extends an arm to proffer a crown. It does not much resemble the crown that King Edward was wearing in the previous scene, but a crown it clearly is. There is no indication who these other two men are, but they must be high-ranking figures, almost certainly representatives of the Witan, the council of the great and good of the land. This would be consistent with those documentary sources which recorded that Harold was elected by the leading men of England.

William of Poitiers, however, has a rather different take on matters, noting that 'on that sorrowful day when the best of kings was buried and the whole nation mourned his passing, he [Harold] seized the throne with the plaudits of certain iniquitous supporters and thereby perjured himself'. Could the two men presenting the crown to Harold be these iniquitous supporters, who are complicit in a hurried coup to grab the crown before anyone can prevent them? Either reading is possible; the Tapestry lets us make our own choice, although the scenes that follow suggest Harold did have considerable support. And whatever the circumstances, Harold does not seem to have hesitated in seizing the opportunity.

We are immediately taken to the next scene (30), where Earl Harold is now King Harold. He sits resplendent on a throne in a shallow-domed hall flanked by two towers reaching right up into the upper border, not entirely dissimilar to the chamber where King Edward received him on his return from Normandy. He is shown frontally, wearing a crown, which does now look like the one Edward was wearing in his final hours, and holding the insignia of royalty, the orb and sceptre. Two men to one side seem to be handing him a sword or brandishing it in his direction, probably the sword of state which is being presented to him. To Harold's right stands Archbishop Stigand, named in the caption directly above his head and shown fully robed and facing out of the Tapestry. An inscription above Harold is unambiguous: hIC RESIDET hAROLD REX ANGLORVM (Here sits Harold the King of the English). So Harold has been crowned. From here on the Tapestry recognizes him as king, referring to him as such on several further occasions. This is crucial, for as far as the inscriptions on the Bayeux Tapestry are concerned, Harold is the legitimate monarch.

The speed with which Harold was crowned following the death of Edward is interpreted in a negative fashion by William of Jumièges, as well as by William of Poitiers, who both see Harold's immediate assumption of power as evidence of usurpation. That said, Edward had been ailing for some weeks, so it would not be surprising if plans were already in hand for his replacement (see pl. 4), and there are other examples of coronations at the time taking place with little delay. Furthermore, on King Edward's death England faced dire threats, not only from Normandy, but from Scandinavia also. England's elite would have wanted the security of being led by a king with authority and an accomplished military leader. The timing was also in Harold's favour. It was common for coronation ceremonies to coincide with major Christian feasts; Edward had conveniently died at Christmastide, so why wait? And the combination of the dedication of Edward's great new church together with his apparently impending death would have meant that all the leading men in the country would have been gathered in Westminster, and it would make practical sense for Harold to be crowned king without delay. But how does Edgar fit into all of this? Harold may have intended to hold the throne for him, but was then persuaded (or persuaded himself) to take the crown in his own right. Could Archbishop Stigand have had a role in this?

Stigand was an important figure in the political landscape but has not featured in the Bayeux Tapestry up to this point. He was an ally of the Godwins, though not so close that he accompanied them in their banishment from England in 1051. He was made Bishop of Winchester in 1047, and after mediating between King Edward and Earl Godwin in 1052 was elevated to Archbishop of Canterbury. New archbishops usually travelled to Rome to receive a pallium (a scarf-like vestment signifying the status of their office) from the Pope. Stigand did not do so immediately, perhaps fearing he might not have received a warm welcome as he controversially held two ecclesiastical sees simultaneously (Winchester and Canterbury). He was not unique in this, and he did receive the pallium later from another Pope, Benedict X, who held office only briefly (1058–59) and was deposed as a usurper. Stigand retained his position for a few years after the Norman Conquest, before being himself deposed in 1070 by papal legates, no doubt to the approval of King William.

Stigand's first appearance in the Bayeux Tapestry in this scene would accord with the version of events offered by William of Poitiers (and others), who stated that it was Stigand who performed the coronation of King Harold on 6 January 1066. It would also fit neatly with a theme of usurpation, by having a usurping king being crowned by an archbishop who wore the pallium of a usurping pope. In fact, by 1072–77, when the Bayeux Tapestry is likely to have been made, Stigand had also been deposed. Seen in that way, Stigand's presence seems an immediate stain on Harold's reign.

However, many modern historians tend to favour the account by John of Worcester who says that it was Archbishop Ealdred of York who crowned Harold king. Ealdred was also guilty of pluralism and was initially denied his pallium by the Pope, but that decision was later reversed when he agreed to give up his second see of Worcester, so he would have cast less of a shadow on Harold's worthiness for the throne. And yet Ealdred is neither named nor shown in the Tapestry. Either the designer is getting his facts wrong, or perhaps is showing that Stigand was present at, but did not actually officiate over, the coronation. After all, if the Bayeux Tapestry was made in Canterbury, it was within Stigand's see and he was an important churchman and magnate, so perhaps it was important to the Tapestry's designer that he was included.

The text in the embroidery does not specifically state that Stigand placed the crown on Harold's head, and he does not appear to be conducting such a ceremony. The Tapestry's scene of Harold's coronation is surprising in that it does not explicitly show him being crowned at all, and neither does the inscription specify this. Some scholars therefore argue that what is being depicted is actually an acclamation, with the king's loyal subjects praising the new monarch as he sits in state in his regalia; in other words, this could be some time after the coronation itself. A possible way of glossing over the speed of Harold's succession following the death of Edward would be to view this as an occasion later on in 1066, when the people came to honour their king.

One line of thought is that Stigand promoted the idea of Harold as successor to King Edward when it became clear that Duke William had aspirations towards the English throne, and that the candidate with stronger claims in bloodline terms, Edgar Ætheling, was too inexperienced to be able to command an effective resistance against such a threat. Stigand did briefly back Edgar as possible king after the

Battle of Hastings, but then switched his support to William. However, it was Ealdred, not Stigand, who crowned the Norman victor as king. So, as with much of the Bayeux Tapestry, Stigand's presence here can be interpreted in different ways.

As for Harold's accession, a fair cross-section of both English and Norman written sources broadly seem to acknowledge that he did have a legitimate claim to the crown. There is a general acceptance that King Edward may well have made him a deathbed promise, and there is also reasonable support for the idea that the English nobility respected this. But from the Norman point of view, however strong Harold's claim might have been, he was still breaking his sworn and solemn oath, and was thus a usurper and a perjurer. And that perspective is fundamental to William's justification for invading England and unseating Harold.

If this scene is one of acclamation rather than coronation, it might also explain the presence of the crowd outside, to the right of the king's chamber (Scene 31). Five men, huddled together and separated from the hall by a tall, slender tower (perhaps the hall's outer walls and reaching up into the upper border), are standing on cobbles, indicating they are outside and not in Harold's immediate stately presence. They apparently are looking in on the event taking place inside through an open door or archway, and all adopt a similar posture, staring at Harold. Rather than pointing at him, their raised arms and open palms convey a sense of praise and wonderment. Perhaps these are the ordinary citizens of London honouring the new occupant of the throne; they are certainly craning their necks forwards to get a good look.

A fiery omen

Another tight group of five men – or perhaps the same ones – appear in the following scene (32), facing in the other direction, with a sixth man standing slightly in front of them. They are most definitely looking at something intently and this time are pointing, but not at Harold; their eyes and fingers are firmly directed towards something in the sky above them. ISTI MIRANT STELLA[M] (These men marvel at the star) is what the Tapestry text tells us, and immediately follow-ing the inscription is the 'star' they are gazing at, high up in the upper border, as no doubt it was high in the sky in reality. A sunflower-like orb trailing fiery tails in its wake forms a dramatic depiction of what was undeniably a dramatic event at the time.

Halley's Comet is named after the famous English astronomer Edmond Halley, who established its average 76-year cycle of appear-ance in the Earth's skies in 1682. In 1066, the comet would have been visible in late April and early May, in other words a few months after King Harold's January coronation. The Anglo-Saxon Chronicle vividly describes the event: 'a sign such as men never saw before was seen in the heavens. Some men declared that it was the star comet, which some men called the haired star.' It was an astronomical phenomenon that transfixed people throughout western Europe.

At that time comets were generally deemed to be associated with change, and often a portent of some evil occurrence, such as famine, plague or war. A recent study of medieval comet sightings has found that they are recorded in the Anglo-Saxon Chronicle eleven times between the seventh and eleventh centuries, and on nine of these occasions their appearance was interpreted as a dire omen in the light of events that followed. This particular astronomical visitation came to be linked to Harold's downfall.

In 1066, the awestruck crowd in the Tapestry watching the comet could not know what would happen later that year, but of course the designer did. There is no obvious break between the two crowd scenes and it does seem they should be viewed together. With this skilful juxtaposition we see Harold's subjects quickly veering from acclamation to acute anxiety about the reign of their new king. This also lends more weight to the idea that the previous scene was not showing Harold's coronation, and that this section could feasibly all relate to April 1066.

So, the comet appears, breaching the upper border and disrupting, perhaps symbolically, the established order of the Tapestry. And the people look on and are worried. What about Harold, though – was he perturbed? Well, maybe. In the following scene (33) we see him, beneath the slightly superfluous caption hAROLD, seated on a throne. He is tilting his head and listening attentively to a messenger who has seemingly just entered the chamber, perhaps rushing in to inform the King of the ominous news of the heavenly arrival. He has one hand on the hilt of his sword, so there is a sense of an element of danger in whatever information he is delivering.

Harold could be learning of the comet, but it is just as likely that other, even more troubling dispatches are being imparted. Below this scene in the lower border is a fleet of ghostly ships – colourless, empty and unmasted, but clearly vessels floating on water.

Three options offer themselves as possible explanations for this curious detail. One is that it shows the marine force that Harold had mustered in readiness for a possible assault on the south coast from Normandy at anchor in London or off the Isle of Wight. He had to stand down this fleet later in the year, both because invasion seemed less likely when the seas were becoming too rough, and as provisions for his seamen were running low. The second option is that it represents the return of the embittered Tostig. In May 1066, and therefore shortly after the comet's sighting, Harold's brother landed on the Isle of Wight with a large fleet provided by Baldwin of Flanders. Tostig raided and then retreated eastwards in the face of Harold's forces. He met up with supporters at Thanet and moved north up the eastern side of the country, eventually fleeing to Scotland. That of course is not the end of his role in this story – he would return one more fateful time. A third possibility is that this is an eerie presage of William's invasion force, which is shortly going to make its appearance in the Tapestry, though in a much grander and more formidable fashion, and certainly a lot more threatening.

So the die is cast. Harold has made his move, for good or ill, and is now king. The arguments for and against his right to rule are, for the moment, over; at this point it is a question of whether he can resist anyone who might challenge his claim. If he can just survive for a year or two, debates about usurpation and legitimacy to rule might gradually become irrelevant should he be able to secure his reign and perhaps establish a dynasty with a son from his new Mercian union. However, the tang of perjury still hangs over everything, and we know what's coming, because we can smell it in the salty air that surrounds those ghostly boats beneath the throne. And with it, for now, any claim by Edgar Ætheling is also fading.

The scene ends with one of those extravagantly curvilinear trees. These have not appeared for a while, perhaps because of the rapid speed of events. It definitely feels that we have come to a moment of pause – a point at which any jongleur retelling the tale a few years after the Conquest would have stopped for an instant to let the enormity of the peril facing England and its crown sink in, and to allow his listeners, the audience viewing the Tapestry, to take a long look at the man who had seized the throne, and wonder at the wisdom of his actions.

CHAPTER 9

WILLIAM RAISES AN ARMY

News of Harold's accession to the throne is not well received in Normandy, where Duke William sees it as an act of usurpation and perjury. He quickly sets about building support for an assault on England, including seeking papal backing for the mission and convincing the Norman nobility that such an enterprise can succeed. William is able to bring together a fleet and a sizeable army, along with the necessary provisions and weaponry, all before the year is out. His fleet then sails in late September and makes landfall near Pevensey on the Sussex coast.

The next inscription in the Tapestry reads hIC NAVIS ANGLICA VENIT IN TERRAM WILLELMI DVCIS (here an English ship came into the land of Duke William), and below it (Scene 34) we see a small, lightly manned ship speeding across deep water with billowing sail. Conditions must have been reasonably good as the helmsman, whose head is almost licked by the protruding tongue of the beast's head carved on the stern post, appears to be engaged in a relaxed conversation with one of the crew. At the bow of the boat another man is preparing for landing, with one arm crooked to shield his eyes from sun or spray, or possibly shouting out, while with the other he probes for the bottom with a long pole.

This is a rather peaceful scene; there are no shields ranged along the ship's gunwales and nothing to arouse any sense of impending trouble. With this moment of apparent calm it feels as if the designer is allowing us a slight respite from the complexities of the preceding political wrangling, or perhaps a different embroiderer, with a lighter outlook on life, was responsible for this tableau. Even the birds and beasts in the lower border look less confrontational than earlier in the Tapestry.

Something unusual is going on in the top border, however, with a man on bended knee carrying a pole. It is not clear what he is up to, but he might be looking out across the sea that the ship is ploughing through, while also gesturing back in the general direction of Harold in the previous scene, though with an open palm rather than pointed finger. The ship itself breaks through into the upper border, with its sail and mast rising right up to the top of the linen. That's because the wavy lines of the sea dominate the lower portion of the main frieze, lifting the boat up into the centre. Such a deep sea has not been portrayed in sailing scenes before this, and there seems to be no obvious reason for it to take up quite so much space now.

The ship makes landfall, with a mariner leaping out barelegged and carrying the anchor through the shallows. Almost immediately, we come to another tree. This tells us that we have left England and arrived in Normandy. Differences in hairstyles between English and Normans seem to become less pronounced as the Tapestry progresses, so it is harder to be sure of the nationality of the men in the boat, but as the text says that it is an English ship it is presumably carrying English sailors, perhaps merchants. It seems safe to assume that someone on the ship is bringing news of Harold's coronation to Duke William. The documentary sources do not provide much information about how William heard of developments across the Channel, though William of Poitiers explains that 'unexpectedly there came a true report, the land of England was bereft of her King Edward, and her crown was worn by Harold'.

But how unexpected was this? To what extent was Duke William anticipating that Harold would turn against him, despite the pact that he probably believed had been agreed between them as they soldiered together in Brittany? Had William become convinced of Harold's honourable nature on their campaign? Did he accept that Harold had some claim to the throne, and how much would he have known about what was going on behind the scenes at court in England? It is all debatable, and of course it is not known what, if anything, Harold discussed with William about the candidates for succession in England when he was at the ducal court. If William believed that King Edward had settled on Edgar Ætheling as his successor, then perhaps Harold's move would have come as a shock. Harold, after all, did not have a particularly strong claim through lineage, and William might have assumed this ruled the Godwin clan out of the running. That said, there was no such thing as a 'designated heir' at the time – what counted in England in the eleventh century was the support base a candidate could rely on, together with their personal determination, whether directly belonging to the royal line or not.

William builds his forces

The case for William's invasion was founded on the apparent promise made to him by Edward the Confessor, reinforced by Harold's oath-swearing, but there is a little more to it than that. It has been noted that William made his son Robert his heir (in Normandy) as early as 1063. That was unusual for Norman dukes, who normally waited until they were approaching death before declaring who should succeed them. It has been seen as evidence that William was preparing for a risky invasion campaign several years before events fell into place, and was making sure his affairs were in order in case things did not turn out well for him. It is probable that he was anticipating taking the throne of England when it became vacant, perhaps considering it predestined, or a sacred mission. One interesting interpretation of the whole Tapestry is that it should be seen as a religious story, with William's adventure essentially being a crusade to punish the oath-breaker Harold and reform the wicked practices of the English church, as exemplified by Stigand. Fresh purpose would have been added when William received the support of the Pope for his mission, but this comes later.

The Bayeux Tapestry does not enlighten us about William's precise thoughts when he discovered that Harold was now on the throne, but clearly he was not happy and it seems he very quickly began readying for war. The text above the next scene (35) tells us that HIC WILLELM DVX IVSSIT NAVES EDIFICARE (Here Duke William ordered ships to be built).

Duke William is seated in a hall on an elaborate chair with a footstool. A messenger, presumably bearing the news of Harold's accession, is on the left, knees slightly bent, arms outstretched towards William. The Duke has his head turned not towards the bearer of bad tidings but the other way, at another seated figure, who is shown looking directly out of the Tapestry – perhaps a sign of a man being decisive. From his tonsured head, this is recognizably a churchman, and obviously a man of status as he is seated in the company of the Duke and on a similar chair. William is shown in profile, which is perhaps to point out that his companion is the more important character at this moment in the story.

That clerical figure has one open hand raised towards William, while with his other arm he points away, either to another man standing immediately next to him, or onwards out of the building. A third person, looking back at the two who are seated, holds a T-shaped axe and is similarly gesticulating away from the throne room and on towards the next scene.

The generally accepted view is that William's seated companion is none other than his half-brother Odo, Bishop of Bayeux. The other man, thought to be a carpenter because of his woodworking tool, is assumed to be rushing away on his master's orders to marshal his men to begin building the required ships. There is a sense of an almost immediate flow of events, from the news reaching William's ear to the issuing of the order to construct a fleet, with Bishop Odo (if it is he) advising on this brisk and direct course of action. It can be read two ways – either William was not expecting Harold to betray him and so had made no preparations and is now responding instantly, or he had anticipated this outcome, and had his carpenters and resources on stand-by ready to start building the ships he would need as soon as he received confirmation of the treachery across the Channel.

William of Poitiers provides some insight into what might have taken place, and what is not shown in the Bayeux Tapestry. First, he tells us that Duke William took counsel with his advisers 'and determined to avenge the wrong by arms and in arms to claim his inheritance'. However, he also states that William's magnates were not initially keen on the project, warning him that it was too hazardous and beyond the resources of Normandy. But William did not listen to these objections, 'as if he knew in advance by divine inspiration what should and should not be done'. So preparations for war commenced. A second interesting comment from Poitiers is that Harold, predicting that William would respond to his assuming the throne in some way, had cunningly sent spies to Normandy. One of these spies was captured and tried to pretend he was not engaged in any subterfuge, but the Duke, with a swaggering flourish, sent the man back to Harold with the message that 'he [Harold] need fear nothing from us, but pass the rest of his days in peace, if in the space of one year he does not find me in whatever place he thinks to be most secure'.

This apparently threw William's magnates into a state of anxiety over the impossibility of readying a fleet in such a short space of time, in addition to the danger of taking on such a wealthier and better-resourced land. William, to paraphrase, would have none of this and told them to take courage because they had right on their side. But we see nothing in the Tapestry of these deliberations and discussions between William and his great lords concerning the wisdom of such a course of action. All we are shown is Bishop Odo seemingly encouraging or exhorting the Duke to forge ahead with the assault. Odo's prominent role in events here makes sense if he was behind the production of the Bayeux Tapestry, because he can then take some of the credit for what would prove to be the correct course of action and also shows him to have had faith in William. By not showing any other key players in the decision-making, the Tapestry avoids having to incorporate the awkward scenario of magnates who then went on to fight with the Duke at Hastings appearing a little lily-livered and hesitant at the start of the great adventure. So Odo comes out of it well, no one else has cause to take offence, and William is seen to be taking advice rather than acting entirely unilaterally. All in all, it is a more diplomatic telling of events than that by William of Poitiers, one that allows Duke William, Bishop Odo and his fighting comrades to emerge from the situation with their reputations intact or even enhanced.

From this point on until the end of the embroidery, Odo appears more frequently. It might perhaps be thought strange that he has not featured more regularly in earlier sections, but that could be explained by a theory that proposes that Odo is being set up as the new hero to Harold's anti-hero. And that opposition only really begins to take shape once Harold has perjured himself, which has now – in the eyes of the Normans – happened. The Bayeux Tapestry has been seen very much in terms of a two-act drama. The first act, ending with Harold taking the throne, sets the scene for the rest, with the consequences playing out from here on and Odo coming into view more clearly. It therefore seems timely to sketch out Odo's history a little more fully.

It is likely that Odo was born in the early 1030s, in Normandy. His father was Herluin de Conteville, a Norman lord, and his mother was Herleva, also the mother of Duke William. Odo probably became Bishop of Bayeux in late 1049 or early 1050, which is before the canonical age and suggests that his half-brother William must have promoted him for the role when so young. Not much is known about what he did between then and the 1066 campaign, and the main evidence for his part in the invasion of England comes from the Bayeux Tapestry. Following the Conquest, he became a key figure in England as King William's deputy and Earl of Kent, and his treatment of his new subjects was criticized in contemporary sources for being overly harsh. The modern view is more nuanced and closer to Orderic Vitalis's assessment of Odo's life and career; he noted that his 'vices were mingled with virtues, but he was more given to world affairs than to spiritual contemplation'. This was not untypical at the time for an aristocrat promoted to senior clerical rank.

As ever, the Tapestry does not really grant us much of a window into the character of the man himself, though the air of authority that he must have exhibited to be so quickly elevated post-Hastings is evident here. In this scene he appears both trusted and decisive, with the Duke seemingly listening to him closely and heeding his advice. After this conversation Odo begins to replace Harold as the hero of the hour in the Tapestry; both the Duke and the carpenter are clearly staring directly at him, much as all eyes have been trained on Harold in the preceding scenes.

Fleet work in the forests

The next scene (36) shows Norman woodsmen and carpenters felling trees and shaping the timber into planks. This part of the story is also told by Baudri of Bourgeuil, the poet who described an embroidery that sounds similar to the Bayeux Tapestry in a work dedicated to William the Conqueror's daughter. He refers to forests being cut down, and ash, oak and ilex (holly) being felled, while pine was uprooted. No trees in the Tapestry are shown being uprooted, but we do see the woodsmen using long, two-handed axes to chop them down.

Work then progresses to trimming the logs into workable timber. The vignette of the man planing and shaping a plank as he stands astride it, with piles of planks already worked behind him, is one that the designer seems to have invested some time in. It is also very similar to scenes showing the construction of Noah's Ark in certain Anglo-Saxon illuminated manuscripts. The Tapestry's depiction includes the interesting detail of the woodsman using a notch in the top of a tree trunk to support the piece of timber as he works on it. Clearly, the correct production of these planks was of great importance for building the boats being assembled in the following scene.

The shipbuilding scene is similarly detailed, though the intermediate stages of manufacture are not shown. Work is being carried out on two craft, one above the other in a vertical arrangement. In the lower half of the frieze, two craftsmen with long beards (perhaps because they are older or more experienced) are bent over a boat and appear to be concentrating closely on what they are doing. Above them, three more men labour, with one worker gesticulating, perhaps angrily, at another. A sense of individual personality emerges, and the various tools the men are using are carefully depicted and indicate the different kinds of work in progress. In the uppermost image one man holds a T-shaped axe and another possibly a drill, while the bearded men below are using a mallet and hand axe. It is not clear whether two boats are being worked on separately, or two separate stages of construction of the same craft are represented, but in these scenes we are probably being shown the story of shipbuilding from living tree to final ship, albeit in a somewhat abbreviated form.

When the ships are finished, they are dragged into the water by five barelegged men hauling on ropes. It is a reminder that this type of vessel was small and shallow draughted, and so could be handled and moved without needing deep water or a built harbour. Two of the boats have carved animal heads attached to the prow posts and all have a line of oar-ports along the gunwales, presumably added in a final phase of carpentry as they are not visible on the ships under construction. As confirmation of what is going on, the caption accompanying this image reads hIC TRAhVNT[VR] NAVES AD MARE (here ships are dragged to the sea).

This short section is full of illuminating details for analysis, and also raises several issues. Using greenwood, freshly felled as the Tapestry implies, has been seen as a questionable method for building ships as it would not have lasted as well in water as seasoned timber. Pre-felled timber supplies could have been used up first, but it does seem to have been standard practice in medieval carpentry to use greenwood for shipbuilding because it was easier to work. Archaeological examples also suggest a tradition of greenwood working. The bigger question is how large a fleet William was attempting to bring together, and whether he constructed it all entirely from scratch, as the Tapestry seems to suggest. Accurate numbers, as with most statistics from the medieval period, are hard to come by. William of Jumièges tells us that the Duke 'hastily built a fleet of 3,000 ships', which seems unlikely because a task of that magnitude could never have been completed quickly. Another, later, source, Geoffrey Gaimar, who was writing in the mid-twelfth century, suggests an even less realistic figure of 11,000 ships, whereas the chronicler Wace gives us the suspiciously precise number of 696. Historians are generally happy to work with a figure of about 600 to 700.

Even that lower figure represents a very sizeable logistical and construction challenge, particularly given the timescale involved. The details of what was achieved have exercised academics considerably over the years, and some amazingly meticulous research has been carried out to try to understand just what might have been feasible given the technological, financial, ecological and time constraints that Duke William was operating within.

The fleet, according to various sources, was ready and gathering together in August 1066. Even if William sprang into action immediately on hearing the news of Harold's coronation in January, that would still give him only six or seven months (maximum) in which to get his invasion project off the ground before the weather changed. It is unlikely therefore that the entire fleet was newly built during that period. The challenges would have been manifold. Not only would the Normans have had to deforest large swathes of their lands to provide the trees (assuming they all needed to be felled if sufficient stockpiles were not available), but they would also have had to transport all the timber to shipyards (again a significant task), and then recruit and resource a substantial force of experienced shipwrights, along with unskilled labourers, to actually build the boats. One estimate is that 8,400 workers would have been required to labour for three months to get the job done. Baudri of Bourgeuil tells us that workers came from all over Europe to build the fleet, but even so, the numbers seem daunting, and indeed, William of Poitiers points out that Duke William's advisers were at pains to stress the difficulties involved in getting everything finished.

It is more likely that the Normans already had some sort of fleet, which they then augmented with further ships hired or purchased from other continental forces, notably Flanders. As noted above, a Flemish fleet had already been deployed against England earlier in the year under the banner of Harold's brother Tostig. Any additional craft required on top of this would have had to be built, and presumably this was a significant enough enterprise to warrant its inclusion in the embroidery.

What sort of ships were they? The boatbuilding scene in the Bayeux Tapestry shows planked vessels, likely clinker-built (with overlapping planks, though carvel construction, with planks butting up, is not impossible, if improbable), with raised prows and sterns (sometimes decorated), and rows of oar-ports along the gunwales. They look very much like so-called Viking ships that were typical across Europe at this time. Throughout the Tapestry, ships are seen under sail rather than being rowed, but presumably they had the flexibility of both modes of propulsion, with oars being used for close manoeuvring near to land or when the sea was still. Scale is hard to ascertain from the way they are represented in the Tapestry, but in terms of size relative to the carpenters working on them they look more like canoes than ships.

In the past few decades our knowledge of shipbuilding and seafaring in this period has been advanced enormously by archaeological finds of Viking Age ships. Particularly informative are the underwater wrecks discovered at Skuldelev in Denmark's Roskilde Fjord. The well-preserved craft found there have been excavated, raised and extensively studied, and have been dated to the eleventh century. Information derived from this research has been combined with findings from other Viking period ships to build and sail several fully functioning replica boats. This has produced fascinating insights into how these vessels would have operated on the high seas as well as on inland waterways.

Such boats would not have been huge – excavated examples vary in length, but the longest are less than 40 m (130 ft) long, and most ships of the day would have been much shorter. They were also narrow, probably not much more than 5–6 m (15–20 ft) across, though some vessels used for other purposes would have been wider and deeper. The excavated examples from Skuldelev show surprising variety. How much uniformity, if any, there was in the types of vessel that made up the Norman invasion fleet is a question that has been debated by historians, and depends of course to some extent on whether they were all built together or requisitioned for the task. Most probably they were a mixture of whatever craft were available (rather like the flotilla that rescued British troops from Dunkirk in the Second World War), but there may have been specific craft for specific tasks.

Wine for the warriors

Building the ships was only one element of the whole enormous logistical operation. William of Poitiers tell us, rather vaguely, that 'With admirable prudence, [Duke] William ordered the provision of ships, arms, men and supplies, and all other things necessary for war; almost all Normandy was devoted to the task, and it would take too long to describe the preparations in detail.' The Bayeux Tapestry provides some hint of the planning that Poitiers seems to have had neither the time nor the inclination to relate. In the next scene (37), pairs of men are shown carrying heavy suits of armour suspended from poles resting on their shoulders, along with bundles of swords, and spears, axes and helmets. These items may have been brought from a storehouse, possibly the small building with four slender columns depicted behind them. Ahead of them, two men visibly struggle to pull a heavy cart loaded with a huge barrel, topped by a row of helmets and bristling with spears. The caption above them reads ISTI PORTANT ARMAS AD NAVES ET hIC TRAhVNT CARRVM CVM VINO ET ARMIS (These men are carrying arms to the ships, and here they are dragging a cart laden with wine and arms).

Contained within this section of the embroidery is a wealth of information, providing a valuable opportunity for social historians to glean details about some of the more mundane aspects of daily life at the time. We learn something about the types of tools that were used for tree felling and woodworking. We see the care with which expensive arms and armour were transported, and that manpower rather than horses or oxen was used to haul the boats and carts. Perhaps men were more readily available, and cheaper, than draught animals, or this was thought to be the safest way to move valuable military equipment. Whatever the reason, the scene also provides evidence about the sort of carts used for transporting goods, with four wheels and raised, slatted sides. Finally, we can conclude that wine was of particular importance to the troops since it is so specifically referred to and clearly depicted. Wine is the only element of victuals shown, so it was obviously a cause of concern to the Normans that they travelled with enough to keep their goblets full throughout the campaign – and perhaps it was also a message to those looking at the Tapestry that William took good care of his troops.

Diverting though it is, this interlude is somewhat inconsistent with the Tapestry's narrative of big men performing great deeds, and also with the dramatic action of the military and naval scenes so far. Why are we being served up this little slice of detail? Presumably because assembling the necessary invasion fleet and supplies in such a short time and with so many players involved was such an enormous logistical challenge, and a seemingly unprecedented one. Other contemporary documentary sources also acknowledge the difficulties of marshalling the ships and soldiers, so there must have been a general awareness of the scale of the undertaking. But it was one that William himself was bullish about achieving. William of Poitiers tells us that in a rallying speech the Duke proclaimed: 'The problem of shipping will not prevent us, because we will soon have enough vessels.' With the benefit of hindsight we know the Norman invasion was possible because it happened, but at the time it must have seemed to many to be a foolhardy enterprise.

The practical, physical preparations were not the only element of the planning for the invasion in the first half of 1066. Spiritual preparation was also taken care of, and this appears to be broadly omitted from the Tapestry's narrative – or at least it is not obviously shown. According to Poitiers (who provides us with most detail for this period, from the Norman side), William petitioned the Pope for support for his venture, which was granted: 'Having sought the approval of the Pope and informed him of the enterprise he was undertaking, the Duke received through his favour a standard, which was a sign of the protection of St Peter, as a result of which he was able to march more confidently and safely against his adversary.'

Orderic Vitalis adds the information that William's request for the Pope's backing was based on Harold's alleged perjury, and that the Duke sent Gilbert, Archdeacon of Lisieux, to Rome to plead his case. Papal support for the Norman Conquest must have been hugely significant, and the exchange of correspondence with the Pope would have taken place at the same time as the ships were being built and the weaponry amassed, yet there is nothing in the Bayeux Tapestry to inform the viewer what was going on. In the following scenes there is a possible depiction of the papal standard, but it is far from clear or unambiguous. There is certainly no textual reference to the Pope in the Tapestry, and neither is there any embroidered scene to emphasize the fact that the Holy See was in favour of William's actions. Why not mention it, particularly when such pains have been taken to show the details of the logistical organization of the project?

Perhaps this is another example of the desire to present a more nuanced interpretation of the story to its intended audience, one that would not offend the sensitivities of the defeated English in the years immediately after the Conquest. Who would want to be reminded not only of being conquered by an invading force, but also of the fact that the enemy had God on their side? A more complex explanation is that it is a reflection of wider political concerns on the continent. Reactions across Europe to William's success in the years after the Conquest were contradictory – while there was admiration for his achievement and the Norman victory, there was also disquiet at the justification for the invasion and the level of violence committed against the English, as well as the potentially morally questionable role of the papacy in supporting it. And although William's relations with the papacy continued to be good immediately after the Conquest, there was a marked decline in cordiality later in his reign as the Pope insisted that King William pay homage and swear fealty to him, something that the Norman was not keen to agree to.

The scenes of preparation end shortly after the unhappy carters struggle to drag their huge barrel of wine, with one further figure more comfortably carrying a smallish sack over his shoulders. It is at this point that the next join in the linen sections falls, marking the end of the third panel. The first joining of panels resulted in a visible error in the alignment of the border lines, and the second came at the moment when King Edward was being laid to rest and the embroiderers may have been forced to squeeze material in. The third join has been made much more effectively, with the border lines matching up precisely and a small clear space between figures, and with no discernible impact on the content of the embroidery.

The Norman fleet sets sail

The next few scenes plunge us back into the progress of the campaign as armed horsemen ride towards the ships, now afloat. With their shields and spears slightly raised in their hands, they look poised for action. A long caption starts above their heads and runs throughout the following scene (38): hIC VVILLELM DVX IN MAGNO NAVIGIO MARE TRANSIVIT ET VENIT AD PEVENSÆ (here Duke William in a great ship crossed the sea and came to Pevensey). It is possible that the first of the riders, mounted on a dark stallion and carrying a pennant banner, is William himself, but there is nothing in the Tapestry to confirm this.

What is not mentioned or shown here is the delay and two-stage embarkation described by William of Poitiers. He tells how William's fleet gathered first at Dives-sur-Mer, a little to the east of Caen, and sat there for a while before moving east along the coast to Saint-Valery-sur-Somme in Ponthieu. William's original intention may have been to make a direct crossing from Dives to southern England, but if so he was forced to change his plans and seek shelter further up the French Channel coast when the weather turned against him.

Poitiers says the ships were detained for a month at Dives, and that some vessels were then lost through desertion and sinking before they reached Saint-Valery, though the Duke concealed these losses to maintain morale. He also notes that William forbade any sort of pillaging or ransacking of the countryside while his army was stranded by contrary winds at Dives, instead paying himself for sufficient provisions for his men. So perhaps the whole phase of preparation seen in the Tapestry was deemed to reflect well on the Duke, showing him to be a magnanimous, fair and painstaking lord, whose strength of leadership was such that he could keep his troops in order even in such testing conditions.

The fleet finally set sail from Saint-Valery on 27 September, voyaging through the night to reach Pevensey the next day. Despite the obvious difficulties and complications the enforced period of waiting would have given rise to, the designer simply shows a reasonably ordered sea crossing. It may not have been considered politic to dwell on potential disharmony in the ranks, nor to give any sense that God and nature were not completely on the side of William and his army.

We also do not see William's troops embarking, unlike when Harold set out from Bosham on his crossing to France. But the group of armed riders must have boarded the boats, as immediately after them, the fleet is sailing away across the water. In all, eleven ships are shown making the Channel crossing. Some are larger than others – probably an attempt to render them in perspective as a fleet stretching out across the water – and some contain both horses and men, others just men. The first ship we see holds ten horses, tightly packed in two groups facing each other, with only their heads showing above the gunwales. They are apparently calm and still, as the sailors actively tend the sails and direct the craft.

Several of the ships have decorative animal figureheads, and two have a line of kite-shaped shields arranged along the gunwales, while others have shields attached to their stern and prow only. All have a central mast and billowing sail in the Tapestry's characteristic triangular form, and some have oar-ports. They are all steered from the stern by a helmsman using a large rudder, who sometimes also takes hold of the end of the sail. In this impressive scene, which fills a sustained length of the embroidery, the ships are once more allowed to take over the upper border, with even the dividing line disappearing. This is a big set-piece moment in the story.

The loading and boarding of William's fleet would no doubt have been a difficult scene to depict in terms of the embroidery, so that may be why it is not shown. In reality, considerable speed and complex organization would have been required simply to assemble all the boats in the right place in the limited window offered by the tides. The task would have been further greatly complicated by having to load horses on the vessels – a problem that has been much discussed by researchers. The Bayeux Tapestry shows them sitting peacefully in the holds of the ships, but surely that must be a simplification. How would a single horse be loaded into a boat like this, let alone the estimated 2,000 horses that William took with him across the Channel? Experiments made with live animals and replica Viking ships have shown it is possible to load horses on to even a shallow-draughted vessel. Specialized horse transport craft may also have been involved, which were modelled on Byzantine designs in use in the Mediterranean. Knowledge of this type of vessel might have travelled with the carpenters who gathered from all over Europe to help build William's fleet.

In the 1050s the Normans had ventured into Sicily and southern Italy, which brought them into contact with new methods and military tactics, but whether these were employed in the invasion of England is open to debate. The Norman fleet probably consisted of a combination of specialized warships (in the event of meeting opposition at sea, though William was probably not anticipating having to engage in naval conflict) and deeper-draughted cargo ships for horses and other provisions, including the wine. It seems likely that some of the ships would have been better suited for the purpose of transport than others.

Although there is not much differentiation in the style of craft depicted in the Bayeux Tapestry, one does stand out. The ship in the middle of the fleet, beneath the word for Pevensey in the text, deserves closer attention. Fully visible and not overlapped by any other craft, it does appear to be the central focus of the scene, with deliberate emphasis placed on it in the overall design. Compared with the others it is also well defended, with shields arranged along its entire length. It may be William's flagship, the *Mora*, which was gifted to the Duke by his wife, Matilda. At the top of the mast is a cross-shaped frame, something not seen on any of the other boats. This, perhaps, is a depiction of William's papal banner. Alternatively, it has also been interpreted as a lantern, which would neatly correspond with the account of the sea crossing recorded by William of Poitiers. He tells us that, in order to avoid the risks involved in a landing by night at an unknown point on the English shore, William ordered that all the ships should anchor around his vessel and wait 'until a fire was lit at his masthead and they heard a trumpet call as signal to resume their voyage'. So the object shown at the top of the mast could be a device for the signal fire, with the trumpeter at the stern of the ship blowing on his horn to give the order for the journey to recommence. In the Bayeux Tapestry there is never any background sky colour other than the cream of the linen and it does not distinguish between day and night – even when Halley's Comet was streaming through the heavens – but we do know that the Channel crossing was made in darkness.

Landfall in England

And so the fleet finally reaches England (Scene 39). According to the Bayeux Tapestry, it was an uneventful voyage and was unopposed. After the ships have landed at Pevensey, the horses are sent ashore: hIC EXEVNT CABALLI DE NAVIBVS (here the horses leave the ships) is the caption above the disembarkation scene. This explicit reference to horses and the careful depiction of them in the Channel crossing suggests that their transport was an important element of the story. The fact that so many animals were successfully and safely carried across the sea was perhaps judged to be a particularly noteworthy achievement. Two horses, apparently none the worse for their trip, are being led off the ship by a barelegged groom in the water, while behind them the mast of a boat is lowered and presumably removed. Nearby is a fleet of unmasted and empty craft, none of which has a figurehead or any fittings; they look not much different from the ones lined up in the shipbuilding scene. There is a tradition that William ordered his beached ships to be broken up, to forestall any thoughts his men might have of making a hasty retreat back to Normandy. Could that be what we see here?

The upper border now resumes with its procession of birds and beasts after the interruption caused by the fleet. Here they all stroll purposefully in the same direction until they are rudely brought to a halt by a single bird poking its head between two of the Tapestry's typical diagonal lines at a somewhat startled-looking lion. No doubt this is to remind us that opposition is yet to come. Below the disembarking horses is a pair of confronted fire-breathing dragons.

The Norman troops quickly establish themselves on English soil (Scene 40), building their first camp at Pevensey. Today Pevensey is a peaceful village with an impressive castle on the East Sussex coast just a few miles from Hastings. Most of what is now visible of its castle dates from later medieval times, but some of the outer walls would have been there when William arrived, and it would have provided immediate shelter and a very convenient base for the invading force. Originally a Roman fortification, it was part of the shore defences against raiders in the fourth century AD, notably Saxons – a reminder that the 'English' were also newcomers once. In 1066 the sea would have come much closer to the defensive walls, as later drainage work has reclaimed some of the land. The castle is not shown in the Bayeux Tapestry, and it is not known if William was making specifically for it, but it is certain that he established himself there before going on to create a second base at Hastings.

It may seem odd that the Normans met with no opposition when they made first landfall in England, but King Harold was otherwise occupied and the local militia may have held back, waiting for reinforcements. As mentioned, according to John of Worcester, earlier in the year Harold had assembled a fleet and stationed it on the Isle of Wight to guard against any potential invasion directed against Winchester, one of his key strongholds. He also had troops positioned at various places along the mainland coast. But by 8 September provisions had run out, the troops had been sent home and Harold had returned to London. William's apparent difficulties with the weather before setting out may well have proved fortuitous for him, as the delay meant that his fleet set sail not long after the English one had been disbanded. If the conditions had been right and given the Normans the opportunity to sail earlier in the summer, instead of being stuck at Dives-sur-Mer, they probably would have crossed the Channel while the English forces were still present. Lucky for William, but luckier still was the fact that while the Normans were making their beachhead on the south coast, Harold had been forced to march north to see off a threat that had suddenly appeared in Yorkshire, some 320 kilometres (200 miles) away. Perhaps God was on William's side, after all?

CHAPTER 10

THE LULL BEFORE
THE STORM

Harold's exiled brother Tostig continues to be a serious problem for the new king. From his base in Scotland he strikes up an alliance with King Harald Hardrada of Norway, who also has designs on the English throne. After initial success, they are surprised by King Harold and his army and are defeated at the Battle of Stamford Bridge. It is a great victory, with Tostig and Hardrada both killed, though Harold is left with the small problem of an approaching Norman army hundreds of miles to the south. As King Harold races back from Yorkshire, Duke William is establishing his position in Sussex. He fortifies his camp and sends out troops to forage for supplies in the local area. It seems he treats the locals ruthlessly, perhaps with the intention that his brutality will provoke Harold and force him to come to battle. Odo is at William's side as the story moves towards the final confrontation.

The Bayeux Tapestry is mute about affairs in England between Harold's accession in early January 1066 and William's arrival at Pevensey in late September. We know from other sources, however, that Harold was kept busy in the first few months of the year contending with his brother Tostig. Having been pushed back from his assault on the English southern and eastern coasts in May, Tostig then moved on to Scotland. There, at the court of King Malcolm, he was able to organize a further attack on England, this time in concert with King Harald Hardrada of Norway. Tostig seems to have been looking for support wherever he could find it. Hardrada brought some 300 ships across the North Sea and joined up with Tostig; it has even been suggested that the Norwegian and Norman invaders somehow conspired together against King Harold, though it is not clear how this would have worked out for them if they had been successful. Could England have been divided into two as it had been in the time of Cnut and Edmund Ironside? Tostig and Hardrada probably landed in mid-September and advanced towards York, sailing along inland waterways. On 20 September, just a few days before William's fleet was finally able to set out across the Channel, they joined in battle against the defensive troops of the northern earls Edwin and Morcar south of the city at Fulford.

The Norwegian army prevailed, decimating the Anglo-Saxon troops, many of whom drowned in the River Ouse. Edwin and Morcar fled, and Hardrada and Tostig entered York victorious, a city with great symbolic significance as it would have been remembered as an important Viking stronghold. King Harold must already have been preparing his forces on hearing of the incursion because he was able to move his own army up to Yorkshire just a few days after Fulford. It seems unlikely this was in direct response to Edwin and Morcar's defeat because mustering and deploying an army from London to Yorkshire in four days would have been an extraordinary feat.

On 25 September, Hardrada and Tostig were forced to fight again, this time a little to the east of York at Stamford Bridge, where Harold's army came upon them with an element of surprise. The Norwegian force was crushed, and both Hardrada and Tostig were killed. Those Norwegians who survived fled back to their ships, though few were needed for them, according to contemporary sources, as their defeat had been so comprehensive and so many were dead. At any other time, such a complete triumph over an army led by one of the greatest warrior kings of the day would have been cause for celebration, and should have secured the kingdom from any further threat of imminent invasion. Not so for King Harold, though, because William was almost immediately on his way, soon landing with his fleet in the south.

This is a part of the story the Bayeux Tapestry does not tell, as we inexorably move towards the climactic clash of Harold's final battle. It has been proposed, however, that events taking place in the north are implied, rather than explicitly shown, by the long sequence in the Tapestry between the Norman landing at Pevensey and the battle at Hastings. The focus of the embroidery in this section is entirely on the Norman establishment of their position.

Foraging for food

After the disembarkation the next caption runs from above the beached ships of William's fleet at Pevensey and on over the heads of several horsemen charging away from the landing site: ET hIC MILITES FESTINAVERVNT hESTINGA VT CIBVM RAPERENTVR (and here the soldiers have rushed to Hastings to seize food). The riders are shown in full armour, apart from helmets, with spears in hand and shields at the ready – they are in enemy territory and prepared for action. The exact number of troops William brought across from Normandy is not known – by William of Poitiers's reckoning it was an unlikely 50,000, but estimates by modern historians put the figure between 7,000 and 14,000. In addition to Normans, there were also men from alliances with other continental lords, as well as some paid mercenaries. It must have been a polyglot army, though dominated by Normans, with all the consequent problems of maintaining discipline and control, perhaps another reason for the Bayeux Tapestry to emphasize how effectively William kept his troops in order throughout the mustering period in Normandy.

Even at the lower end of the range of numbers of troops, that would be a lot of mouths to feed, both human and animal. Although the Duke had been very concerned to ensure that his men did not plunder the countryside when they were stationed in his territory in Normandy, he had no such qualms about their behaviour in England. Whatever food supplies they had brought with them would surely not have been sufficient to keep a large army fed for even a brief time, let alone an extended period. As far as is known, there was no system for bringing in provisions from behind the lines, so it was a case of taking what was needed from the surrounding territory. More than that, though, William had to entice Harold south, and what better way to do it than by ravaging his lands and his people. This was, after all, the heartland of Harold's original domain as Earl of Wessex.

Foraging for food must have been a major occupation for the Normans, and this is what the next part of the Bayeux Tapestry is taken up with. Resistance from the locals would have been an ever-present danger, though it is not clear whether the non-military characters shown are Normans looking for supplies or Anglo-Saxons trying to protect their possessions, or a mixture of both. In the next scene (40), ahead of the armoured knights on horseback is a sequence of several men in civilian clothes. The first wields an axe, while a smaller figure beside him is leading a sheep. They are possibly defending their livestock, including a rather crumpled (some have said drunken-looking) cow behind them, or the man with the axe may be attempting to butcher the animals. A third man, with a sword fastened at his waist, is carrying something that defies easy explanation, though many have tried. It looks like he is holding a transparent disc in front of his face, which has been interpreted as a coil of rope or a barrel (see pl. 11) – it is hard to make sense of what it might be. Whatever is intended, it has almost certainly been borrowed from an illumination in a late Anglo-Saxon copy of the *Psychomachia* of Prudentius (British Library, Cotton Cleopatra C. viii), which itself is an imprecise version of an earlier image of a labourer carrying a boulder. Behind this man someone is more obviously making off with a pig over his shoulders, again armed with a sword and so ready for any trouble, while another man, his heavy axe resting loosely over one shoulder, holds the reins of a small packhorse or pony loaded with a saddlebag.

There were reasonably rich pickings to be had, clearly, but also a lot of men to be fed. Between the two last figures a knight wearing armour sits astride his horse, seemingly at the heart of the proceedings. The responsibility for the supply task may have fallen to this man. HIC EST VVADARD (Here is Wadard) reads the simple caption above him.

Wadard has been identified as another of Bishop Odo's men, and here he is, with no other knights accompanying him, possibly in control of an important element of the invasion logistics.

The Normans feast

Following the search for provisions, a semblance of everyday life resumes as the Normans cook and feast, and the atmosphere becomes almost jovial. hIC COQVITVR CARO ET hIC MINISTRAVERVNT MINISTRI (here is the meat being cooked and here the servants have served it up) reads the next caption (Scene 42), and we see men tending to a large cauldron suspended on poles over a blazing fire, while above is a line of what are presumably pieces of meat on skewers or spits ready for cooking. One researcher has suggested that kebabs of this kind were unknown in either England or Normandy at this time, which led to a questioning of whether the Bayeux Tapestry as it survives is actually the same one that was recorded in medieval times, and, if so, how much has been changed by later restoration work. Cooking meat on skewers in this way would seem a logical method, however. Another cook is turning various foodstuffs on a flaming grill with a large fork and placing them on a dish. The cooking apparatus in both cases is portable, highlighting the preparations, attention to detail and enormous resources that were involved in getting the Norman army over the Channel, set-up, established and fed.

Once cooked, the meat kebabs are handed out to the waiting soldiers, who sit in two groups (Scene 43). The men serving the food hold bundles of skewered meat and stand before a rather basic structure consisting of two towers linked by a slightly arched roof. Another join in the Tapestry's linen base falls just after the first tower. Next, a band of four men has made a makeshift table from upturned shields to eat their banquet from, though it is also possible they are preparing food. In front of them is an array of bowls, cups and utensils, which they seem to pick up and sort. One man is blowing a horn, perhaps summoning others to dine, and his companion seems to rise from the table as if moving on to the next scene, encouraging us to hurry along.

The Tapestry now presents us with an impressive feast being enjoyed by a group of diners seated around a semicircular table groaning under the weight of a great range of foodstuffs, including a couple of fish. In front of the table a rather fine-looking pie is being ceremoniously presented by a servant on bended knee with a cloth draped over his arm. Above them the caption reads hIC FECERVNT PRANDIVM ET hIC EPISCOPVS CIBV[M] ET POTV[M] BENEDICT (here they held a feast, and here the bishop blesses the food and drink). The bishop in question is none other than Bishop Odo of Bayeux. The lettering of this inscription now alternates in colour, a feature more commonly found in continental art, and it must have some relevance, though exactly what is unknown. Perhaps it marks the work of a new embroiderer, or embroidery team, or even reflects the fact that there is a shift in the narrative.

And there sits Odo, in the middle of the men gathered round the table, his tonsure unmistakable, while a diner next to him gestures up to his name written in the following inscription. Odo blesses the food (as the text above him says), while the rest of the party eats. None of the other figures is clearly identifiable or identified, but one diner is of interest. Of seemingly venerable years, with a flowing white beard, he is seated beneath the word *hic* and sips from a bowl or flat-rimmed cup, talking to a man at the end of the table. He seems familiar – he looks a little like King Edward. That is impossible of course, but might the Tapestry designer be suggesting that Edward was with the feasting Normans in spirit? There is an extra twist to this interpretation, however. He has one hand resting on the table with his arm jutting out abruptly at an angle, his elbow almost in the face of the man next to him, who might be Duke William himself. We cannot be sure, but he does look very much like the Norman Duke of earlier scenes. Given that the Bayeux Tapestry is extremely inconsistent in its portraiture of individual characters, this is pure supposition, but is the possible Edward figure elbowing 'William' out of the way, as he had done on the issue of the succession? Might the Tapestry designer (or even an embroiderer) be reminding us that Harold was ultimately Edward's choice as his successor?

Many scholars have noted that this feasting scene in the Bayeux Tapestry is almost certainly copied from an image of the Last Supper in the St Augustine Gospels, a sixth-century manuscript known to have been owned by St Augustine's Abbey in Canterbury by the eleventh century. Tradition has it that it was brought over by St Augustine himself in 597, and it is still used in the ceremony to consecrate new archbishops of Canterbury. In the Tapestry, Jesus is replaced by Odo, with very clear connotations that would have been as obvious to the contemporary viewer as they are today; it could indeed be seen as a radical and provocative move, which is especially interesting since it seems Odo and William fell out after it was suspected that the bishop had his sights on the papacy. It is also one of the clearest examples in the Bayeux Tapestry of the influence of known manuscripts that were in the Canterbury scriptoria at the time.

It is quite likely that this is not simply a case of the Bayeux Tapestry designer borrowing a convenient scene of feasting from an illuminated manuscript and dropping it into his design. One suggestion is that the overtly religious overtones are specifically intended to stress that the Normans, under Odo's guidance, are dining with God on their side, and that their victory in the ensuing battle is divinely ordained. The multicoloured lettering may have some significance in this respect. A contrast has been drawn between this feast, with the religious implications in the way it is portrayed, and the secular setting of Harold's Bosham drinking party, with the sinful English set against the righteous Normans, who are feasting, metaphorically, in the presence of Christ. There might be something to this, but it is also true that the Normans appear to be having as good a time at their feast as the English were earlier. What is undeniable is that Odo is the focus of our attention here, and is being presented as a model lord who takes care of the physical needs of his followers, with generous amounts of food and drink (even in such challenging conditions, with the help of his man Wadard), while also ensuring that they are spiritually nourished.

Council of war

Odo is depicted as not only a man orchestrating a fine feast for the troops, but also a key player in the leadership of the entire endeavour, as before when he seemed to advise William on constructing an invasion fleet. In the next scene (44), the words ODO EP[ISCOPV]S (Bishop Odo), WILLELM (William) and ROTBERT (Robert) are written above the heads of three seated men, so the bishop is finally categorically identified by name, as is William. Robert, who has not previously been distinguished in the Tapestry, is a common name, and there were several important Roberts in William's retinue. The balance of probability, however, is that this is William's other half-brother, Robert, Count of Mortain, the full brother of Odo. The men sit in council within a small triangular-roofed structure, sharing a cushioned bench with footstools for comfort. The throne-like chairs of previous scenes have become a little more basic (they are on military campaign, after all), but even so the brothers are portrayed as men of status. The building they are seated in is harder to interpret. Clearly made of stone, it could not have been constructed this quickly by William's army, and is unlikely to be of a type then existing in Britain. In fact, its classical features betray it as being directly borrowed from art, with little attempt made to reflect reality on the ground.

The Duke, centre, is flanked by his two advisers. Both William and Robert bear swords, while Odo, weaponless, appears to be explaining something to an attentive William. The Duke's head is turned towards Odo, who is shown with one hand palm open and the other pointing. Robert looks on from the other side, almost drawing his sword from its sheath and seemingly on the point of taking his leave. Presumably this is a council of war, and, crucially, Odo is once more in a commanding role, almost instructing William what he should do. The presence of the other brother is interesting. Robert is not a figure who has received much attention in Tapestry studies, but his role in the battle has recently been stressed, as has the fact that he and Odo (full brothers) had a strong relationship. This was demonstrated by the fact that Robert apparently energetically argued for

Odo's release from prison after his fall from grace in 1082. If, as is likely, Odo was the guiding force behind the Bayeux Tapestry, then naturally he would have wanted to give his brother Robert a prominent role. One suggestion is that Robert's active pose is to demonstrate that he is responsible for the work that takes place in the next scene. He is poised to spring out of the council to put into action the plan under discussion, namely to build a castle at Hastings.

Building castles

The following scene (45) is captioned ISTE IVSSIT VT FODERETVR CASTELLVM AT [sic, for AD] HESTENGA (This man has commanded that a castle should be dug at Hastings). It is not clear exactly who 'this man' is, and an alternative translation of the word ISTE is 'the latter', so it could be Robert of Mortain who is doing the commanding. A standing figure appears below ISTE, presumably the man in question, whether Robert or not. He wears a long cloak and holds a standard with pennant (decorated with a cross) in one hand, while pointing with the other to his workmen. He has a more elaborate hairstyle (or perhaps is wearing a hat) than the majority of people in the Tapestry, with a full head of hair consisting of layered locks slightly raised and swept back. Admittedly this does not look much like the close crop that Robert was shown with when seated in council with William, but perhaps it is because he is outside, buffeted by the wind, as he directs his men in the construction project.

Or perhaps the embroiderer of this part of the Tapestry wanted to introduce greater individuality and a hint of humour into the narrative. The depiction of the workmen responding to the overseer's instructions is one of the more characterful episodes in the entire length of the embroidery. We see four men in a row, all brandishing triangular shovels and spades. The first looks back over his shoulder to the overseer, possibly with a slightly insolent air, almost juggling with his tools, while the man in front of him awkwardly raises his shovel in his left hand towards the word *foderetur* (dug). The two others ahead are engaged in either a straight fight, hitting each other on the head with their tools, or a bit of horseplay. The scene definitely has the air of a slapstick interlude; even the long-necked birds in the upper border seem to be in on the joke, laughing at the action, and it is not too much of a stretch of the imagination to invest the two cawing birds in the lower border with an amused attitude also.

Why this element of levity is included is hard to guess. Perhaps it is just an embroiderer indulging in a moment of personal expression that slipped past the designer's attention. Or it could be more laden with significance, reminding us that although the Normans had to fortify and defend their position, they were still confident of success given the divine protection they boasted. But then it is back to business, as another standing figure, perhaps the same commander, again wearing a cloak and holding a staff and pennant and pointing up towards the inscription with his free hand (though now with a less elaborate hairstyle), supervises a busy construction scene.

What follows is a fascinating section of the embroidery for enthusiasts of early castle technology. The gang of workmen (now five of them), are no longer fooling around and are knuckling down to some serious digging. All, that is, except one man, closest to the cloaked individual, who appears to be absent-mindedly dropping some stones on the head of a labourer hard at work with a pick.

The workmen are using their pick-axes and spatula-shaped shovels to throw up a rounded motte made up of different coloured bands. A wooden fort has been erected on top of it, with what appears to be a plank-built palisade. The word CEASTRA (castle) is centred above it, and almost linked to the word for 'Hastings' in the preceding scene, so we are in no doubt as to what it is, or where we are. It is similar in form to the sort of defensive structures shown in the Brittany campaign earlier, though not nearly as elaborate, so is this an indication of the Normans bringing new ideas about fortification to England?

Archaeologists have not identified any clear-cut evidence for an earthwork of this type in the area, but given the very brief time available to raise such a structure, it would not be surprising if it were ephemeral. The generally accepted view is that it would have been established within the existing defences of the Iron Age hillfort at Hastings, and therefore not necessarily on the same site as the later medieval castle. Wherever it was, the embroidery and the documentary sources both agree that a castle was constructed at Hastings (and possibly also at Pevensey), and it would have been something completely new for the locals, if any of them were in the vicinity to see it. There had been no tradition of building motte and bailey castles in Britain before the Normans arrived, so it would have been an unfamiliar and no doubt alarming development.

War draws near

Perhaps it was within the safety of the walls of the new motte that the following scene was enacted, as Duke William finds out why Harold has not engaged him in battle sooner. HIC NVNTIATVM EST WILLELMo DE hAROLD (Here news is brought to William about Harold) reads the caption above the image. A seated William, holding a standard with a pennant on it (which some have interpreted as the papal banner), is receiving word from a cloaked and armed messenger, apparently delivering important information. Both their spears penetrate the inscription, which seems squeezed into the space above them; William's name has even had to be abbreviated in an unusual way to fit it in.

Precisely when news of the events in the north reached the Norman troops on the south coast is not known, but William of Poitiers tells us that a messenger came to the Duke at his base in Hastings to inform him that Harold had won a mighty victory against the Norwegian king and his own brother Tostig, and was now on his way to deal with the Normans in the same way. This, it is easy to imagine, is the news being imparted here. The Bayeux Tapestry does not name the messenger, but through a reference in William of Poitiers he has been identified as Robert fitz Wimarch, a Norman who had originally come to England in King Edward's retinue. Since he is shown as a man of status (he wears an impressively large cloak), perhaps the two stories can be linked. Poitiers puts a very bold speech into the mouth of Robert, cautioning the Duke that he would not win against Harold and that he would be well advised to 'stay within his defences for the time being and not give battle'. William does not take kindly to the tone of the message and sends Robert back to Harold with very short shrift, saying that he will not seek the shelter of walls and will do battle as soon as possible. Even the borders in the Bayeux Tapestry seem to feel the force of William's anger, with the birds at the top almost blown over by it.

It may have been William's fury at the impertinence of Harold's message that led him to increase the ferocity of his campaign of devastation against the local lands and people, including now burning down their houses. hIC DOMVS INCENDITVR (Here a house is burned) is the caption above the next scene (47), and the brutality of the act depicted is very evident. What looks like a fairly imposing structure, perhaps of two storeys, is being torched. Two Normans, here in civilian dress, are thrusting their flaming braziers at the building and have successfully set the roof ablaze, with the flames licking the upper border of the Tapestry. This may have been a military tactic to provoke Harold into making some response and compel him to engage William in battle sooner rather than later. But to complicate matters, it has been suggested that this is not a scene of Normans burning down the house, but rather a representation of an Anglo-Saxon scorched earth policy, as the inhabitants destroy their properties to prevent the Norman invaders obtaining food. One of the later sources does hint at such a strategy, but the fact that it is a house rather than foodstuffs being burnt somewhat argues against this. Whoever is responsible for the act of violence, the real power of the scene lies in the two figures we see fleeing the burning house. A woman wearing a floor-length, wide-sleeved gown and a veiled head-piece leads a boy away from the carnage by the hand; her other hand is open, perhaps imploring for mercy. The woman is not named, and her diminutive stature in comparison to the torch-bearing men suggests we are not supposed to recognize her as anyone of particular political significance, but her plight and apparent innocence underscore the abhorrence of the event and William's callous cruelty.

Even given the limitations of the artistic medium in which they were working, the designer and embroiderers have succeeded in encapsulating the desperate situation of the refugee. Perhaps it is because we are familiar with similar images today from conflicts around the globe, but there does seem to be a great deal of emotion invested in this scene. The people working on the Bayeux Tapestry, if they were English, might even have had first-hand experience of such horrors themselves. It is one of the rare moments in the whole embroidery that forcibly reminds us of the true impact of what must have been a very bloody and tumultuous sequence of events for the ordinary people of England. The woman's clothes have been interpreted as an indication that she was someone who was reasonably well-to-do, perhaps the wife of an Anglo-Saxon noble. She is the third, and last, clothed female we see in the main frieze of the Tapestry, and if there is truth in the suggestion that women are shown at key moments in the narrative, it is fair to say that this is a real turning point. Immediately after this scene comes an architectural vignette, thought to be a representation of the town of Hastings; it is a complicated structure consisting of various elements, with an open door inviting us to pass through it to what follows next. And then we are unmistakably in battle mode.

Most of the people portrayed from here on are wearing armour, and most are fighting, being killed or are already dead. The final quarter of the Bayeux Tapestry is all about the battle. The slash-and-burn strategy has done its job, and Harold has been given little choice but to exhort his men to follow him to Hastings and make a stand against the invading Normans.

CHAPTER 11

THE GREAT BATTLE

On 14 October 1066 the English and Norman forces finally meet. The English occupy the higher ground on a hill a few miles from Hastings (at the place now known as Battle), and the Normans advance to meet them. The English fight on foot, forming a shield-wall to fend off their enemy. The Normans attack on horseback, and in addition have a strong force of archers as well as infantry. William's army is not just made up of Norman troops, but also includes a sizeable section of Bretons and others.

The Battle of Hastings is fairly well attested in several sources, so we know its critical moments, including a feigned retreat by the Normans which successfully draws the English off the hill they are on and into a more vulnerable position. The battle is closely fought, but in the end the Normans win the day, and King Harold himself, along with his brothers, is killed. At that point the Bayeux Tapestry concludes, though the story of the Norman Conquest is far from over.

A battle-ready figure stands outside the open door of the structure representing Hastings, and the caption above him reads hIC MILITES EXIERVNT DE hESTENGA ET VENERVNT AD PRELIVM CONTRA hAROLDVM REGE[M] (Here the soldiers have gone out from Hastings and come to battle against King Harold). The man wears armour from head to foot, from his conical helmet with nose piece, to a body-length hauberk that stretches down to his knees and what looks like mail leggings right down to his feet. Tassels or ribbons hang from his neck and helmet, and he has a sword at his waist. In one hand he holds a spear with pennant and he is pointing with the other. This, it is generally agreed, is Duke William. He is engaging with an unarmoured man leading a stallion, presumably the Duke's groom bringing him his mount so that he can join his cavalry as they move out of Hastings.

Three stylized trees with interlaced branches, the central one with a very odd rounded upper trunk, make up a little copse, which is surely intended as a major punctuation point in the story. Directly after the trees is an array of Norman riders (Scene 48), ten of them closely packed, steeds tensed and ready to move off. They also are wearing helmets and armour, with their spurred feet in the stirrups, and are holding spears and shields. From the details shown it is even possible to see how their shields are gripped by a strap, presumed to be leather, on the reverse side. Their armour is identical to that worn by the standing Duke William, though they lack ribbons on their helmets, and below the knees they seem to have the usual leggings worn by men in the Tapestry, rather than the protection of mail. One curious feature of their armour is the square 'patches' on their chests, which will be examined later. On the whole this is a very full and meticulous piece of stitching, but it looks like the embroiderer ran out of time, patience or interest because the shields of the two soldiers at the front are not filled in with colour, in contrast with their companions. Perhaps this is because this scene falls right at the end of a linen panel, with the join with the next one running, almost imperceptibly, through the head of the leading rider's horse.

At the start of the succeeding panel, the riders gather pace – the horses spread out and their gait increases from trot to gallop, but before we follow them, there are some curiosities in the borders that demand our attention.

Below the scene of William and his groom is a pair of confronted deer (or similar), but with their heads turned back, away from each other. They are followed first by two squawking birds and then a pair of lions with rather human expressions looking straight out of the

Tapestry. In the upper border, things become a little stranger. Just as the troops on horses appear are two more occurrences of human nudity. In the first of two pairs of naked people, a long-haired and we assume female nude, stretches her arms out towards an obviously male figure with testicles plainly visible. He is holding a large axe over his shoulder, and also offering what looks like a small bag to the woman. After a pair of birds, another two nudes appear: a man with a prominent moustache and a woman seem to be rushing towards each other, either to fight or embrace. They are followed by a donkey eating grass, two drooping plants and a possible wolf. It is hard to make out what, if anything, this all might mean.

Matters have moved on significantly in time and space now. All posturing is over, and the rest of the Tapestry is devoted to what takes place on 14 October 1066, the day of the great battle. The armies met not at Hastings itself, but 11 kilometres (7 miles) northwest on the hill that was to become the place named Battle. Then, as now, the engagement was of such significance for the history of the English nation that it needed no other name. King Harold, according to William of Poitiers, was so enraged by reports of the devastation around the Norman camp at Hastings that he resolved to undertake a night attack and catch his enemy unawares. William of Jumièges, on the other hand, has it that the Norman Duke was ready and waiting for Harold's night attack and had his army stand to arms from dusk till dawn the night before.

The Bayeux Tapestry does not help much in establishing the exact order of events, though perhaps in this it follows Jumièges more than Poitiers, as the Normans appear to be advancing in good order from Hastings, and are well organized and disciplined, rather than being taken by surprise by the English. This is itself somewhat confusing as it is assumed that on the night before the battle the two armies were encamped within sight of each other. Both the imagery and the inscription before and above the advancing Norman cavalry suggest that they went directly from Hastings to fight, but presumably this is artistic licence on the part of the designer.

The Norman riders begin to pick up speed. Two of the horsemen now have banded leggings and the pennants on their spears flap in the wind. One of the banners is semicircular, with what looks like a small bird on it, the other is decorated with a cross. But then the pace of the horses slows again as we reach another important moment. The caption above the next few horses is HIC VVILLELM DVX INTERROGAT VITAL SI VIDISSET EXERCITV[M] HAROLDI (Here Duke William asks Vital whether he had seen Harold's army), and the scene (49) is composed of two Norman knights meeting another coming from the opposite direction. Those travelling forwards wear mail covering their entire bodies, including their lower legs, but they have no shields and hold a mace and a club respectively rather than spears. The more advanced of the two is pointing at the rider who is approaching at speed from the right. This incoming horseman, holding a spear and shield and without the lower leg mail, points back over his shoulder, onwards along the Tapestry, directing us to the next scene.

The foremost horseman wielding the club is probably Duke William, who is speaking to Vital, the rider arriving from the other direction. The man behind William, holding a mace, could be one of the Duke's brothers, either Odo or Robert, although he is actually below the word Willelm. Vital, who must be an advance scout of the Norman army, is apprising William of the lie of the land, and his gesticulation suggests that his answer to the Duke's question as to whether he has seen Harold's army is 'yes, over there'. Vital has been identified as another of Odo's men (along with Turold and Wadard seen earlier), and is one of the less exalted figures in the story who nevertheless receive recognition in the Bayeux Tapestry. Less important Vital may be, but his role in the narrative is crucial because it tells us that William is informed of Harold's deployment and not caught unawares by it, suggesting that the English did not have the benefit of surprise on the day. According to the Anglo-Saxon Chronicle, it was Harold who was surprised by William's appearance, though that, as soon becomes apparent, seems even more unlikely.

The Norman cavalry troops press on (Scene 50), forewarned about the enemy dispositions, and seem to progress up over raised ground, perhaps a hillock. One of the knights is helmetless and we can see a mail covering, known as a coif, over his scalp, while a second holds a pennant-banner in his hand. The knight in front seems to be pointing his shield towards or through another group of stylized trees occupying the downslope of the hill they have ridden up. Beyond the trees a man faces the riders with one hand raised, and the next caption reads ISTE NVNTIAT HAROLDVM REGE[M] DE EXERCITV VVILELMI DVCIS (This man gives news to King Harold about Duke William's army). So this is an English lookout informing Harold of William's approach. He is on foot, but other than that his arms and armour are very similar to the Normans'. Having spotted the advancing enemy, it seems he turns and runs hurriedly back to report what he has seen to Harold, who must be the extravagantly moustachioed horseman with a red shield. This is the last time in the Bayeux Tapestry that any of the English are shown mounted, perhaps not a true reflection of the reality of the battle but a way for the Tapestry designer to distinguish the Normans from the Anglo-Saxons.

Both armies now know where their adversaries are deployed, and we cannot be far from the first engagements. Presumably, then, we have reached the early morning of 14 October, and we must be on the field at Battle. William of Jumièges says that Duke William marshalled his squadrons into formation at dawn and that the first fighting occurred at 9 a.m. There is nothing to tell us the time of day in the Bayeux Tapestry, but we can almost sense the early morning mist, even if it is not actually depicted, beginning to lift as the hour of battle draws near.

Arms and armour

Before the action commences, it seems an apt moment to consider exactly what we are shown by way of arms and armour in the Bayeux Tapestry. Military historians have taken considerable interest in these battle scenes and how they help further our understanding of what eleventh-century warfare was like. According to one count, 79 figures are shown in body armour in the embroidery out of a total of 201 armed men, and that offers a marvellous pictorial resource. As noted, there does not seem to be much difference between the way the armoured Normans and the armoured English are represented. How far the designer was attempting to reflect what the warriors actually wore is a subject of debate. To take helmets as an example, everyone is protected by the same conical headpieces. They generally seem to be constructed of four sections, of which we see just two parts of one side, generally held together by bands (shown as lines) going over the helmet; sometimes the halves are coloured differently in the embroidery. In addition, there is a nose guard and usually a band around the rim. The Tapestry's helmets seem to match quite closely surviving contemporary examples and those depicted in art (such as on coins), which were constructed of different sections held together by metal bands, although some helmets would have been hammered from a single metal piece.

Armour is also broadly uniform across the Bayeux Tapestry, with warriors on both sides wearing what look like mail suits, or hauberks, which were seen earlier being carried on poles during the Norman preparations for the invasion. These would have been heavy (though the weight would be distributed when worn on the body) and expensive, and were probably worn over a leather base garment to provide some padding and comfort. Although the armour is generally similar, there are several curiosities. A small academic sub-discipline exists to address the question of whether the hauberks extended down to become mail trousers. They certainly look like this in the Tapestry, but numerous scholars have noted that wearing mail trousers would have been very uncomfortable, particularly when riding horses. The general view is therefore that this is a mistake of understanding on the part of the designer (or we are just not seeing them as he intended) and that in reality these trouser elements would have been open sided. It was once argued that this apparent error in detail could be explained by the fact that the designer either had experience only of English armour, and that as English soldiers tended to fight on foot rather than from the saddle they may have worn full mail trousers, or that he drew his depictions from art that he did not quite understand and so had not grasped exactly how these garments were worn. The likelihood, however, is that the Anglo-Saxons and Normans wore similar armour (as the Tapestry suggests), and the English probably did also ride in battle, though not commonly. Sometimes warriors are shown with further mail leggings that go right to the ankles, but this is limited to just a few people, of whom William seems to be one.

Another aspect of armour that is regularly debated by scholars of the subject is the chest plate, the square 'patch' that features on the breast of several figures, including William and Harold. While it is not absolutely clear what these patches represent, some sort of reinforcement in this vulnerable area seems likely. The fact that it is higher-profile figures who tend to be shown with them could indicate that they were somehow more expensive elements of the warrior's equipment and had greater status, although the Tapestry is not consistent in depicting the device. One view is that they might be ventails, mail patches that could be tied up to protect the neck, or left down, as they are in the Tapestry. But if this is the case, none are shown in use in this way. Although the hauberks look broadly similar throughout, details of how the armour is depicted do vary, with several styles of triangles, squares, circles and scales. Different motifs seem particular to certain parts of the work, suggesting it was a directive of the designer, or even agreed between the embroiderers working on an individual section.

No arms or armour have been recovered from the site of the Battle of Hastings (although an axe, reputedly associated with the fight, is now in Battle Museum, though it is neither necessarily a weapon of war, nor even contemporary with the battle), and indeed little extant eleventh-century armour is known. The reason for the poor survival of arms and armour on battlefields is that, being items of value, most would have been recovered, as is shown later in the Tapestry. Even if some was left behind, much of it was made of iron and would therefore have corroded over time.

Although in the Bayeux Tapestry the majority of those engaged in the battle are well armed, the reality may have been different. William, his closest followers and elite troops will have had war-gear similar to that depicted, and so would their own men. However, there was no standing army as such, and some men may have been responsible for providing their own arms. Many of those fighting on the day, especially given the magnitude of this battle, may not have been so well protected and their equipment could have been more rudimentary. This is probably particularly the case for the Anglo-Saxons, whose ranks may have been supplemented by the local population. Such men would have had to defend their lands and themselves with whatever they happened to possess. The Normans, on the other hand, would have been selected for war and may well have had more support in terms of their equipment. The fact that both sides appear similarly protected is significant in terms of the assessments by military historians of whether one side had a technological advantage over the other in the fight. From the perspective of armour, it would seem not. But there are other elements of technology and tactics that do seem to have been different, as discussed later.

What is going on in the borders from the beginning of this phase of the action is also of interest. In general, the pattern of paired animals, often birds, continues, and there are also more fantastical beasts. However, some depictions are not so conventional, especially, though not exclusively, in the lower border. For example, as the Normans are galloping from Hastings, we see a bird and a hare, but is one chasing the other? Beneath the Norman scouts a donkey is eating straw, with a spotted creature looking on through one of the diagonals. Later on, a number of animal heads peer out from what is interpreted as a cave, with a four-legged creature (perhaps their mother) standing before them. Further on again, another spotted animal seems to be making off with a bird (perhaps a duck) in its mouth, and ahead of it is a beast with what could be a mouse in its jaws. What these miniatures, and others before them, represent is unclear, though some scholars have invested them with meaning. Perhaps they are simply comments on the pursuit shown above, or the embroiderers, who may have been free to choose, copied them from exemplars either at random or with some unknown purpose. We can only guess.

Duke William exhorts his troops

After Harold has learnt of the approach of the Norman army, the next scene (51) is captioned by an enormously loquacious inscription: HIC WILLELM DVX ALLOQVITVR SVIS MILITIBVS VT PREPARARENT SE VIRILITER ET SAPIENTER AD PRELIVM CONTRA ANGLORVM EXERCITV[M] (Here Duke William exhorts his soldiers to prepare themselves manfully and wisely for the battle against the English army). This is a large number of words for the embroiderers to fit in, so the text extends over a fair length of imagery, which itself seems also to stretch out.

The first two words, Hic Willelm, frame the head of the first mounted figure after a chapter-dividing tree. He holds a club, is pointing purposefully to this caption and is wearing mail armour right down to his feet. So all the indications are that this must be Duke William, in the act of exhorting his men as the caption tells us. The next soldier along is looking back at him, presumably listening to his leader's instructions. This rider is noteworthy more for an error in the embroidery than anything else, because his helmet is shown behind his mailed coif, rather than on top of it. There are a number of mistakes in the Bayeux Tapestry, but this one is particularly striking, perhaps matched only by the misalignment of linen panels near the beginning. The errors are useful in themselves as they are an indication that the designer might not have been so closely involved in the project at the stage when the embroidery work was being done, as surely such blunders would have been easy to correct.

A line of mounted soldiers, with William's encouragement no doubt still ringing in their ears, is now shown riding at speed, spears readied, shields raised, pennants flying. Paired birds and animals in the borders seem to be chattering excitedly as the momentum gathers, and towards the front of the riding party are the beasts in the lower border with prey in their mouths, perhaps alluding to the fact the English are now in sight and will soon be caught. In front of this group of horsemen, we have our first sight of the Norman archers. Four of them on foot, one in full armour, are running forwards, with full quivers and arrows fixed in their bows ready to let fly.

The presence of archers is significant because it corresponds with the account by William of Poitiers of Duke William's tactics. According to Poitiers, William split his forces into three, with each division attacking in formation – first archers, followed by cavalry and then heavy foot soldiers. There are several references in the documentary sources to the Normans using crossbowmen, but these are not shown in the Tapestry – the archers here are longbowmen. The idea was that the archers would wear down the enemy, then the charging cavalry could smash through the English defences and the foot soldiers would mop up individual foes in hand-to-hand combat. The overall effect of this is not quite achieved in the Bayeux Tapestry because no Norman infantry appear at this stage. In front of the archers are yet more riders, spread out across the height of the frieze, perhaps to indicate a change in formation as they near the enemy. The riders charge over another seam, where the sixth linen panel meets the seventh (the join is well disguised), and then finally the forces engage. It has been a very long build-up to the attack by the Normans, which occupies a fair length of the embroidery, but it successfully conveys an atmosphere of mounting tension as we follow the action, and demonstrates that the Norman army was a substantial one.

As the vanguard of the Norman cavalry charges into the ranks of the English defence we see the first casualties of battle. They are being trampled by the horses, as one man has a spear embedded in his chest and another is pierced through the heart perhaps. Mail armour did not always provide sufficient protection, and may even have hindered the escape of the wounded. At this same moment two paired birds in the lower border also appear to have tumbled over, and they are the last creatures (apart from a dead horse) to feature in this border. From this point on for several scenes, the space is reserved for the grisly carnage of the fallen in battle, and is strewn with bodies, body parts and abandoned weaponry, the grim consequences of the battle.

In the main frieze, the Norman cavalry now hits the Anglo-Saxon shield-wall, famed in accounts of the battle. The shields of the English are peppered with arrows, while overhead spears fly in both directions and a mace hurtles through the air towards the Normans. This scene, both evocative and terrible, demonstrates the essential difference between Norman and English tactics – the Normans fought on horseback, the English preferred to stay on their feet. A reference in the Anglo-Saxon Chronicle for 1055 tells of Earl Ralph of Hereford (of French extraction, and nephew of Edward the Confessor) failing against the Welsh as he had made his men (Anglo-Saxons) fight on horseback 'against their custom'. Although there is evidence that English forces did sometimes fight from horses in the period before Hastings, as in the account above, it seems that generally they fought on foot.

This may sound like a certain backwardness in technique, but it could also have been about making a statement of defiance – there would be no retreat once a position had been established. Certainly, since it is recorded that the English had the higher ground in this battle, a defensive formation could well have been seen as the most sensible tactic, especially given the fact that the Normans had to attack and win at their first attempt. William could only reasonably expect to have one chance to defeat Harold, as he could not sustain an army in England indefinitely without gaining significant territory.

The English defence, the shield-wall, took the form of locking shields together – usually thought to be round shields, rather than the kite-shaped ones of the Tapestry – to create an impenetrable wall through which arrow, spear and horse could not pass. In terms of weaponry, the English here are for the most part holding spears (see pl. 13 and 14), which they are either thrusting or perhaps throwing at the enemy, though one man at the back wields an axe. This is not one of the huge, long-handled axes seen before, which are regarded as indicating status. Such massive axes do appear later in the battle, in association with men fighting with King Harold and his brothers, so perhaps these first troops were not the elite housecarls, the quasi-professional household guards of the great men of England. There is also a single archer, who is not wearing armour and is the only Englishman shown with a bow in the Tapestry. This shows that bowmen were not exclusive to the Norman ranks, though they perhaps were not so decisive in this battle for the Anglo-Saxons.

The direction of flow of the Bayeux Tapestry becomes looser now, as the English are shown fighting back to back, with another Norman cavalry attack riding in from the right. We can almost hear the screeching of the birds above them as they crane their necks down towards the action, unable almost to remain within the confines of the border. One English soldier is shown dramatically tumbling forwards from the defensive line under the hooves of a Norman horse, while decapitated bodies are scattered in the lower border. At this stage it is still hard to get any sense of who might be winning.

The battle hangs in the balance

The fortunes of each side soon become a little clearer in the following scene (52), in which another troop of Norman horsemen charges into a group of English warriors from both sides. The embroidery now makes the English defences look distinctly fragile. No longer are the English soldiers ranged tightly together, shields locked in close defence. Instead, they seem to be engaged in wild hand-to-hand combat, with their flanks defended by men swinging two-handed axes. Within the 'wall' a warrior is shown slashing with a sword, while his round shield held in front provides him with individual protection. A second warrior, with a similar shield and a noticeable moustache, is attempting to thrust his spear into a charging horseman, but is also on the receiving end of his opponent's weapon, which looks like it will plunge straight into his face. In the midst of all this, two other English warriors tumble down, almost as if in slow motion.

Clearly, the English lines have been penetrated by the Normans. A rider separates this first knot of English soldiers from a second, where an axe-wielding man, seemingly struck by a Norman lance, battles desperately as his comrade, mortally pierced, falls beside him, dropping his pennant to the ground as he dies. The caption tells us that the scene portrays the death of Harold's younger brothers, Leofwine and Gyrth: hIC CECIDERVNT LEVVINE ET GYRÐ FRATRES hAROLDI REGIS (Here fell Leofwine and Gyrth, the brothers of King Harold); the Old English Ð (for 'th') in Gyrth betrays an Anglo-Saxon hand in the writing of this inscription.

It is not entirely clear which figures are Leofwine and Gyrth in this dramatic image of tumultuous action, but it is likely they are depicted below their names. Leofwine would then be the axeman (and possibly also the second man falling down) and Gyrth the moustached warrior with a round shield being impaled through the face. This is a critical incident – not only were these two men leading earls of England, and among Harold's closest supporters, but it is also possible that, should Harold die and they survived, they might have been seen as king-worthy. It was significant therefore to show that they had been killed to preclude any possible later resistance to Norman rule. One intriguing consideration relating to this is that Edgar Ætheling is not shown at Hastings, presumably because he did not fight there, but would the Tapestry have shown him if he had? Some of the documentary accounts place the deaths of Harold's brothers towards the end of the battle, so the Bayeux Tapestry diverges from them, highlighting the difficulty of interpreting the different sources for the battle that survive.

With these scenes the Tapestry designer has taken us straight into the heart of the fighting, and some of the earlier stages of the evolving battle recorded in the documentary sources have not made it into the embroidery. We are not shown, for instance, how King Harold managed to take possession of the high ground of the battlefield, then plant his banner and set up his other standards, before sending the horses away and letting sound the trumpets of war. Neither have we seen how Duke William sent his troops in an orderly advance, led by bowmen, or how his three divisions of Frenchmen, Bretons and

5 TOP Bayeux Cathedral today. This is largely a thirteenth-century structure built in the Gothic style, but within some parts built by Bishop Odo can still be seen. Odo's cathedral was consecrated in July 1077.

6 ABOVE The nave of Bayeux Cathedral, with a replica of the Bayeux Tapestry hung around it. It is not known if the embroidery was displayed in the cathedral in the 1070s, though by the fifteenth century there was a tradition of doing so.

7 TOP William as king of England in Matthew Paris's *Historia Anglorum* (A History of England), dated c.1250–55. William is perhaps holding aloft Battle Abbey, which he had built in penance for the slaughter at the Battle of Hastings.

8 ABOVE Illustration from the *Les Grandes Chroniques de France* (BL Royal MS 16 G VI), 1332–50, showing Duke William of Normandy defeating the French in battle, and sending a herald to King Henry I. As William's power grew his relationship with the French king, his lord overlord, became more complex.

9 TOP Mont-Saint-Michel today, with the great abbey on the summit. Twice daily the town is cut off from the mainland by the tide, though a road now provides a permanent crossing.

10 ABOVE The burial of King Edward in the *Life of King Edward* shows the ceremony surrounding the death of a king, with both secular clergy and monks in attendance.

11 TOP It is almost certain that the Tapestry's image of a man carrying a rope or barrel was copied from a similar drawing in a late Anglo-Saxon manuscript of Prudentius' *Psychomachia* produced at Christ Church, Canterbury.

12 ABOVE Harold and Tostig fight one another when boys, as shown in the *Life of King Edward*. Their quarrel unnerves King Edward, but their father, Earl Godwin, is less concerned. The two brothers' relationship would come to define 1066.

13 TOP A band of men in the Junius 11 manuscript carrying spears comparable with those depicted in the Bayeux Tapestry.

14 ABOVE Although it would not have been known to the designer of the Bayeux Tapestry, the lone archer shown on the eighth-century Franks Casket is very much like one depicted in the Tapestry within the Anglo-Saxon shield wall.

15 TOP Finally, King Harold is killed (Scene 57). This is perhaps one of the most famous scenes in the Bayeux Tapestry, yet it remains enigmatic, for is Harold the figure with the arrow in the eye, and is it certain that it is an arrow at all? Despite this, the English fight on.

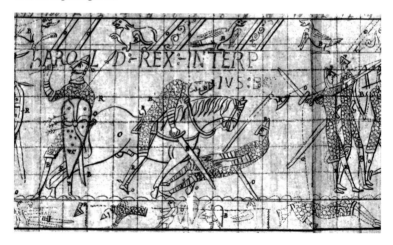

16 ABOVE Antoine Benoît's 1729 engraving of the Bayeux Tapestry appears to show the figure with the arrow in the eye in fact holding a shaft, possibly of a spear. **17 OPPOSITE** Charles Stothard, in his 1819 watercolour drawing the Tapestry, has added flights, so that it becomes an arrow. Perhaps Stothard's drawings influenced restorers of the embroidery in the nineteenth century.

18 TOP The Tapestry as exhibited in the Queen Matilda Gallery in the Hôtel de Ville, Bayeux. It was here that the embroidery was first put on public display in 1842.

19 ABOVE German officers examine the Bayeux Tapestry in the Second World War. During the German occupation of Normandy, a research team made a full study of the embroidery as the Nazis were interested in art works associated with the history of Germanic peoples.

Normans went forward having been heartened by the solo antics of a brave jester called Tallefer, who juggled swords in front of the English lines and then decapitated the soldier who rode out to challenge him, as described in the *Carmen de Hastingae Proelio*.

After the deaths of Gyrth and Leofwine there is a sense of the battle hanging in the balance (Scene 53). The next caption reads hIC CECIDERVNT SIMVL ANGLI ET FRANCI IN PRELIO (here English and French fell together in battle). A Norman soldier springs out from behind a horse and attempts to decapitate an unsuspecting Anglo-Saxon, who turns round as the head of his axe flies from its shaft. Next to him, an Englishman buries his axe into the head of a horse, as its rider tries to slash his sword down on his attacker. Men fall with twisted limbs below, and a severed head lies on the ground without its body. Even in cartoon style, the detail is gruesome.

The furious action continues with Norman knights and horses tumbling with neck-breaking force as they appear to cross a water-filled ditch. One horse falls dramatically backwards, its rider thrown head first into the water or marshland, while another horse is caught by the Tapestry in an extraordinary position, tipped over vertically, with its bent head and neck resting on the lower border and its back hooves touching the upper one. When compared with the documentary accounts, this is a difficult scene to place in the sequence of events. There is a famous moment, known as the Malfosse incident, which is described by numerous sources in slightly different ways. What seems to have happened is that Norman horsemen, charging after fleeing English, were surprised by a concealed ditch, causing the horses to stumble, and many lives were lost. That looks like what the Tapestry is showing, but according to most other sources, the incident occurs at the end of the battle, when the English are in full flight, so it does not sit correctly in the chronology here, where the fighting is far from done.

Of course, there may have been more than one ditch and more than one such episode, or it could be that either the Bayeux Tapestry or the other sources have got events mixed up. Either way, the embroidery very effectively captures the drama of a moment when the Normans encountered considerable problems with an unexpected hazard in the landscape. But next it is the English who are clearly in trouble. Several men are holding out, somewhat desperately, on a hillock. No longer in formation with interlocking shields, they are not wearing armour of any kind and perhaps are the levy of lesser men who cannot afford good mail. They seem badly defended against a cavalry charge attacking from the left. One of the two horsemen is pitching forwards as an Anglo-Saxon on the ground is bravely loosening the girth of the horse's saddle. Three of the defenders on the hill throw their spears down at the Normans, while another two plunge forwards into the melee below. At ground level two men appear to flee, though rather indecisively, as if feeling surrounded and with nowhere to escape to. One, with an axe, runs right but looks back, while his companion with a spear seems to be suddenly stopped in his tracks by something, with his free hand covering his mouth, or perhaps he is calling out. In front of him are Norman knights charging from the opposite direction, who are being observed by the last man on the hill, his foot resting on another stylized tree that ends this scene. The pace has been relentless, but the tree marks a stop, allowing us to breathe again, if only for a moment.

The tide turns

The two fleeing Englishmen facing the next mounted charge might instead be goading or taunting their attackers with their hand gestures if they thought the Normans appeared to be losing heart. The chroniclers tell us that the battle raged all day, and William of Poitiers talks of the Duke's army falling away in the face of steadfast resistance by the English. Luckily for the Normans – according to the Tapestry's narrative at least – they have Bishop Odo, whom we see dressed in a hauberk covered with a triangular chequered pattern and holding his baton aloft (Scene 54). As the inscription tells us, he is encouraging the men: HIC ODO EP[ISCOPV]S BACVLV[M] TENENS CONFORTAT PVEROS (Here Bishop Odo, holding a baton, cheers on the young men). The action becomes more confused now, as Odo rides in one direction (to the right), while two Normans charge behind him in the other, towards the English. The sight of a churchman in the bloody heart of a battle might seem surprising today, but it was perfectly acceptable by the norms of the time for the bishop to be wielding his mace at an opponent.

One interpretation of this scene showing the 'young men' on horseback being encouraged by Odo is that it was part of a calculated tactic. According to this theory, the Normans, having failed to entice the Anglo-Saxons from their defensive positions, organized a feigned flight to draw them out. Previously, it seems the English had broken ranks to pursue fleeing Bretons who had begun to give way, possibly in a real retreat, which then inspired William to do something similar intentionally. This tactic might have been learnt by the Normans in Italy and Sicily, and then employed by their kin in England. Others have doubted whether it would have been possible to deliver such a manoeuvre successfully in the confusion of battle. Whatever the case (feigned flight or not), the Anglo-Saxons did leave their defensive positions at Hastings, exposing themselves to attack and defeat.

Odo's intervention at this point in the battle is not mentioned in any accounts other than the Bayeux Tapestry, which is one of the reasons why it is thought likely that he had a hand in its creation. The next moment depicted in the embroidery, however, is one that is reported by other sources. Duke William is shown deliberately raising his helmet so that his men can see him (Scene 55). William of Poitiers describes how a rumour went round the Norman forces that the Duke had been killed, threatening to send his troops into headlong retreat. William, supposedly noticing that the English had left their lines in pursuit of the fleeing Normans, raised his helmet to show that he was still alive and told his men to turn around and renew their efforts.

The caption is unequivocal: hIC EST DVX VVILEL[MVS] (here is Duke William). This text sits above the image of the Duke, in full armour on his galloping horse, as he lifts up his nose piece and looks backwards over his shoulder, apparently in accord with Poitiers's account. The horseman behind him (to the left) seems to be raising his sword in some sort of acclamation, and to make absolutely sure there can be no misunderstanding, the man in front of the Duke, with a prominent moustache and chest piece, points directly at William's head with one hand and grasps an impressive standard in the other. This was clearly a critical moment in the battle, when William demonstrates his bravery, strength of leadership and initiative in order to turn the situation to his advantage. It is also a moment that anyone hoping to be held in high repute after the battle, and wanting their name to be remembered, would wish to be associated with. And that brings us to the identity of the man who is pointing at the Duke. The surviving text in the upper border above him appears to read E...TIVS, but there is a gap between the E and the other letters where a patch has replaced a section that was torn away at some point. Scholars have argued that the word originally read EVSTATIVS, that is, Eustace.

The most likely candidate for a Eustace is Count Eustace II of Boulogne, who in 1051 had been involved in the dispute with the Godwins in Dover. It is certain that he fought at Hastings, and it seems he was also renowned for his extravagant facial hair – his nickname was 'al gernons', the moustachioed. So it would seem fairly conclusive that this is indeed Count Eustace, which has led some academics to promote the idea that Eustace may have been the patron of the Bayeux Tapestry, especially given the key role he seems to be accorded at this pivotal point in the story. But, as always with the Tapestry, an extra element has to be taken into account.

In the early nineteenth century, Charles Stothard was sent by the Society of Antiquaries of London to make a full-scale drawn copy of the Bayeux Tapestry, so that coloured engravings could be created and sold to scholars and antiquarians of the Society. It appears that Stothard decided to restore the Tapestry in his drawings to the condition that he believed it was in when it was first documented by researchers almost a century previously. He did this by joining up the dots in the form of needle holes that he could see on the original, and perhaps also reinventing some images. Almost certainly the Bayeux Tapestry itself was then physically restored on the basis of Stothard's drawings, though not necessarily in accord with the original medieval work. Notoriously, Stothard also removed at least one small piece from the Tapestry. A fragment was for a time in the collections of the South Kensington Museum (later the Victoria and Albert Museum), London. Plaster casts were also made, which are now held by the British Museum and the Society of Antiquaries.

A recent study of the Eustace question has pointed out that the E...TIVS text as it survives today may well have been substantially altered by antiquarian restorations based on Stothard's pen and ink drawings, no doubt influenced in turn by his knowledge of the Conquest story. The moustache of the figure also seems to have grown in size when compared with the Stothard drawings. While Eustace is recorded in the documentary sources as being present at the battle, his involvement in this episode is not mentioned. Doubts have therefore been raised as to whether the figure is in fact Eustace, or someone else entirely. And that someone else, it has been proposed, is Robert of Mortain, Duke William's half-brother, the man shown in the Tapestry in the company of William and Odo in the early phases of the campaign on English soil. Following this line of thought, the 'E' is really an 'R' and the rest falls into place: ROBERTVS.

It is notable that from about this point onwards, the lower border changes; instead of a charnel house of corpses it is now occupied by a steadily advancing rank of archers, all marching forwards in unison. They are somewhat under-embroidered, with an almost complete lack of colour infilling, apart from a couple of exceptions. Whoever was in charge of sewing this part perhaps ran out of time or patience to complete them. This area also might have been heavily restored, so further study is required for it to be properly understood. Nevertheless, they are clearly archers, and no doubt an indication of the importance of William's bowmen in the eventual outcome of the battle. It is about halfway through this line of archers, and just after the horse of the 'Eustace/Robert' figure that the join falls between the seventh and eighth panels of the Tapestry.

Following William's demonstration that he is still alive, thus reviving hope in the hearts of his soldiers, it feels like the battle has swung decisively in favour of the Normans. Not only are the archers below rushing forwards, planting their quivers in the ground and then loosing off volleys of arrows, but the horsemen are also once more charging into the fray with renewed vigour. hIC FRANCI PVGNANT ET CECIDERVNT QVI ERANT CVM hAROLDO (here the French fight, and those who were with Harold fall) reads the caption extending above their heads as they assault the English infantry (Scene 56). The Anglo-Saxons here are wearing full armour again, but are much more scattered and less well organized than before, as they are attacked from all sides. The caption seems to suggest that these are the elite troops around Harold – the final line of defence. Arrows liberally bristle from their shields, and though they are fighting bravely with their battle-axes, they are being slaughtered. On the left, an Anglo-Saxon has miscalculated his sword blow, exposing himself to a mounted knight. Behind him is an axeman, another with a spear and a third falling to the ground with an arrow in his face. Facing the other direction, a man with an unusual oval shield (either a rendering of perspective or just a badly embroidered kite shield) is about to be decapitated by a Norman sword before he has time to bring his axe down on his assailant, who himself carries a shield with an elaborate motif and is out of his saddle. Beneath them in the lower border, dividing the line of Norman archers, is a dead Anglo-Saxon with a round shield.

Then, in a particularly graphic and brutal scene, a man in civilian dress has his head split open, with blood (represented by lines) spurting from his head and stomach. Even though directly above this unfortunate victim is the inscription 'Harold', it is improbable that this is supposed to be the King, but rather is one of his close entourage. The precise course of events leading up to this climactic point in the battle is not completely made clear in the Bayeux Tapestry in its rush to reach the finale. Some documentary sources talk of several feigned retreats by the Normans, which drew the English away from their defensive positions and allowed the Norman cavalry to wheel round and mow down their reckless foes. The arrows of the Norman archers were also said to have proved particularly decisive in breaking down the English resistance. We do know that the battle was long and bloody, and the Tapestry does not flinch from the gore, but it is less forthcoming in terms of the details of military strategy.

The death of Harold

With Harold's companions dead, we come to the moment of reckoning. The brutally bald text hIC hAROLD REX INTERFECTVS EST (here King Harold has been killed) tells us what we have been anticipating for a while (Scene 57). To anyone viewing the Bayeux Tapestry, then as now, it is obvious that this is the end, but the drawn-out and mercilessly detailed depiction lends an air of pathos to the English king's last stand. In this, one of the most famous scenes in medieval art, we see the figure of a man with a full moustache clutching an arrow that appears to be lodged in his eye. All around him, men are falling.

At this point, the crux of the entire battle, which perhaps was over all too quickly in reality, it seems the Tapestry designer may have tried to slow time down and show us more than one moment in the same event, making this part of the Tapestry in effect a series of time-lapse vignettes rather than what would now be regarded as separate still photographs. It is a scene that needs to be read from both sides, with the central small knot of English troops being subjected to an assault by the Norman knights left and right. On the left of the group, standing behind a valiant defender with his shield, is the standard bearer holding the dragon standard of Wessex; in front of them, another figure, but presumably also the standard bearer, is falling forwards, dropping the standard and about to be trampled by a Norman horse. To the right, a man is felled by an incoming horseman, his axe flying from his hands, and then a further group of warriors tries desperately to hold off the spear-wielding cavalry, but to no avail, as we see them being mown down one by one, falling like tumbling acrobats in front of us.

In the centre is the figure clutching the arrow, and the question is whether this is in fact King Harold with the fatal wound. Certainly, the word Harold appears written on either side of his head, and this, as we have seen before, is the way the Bayeux Tapestry identifies named individuals. It is also quite possible, as most historians believe, that the figure being cut down by the sword of the advancing horseman immediately to the right is Harold too. In which case the designer intended the two figures to represent the English king at different stages of his death, first receiving an arrow wound in the face and then being slashed and falling down. This time-lapse representation of the death of Harold would mirror the way the standard bearer also appears to be shown alive and in the throes of his death within the space a few centimetres of the embroidery. It is after the banner pole of the first standard bearer that the divide between the eighth and ninths panels falls, a join that was unknown until 1982, so well disguised is this seam.

Interestingly, the closest contemporary documentary sources to the battle do not refer to Harold being killed by an arrow (see pl. 15). William of Jumièges says that Harold fell 'covered with deadly wounds', while the *Carmen de Hastingae Proelio* describes him being felled with blows that variously 'cleaved his breast ... smote off his head ... pierced the inwards of his belly ... and ... hewed off his thigh and bore away the severed limb'. It is not beyond the bounds of possibility to correlate these accounts with an interpretation of this scene as showing King Harold receiving several final blows.

The story of Harold's death by an arrow only starts to appear in later documentary sources. The monk Amatus of Montecassino, in a geographically wide-ranging history of the Normans written in the 1080s, mentions Harold's eye being gouged out with an arrow, though some scholars consider this to be unreliable, as the only surviving version of the text we have today was written 250 years after the original. Baudri of Bourgeuil, writing a few decades after the Conquest, does describe Harold dying by a lethal arrow, and references to this then become progressively more detailed as time goes on. This could be a case of the documentary sources following the lead of the Bayeux Tapestry.

There is also, of course, a lively debate over whether the Bayeux Tapestry originally showed Harold being shot by an arrow in the eye at all. It would have been a stroke of very bad luck to have received such a precise injury as in the Tapestry. Comparison with the earlier drawings of the embroidery, however, has revealed that, as with the Eustace scene, restoration work has been carried out here. Originally, it seems, the Tapestry may not have shown an arrow piercing the eye, but rather a spear passing just over the figure's helmet (see pl. 16 and 17). That would be a significant difference. And research has further ascertained that it is not an isolated example in the embroidery. At least seven arrows now visible in the embroidery seem to have been added since the eighteenth-century drawings were made, in other words during the nineteenth-century restoration work. In Charles Stothard's drawing the shaft has flights attached, turning it into an arrow. The inference then is that the Tapestry was altered in the restoration to fit more closely with the believed circumstances of Harold's death. That does not, of course, preclude this figure being Harold, but it does cast doubt on whether the Tapestry designer intended to show him meeting his end in this way.

What can we learn about Harold in his final hours? There is no sense of him exhibiting cowardice or behaving dishonourably, and he is granted the good death of a soldier in battle. It could be read as a glorious last stand against his enemies, surrounded by his few remaining followers, in the tradition of other great warriors of this period, such as Ealdorman Byrhtnoth (in the Battle of Maldon) and Beowulf (though fictional). Any moralizing about his perfidy and perjury that there may have been earlier in the Bayeux Tapestry ceases when the battle begins to rage, as the designer focuses unsparingly on the violence and ferocity of the fight. In essence, Harold dies a hero's death. By extension, perhaps, the Anglo-Saxons are also allowed to emerge from the battle with some sense of honour in defeat.

Though the manner of his falling may be in doubt, Harold's death does seem to bring English resistance to an end. Already in the lower border the Normans are reaping the rewards of their victory, with the bodies of the dead being stripped of their weapons and armour as the winners' booty; hardly a trace will be left in the ground as a record of the cataclysmic event. There is even a possible touch of levity among the horrors of the bloody day as two men seem to be wrestling over possession of a shield they both want.

But the day is not yet quite done, as the Bayeux Tapestry has one final (existing) scene (58), which is prefaced by the caption ET FVGA VERTERVNT ANGLI (and the English have fled). We see five triumphant Normans, including a mounted archer, spurring their horses on to chase the fleeing English. The embroidery here is badly damaged and has been subject to much restoration, not all of it necessarily sympathetic to the original. Among the ragged patchwork as the Tapestry peters out, and after a heavily stylized tree, the action splits into two registers. The upper section shows unarmoured men making a bid to escape the field; three of them are carrying strange clubs ending in four bosses, while one has been fortunate enough to procure a horse. One of these fleeing Englishmen is pierced in the eye by an arrow; it too, like Harold's, seems to be a later addition by restorers. Below them, two slightly exotic-looking horsemen seem to be brandishing flails towards a figure who is in some way bound up, perhaps to a tree. Presumably this is the victors exacting harsh justice on the losers.

A final odd addition to the surviving scene here is the naked man among vegetation in the lower border. As the rest of the border is missing from this point onwards, it is not possible to know whether there were further curiosities or anything that might help explain his presence, but similar motifs occur in contemporary art.

The end of the story?

And so we have reached the end – the Normans have won, the English are vanquished, Harold is dead, and the throne is William's to seize. It is an abrupt conclusion. The aftermath of the battle is not shown in the Bayeux Tapestry, so we do not learn of one more English last stand among the trees, nor are we told how Harold's body, almost unrecognizable, was buried in an unmarked grave. Also, we see nothing of the Norman army's subsequent rampage through the southeast of England and advance to London, or Duke William being crowned king of the English in Westminster Abbey on Christmas Day 1066.

Or at least we do not see any of this in the embroidery now. It seems certain that some scenes have been lost through the damage caused by the winding and unwinding of the Tapestry over the years. We cannot be sure what is missing, but a widely held view is that it would have shown some of the events outlined above in the run-up to the coronation of King William, and perhaps also depicted him seated on the throne, in a mirror image of King Edward at the start.

If that were the case, it is unlikely that much attention would have been paid to the brief show of support by some of the English for Edgar Ætheling, the forgotten prince, to become king after the English defeat: 'Archbishop Ealdred and the garrison in London wanted to have Prince Edgar for king, just as was his natural right', says the Anglo-Saxon Chronicle. Given Edgar's absence from the Bayeux Tapestry up till now, it is not plausible that whoever was driving the narrative would have authorized any account of him precisely at this moment of resistance. English opposition to the new Norman regime continued for years, but William maintained his grip on the throne until his death in 1087, ensuring his dukedom and the crown passed on to his heirs. Robert Curthose became Duke of Normandy, and William II, Rufus, became King of England.

From this perspective, the Bayeux Tapestry has somewhat skewed our understanding of the Norman Conquest. It shows it as being the result of a clash between just two men, Harold and William. Despite the damage, the embroidery has in this way done one of its jobs with great success, which is to write the later English resistance to the Conquest out of the story, and to expunge from the record any conflicting claim to the throne that William had won by his victory at Battle. It has very effectively persuaded generations that Harold usurped the crown that was rightfully William's, and then paid the price (though with honour intact at the end perhaps). It is what is missing from the narrative that is perhaps most interesting to consider next, as it is time to examine the long and far-reaching legacy of the embroidery.

CHAPTER 12

THE BAYEUX TAPESTRY AND ITS LEGACY

The Bayeux Tapestry is a unique historical source for unravelling the circumstances surrounding the Norman Conquest of England in 1066 and the events that led up to it. It provides a version of the past that people today can still relate to, particularly because of its 'comic-strip' style. We can understand, in broad terms, the story it tells, and it helps that some of the events and characters are, to a greater or lesser extent, familiar. Other narratives of the period exist, referred to throughout this book, including the Anglo-Saxon Chronicle and the histories of the two Williams, Poitiers and Jumièges, but compared to the Tapestry these are rather terse and dry, or hard to understand. Surviving Norman buildings, such as the great castles and cathedrals, provide a background to the story, but can be complex to interpret. Even the site of the great battle itself, dare we say it, though evocative, does not relate the events that happened there as clearly, powerfully or imaginatively as the Bayeux Tapestry.

Its art, though superficially simple and stylized, and in a sense archaic, has stood the test of time well, ensuring that the Bayeux Tapestry still exerts a strong fascination today. We can see who is doing what, and the captions (when translated) do not require a great investment of time to read or understand. Oddly, although the Bayeux Tapestry was worked almost a millennium ago, it somehow feels quite modern. There is something about the scene-by-scene format of the embroidery that encourages us to view it almost as a series of photographs. It fixes precise moments in history very effectively, which means that it has become imbued with far more literal power than perhaps even the original designer intended. Although most people today understand that photographs can be framed, composed and manipulated to produce a very specific view of an occasion, we still tend to trust them as accurate witnesses to events. Because the Tapestry has a similar photographic quality, framing episodes and the actions of characters within them, we take it at face value, as the way things actually happened at the time, much more so than the documentary accounts, which we tend to assume come freighted with their own internal biases.

Historical legacy

In this way, one important legacy of the Bayeux Tapestry is how it has shaped our view of history and what happened in 1066. Reading it literally, the Battle of Hastings and the following Conquest of England might seem the result of a simple binary fight between two men – King Harold II of England and Duke William of Normandy. Because William was the victor, the implicit suggestion is that Harold was somehow not throne-worthy, and that William won by both might and right. The Bayeux Tapestry does not offer an absolute answer to the question of Harold's right to reign, aside from acknowledging the fact that he was king. Nonetheless, there is an undercurrent in the story that Harold, in making some sort of sacred oath to William, may have perjured himself. This does not necessarily mean that the Tapestry wants us to believe that Harold lacked a legitimate claim to the crown, but rather that he had compromised it by (apparently) agreeing to support William. The more serious issue for Harold was that he had lied under oath.

Such a straightforward presentation of the situation as a head-to-head clash does not allow for any nuance or complications, and writes other significant figures out of the story (one exception being Bishop Odo). Tostig and Harald Hardrada, and their invasion of northern England, for instance, are entirely absent from the embroidery, and this is significant because Hardrada could have been a throne-worthy figure himself; he certainly would have found support among Anglo-Scandinavians in northern England. The fact that the Norwegian king died at the battle at Stamford Bridge meant that by the time the embroidery was made he no longer presented a threat to King William, the Conqueror. In which case it might not have been too impolitic to have included him in the Tapestry's tale. However, it would still have clouded the picture of a binary conflict between Harold and William.

One fascinating fresh piece of the jigsaw, highlighted in a recent biography of Edward the Confessor, is that (through the complexities of the European dynastic situation) Harald Hardrada was likely to have been the uncle (by marriage) of Edgar Ætheling. Edgar's mother Agatha was probably the daughter of Iaroslav I of Kiev, and another of Iaroslav's daughters was married to Harald Hardrada. That raises the tantalizing possibility that Hardrada was actually invading in support of Edgar, which again would explain why he would not be a welcome addition to the Bayeux Tapestry's narrative.

The failure of the Bayeux Tapestry to include any reference to Edgar Ætheling is of greater consequence in terms of its legacy. In the eyes of many at the time, Edgar was the strongest claimant to the throne in terms of his lineage, being the grandson of King Edmund Ironside (King Edward's half-brother). His age and inexperience weighed against him, as did his likely lack of a support base in England given his lifetime in exile. Even so, for Edgar to feature in the Tapestry would have required some justification for why both Harold and William had wrested the throne from him. Edgar survived the Norman Conquest, rebelled and was then rehabilitated into William's court. So presumably he continued to be a figure around whom English support against the Normans could potentially have crystallized when the Tapestry was under production, and it is not hard to understand why, in the context of the immediate post-Conquest period, his exclusion makes sense.

What is surprising, however, is that even at this distance in time the absence of Edgar from the narrative of the Norman invasion remains with us. We still tend to see the Norman Conquest as the

Bayeux Tapestry presents it, with little room for Edgar. That is not to say that historians do not consider Edgar Ætheling (and the other possible claimants to the throne in 1066) in their research, but it is the story told in the embroidery that tends to prevail in popular understanding and representations of the events. While Edgar's importance in the Conquest story is familiar to academics, there is no place for him in the narrative for most people beyond scholarly circles.

The enduring reach of the Bayeux Tapestry means it still dominates the conversation about the Conquest story. Its presentation of events as a direct clash between William and Harold sees Harold first built up as a figure endowed with laudable qualities including martial prowess, bravery and piety, but who is then let down by his own actions. Nevertheless, he is still a worthy adversary for Duke William, who is shown as a decisive military leader. However, although the embroidery's images and story may seem – on the surface at least – clear, it is also opaque and noncommittal in almost every aspect, and can permit a range of interpretations according to an individual's point of view and sensibilities. It grants a certain sense of Anglo-Saxon honour in defeat, while also lauding the achievement of the Norman victory. That was the case back in the later eleventh century, and is even more so now, as we struggle to put ourselves into the mindset of those living in the post-Conquest period. It is the Tapestry's genius, really – for almost its entire length it is like a modern politician avoiding answering a difficult question. But at the same time, it did perform the function of heading off any speculation as to whether William had a stronger claim to the throne of England than anyone else – in fact, perhaps no one at the time entirely understood all the circumstances. Seen in that way, the Bayeux Tapestry is quite factual, simply presenting things as they were, without trying to give one single perspective and allowing for many views to be accommodated.

Given all the Tapestry's hedging what can we conclude about it? As far as the evidence available permits us to judge, the Tapestry was designed and made in Canterbury, by English embroiderers, within a decade of the events it describes. It was almost certainly completed by 1077, in time for the consecration of Bayeux Cathedral, probably on the orders of Bishop Odo, but not necessarily for specific display – it might be imagined that it was left up to the cathedral authorities to decide what they actually did with it. Odo's motivations in this project included self-aggrandizement in the eyes of his contemporaries, and possibly also of God (hence the gift to the cathedral), a desire to please and praise King William, to acknowledge the success of the Conquest (and, coincidentally, thank God), and promote his own actions and those of his followers. As many have pointed out, this explains why both Odo, and Bayeux, are so prominent in the story.

Assuming Odo is the key player in the creation of the Tapestry, this still leaves room for a possible role in the production or design of the Tapestry for Abbot Scolland, formerly a monk at Mont-Saint-Michel and from around 1072 Abbot of St Augustine's, Canterbury. While he has been cited as a potential important figure in its production, his role might simply have been to make Canterbury's libraries available for consultation for drawing designs for the embroidery. If so, this might help date the Tapestry to between 1072 and 1077. The designer of the Tapestry certainly seems to have borrowed heavily from contemporary manuscript illuminations for aspects of the design, supporting a Canterbury provenance.

The Tapestry's intended function was potentially quite simply as a piece of impressive art to document an impressive story. Although it has been seen as a justification for William's invasion of England, on the basis of the perjury of Earl Harold and the latter's subsequent usurpation of the throne, the Tapestry's account is, as noted, fairly balanced. That is not to deny that there are various places where the designer (or an embroiderer) has inserted artistic devices and mechanisms for the purpose of commentary. Images in the upper and lower borders sometimes have implications that inform, or allude to, the main narrative, though it is debatable how far this can be taken in every instance. On the whole, such artistic devices serve to increase tension – most of the Tapestry's border animals, for instance, confront or fight each other.

As it is apparently such an even-handed account overall, it is unlikely, as has been suggested, that the Bayeux Tapestry contains any deep subversive message or code that supports a pro-English standpoint. Those viewing it who were not supposed to be able to see such hidden meanings would not have been so easily fooled. And who was the likely intended audience? It is hard to say, but as it was probably designed for Bayeux Cathedral's consecration, it could have been seen by the great and the good of the new Anglo-Norman secular and clerical hierarchy of the time, many of whom would have had direct experience of the events of 1066. Quite possibly a narrator was expected, and required, to guide the viewers through the Tapestry, whether that was when it was periodically hung, as in later times, or just rolled out.

The fact that the Tapestry was probably designed for initial display at the consecration of Bayeux Cathedral does not rule out the idea (if perhaps unlikely) that it could have been taken around other ecclesiastical and secular venues. The absence of heavy gold thread in its design makes it more portable than such a long embroidery might otherwise have been, though its length does limit its potential for travel and display somewhat. However, it is possible that it was just the act of making and presenting it that was of importance, and it was then kept in storage and only brought out on certain occasions or maybe not often at all, hence its generally good state of preservation to this day. There is probably not much missing from the beginning of the Tapestry, though this part has been heavily restored, but the general consensus is that the end has lost scenes, which most likely would have depicted William's coronation in London – assuming the embroidery was actually completed at all.

Cultural legacy

One of the most long-lasting historical legacies of the Tapestry is to continue to exclude Edgar Ætheling from the picture. By not making any reference to him, or any other contenders for the crown in 1066, the Bayeux Tapestry has imposed boundaries around the popular perception of the story. So perhaps someone should embroider a new 'tapestry' that stitches Edgar back in. That is not a wholly implausible idea, because one of the other legacies of the Bayeux Tapestry has been to inspire a whole raft of imitations, replicas and remakes. There are people who have imagined new endings for the Tapestry, others who have created replicas of the whole thing, and some who have made embroideries, even tapestries proper, in style and substance similar to the original, but telling different stories. And on top of that, the Tapestry has an astonishing modern cultural influence and value, having been used for all sorts of serious, and less serious, contemporary and political commentary.

The history of reproducing the Bayeux Tapestry goes back a long way, to the point at which its very existence resurfaced among the academic community three hundred years ago. As noted in the introduction, at the beginning of the eighteenth century, Nicolas-Joseph Foucault, a French man of letters, had a drawing of the embroidery made for him. This did not include any information about the original work that it reproduced, so after Foucault's death it was something of a mystery until Bernard de Montfaucon established by 1730 that it was the embroidery held in Bayeux. Two facsimiles of the Bayeux Tapestry were then made, and by the 1750s there were also English copies. Indeed, realizing that the Tapestry might be an English product, it was important for the British to have 'their own' copies. That led in the early nineteenth to Charles Stothard being sent by the Society of Antiquaries of London to make his accurate reproduction drawing of the Tapestry.

With increasing public awareness of the existence of the Bayeux Tapestry in Britain, nineteenth-century tourists began to make their way to Normandy and record their observations, so that some documentary accounts now also accompany the pictorial narrative. Hudson Gurney published his description in 1817, Dawson Turner in 1818 and then Thomas Frognall Dibden in 1821. It is from these reports that we learn that the embroidery was in a parlous state at both ends from being stored on a rolling device which allowed it to be unwound for visitors to view on request. It was only in 1842 that it was put on permanent display in a room in the town library (see pl. 18), and then in 1913 in the former Deanery.

When photography came of age it was soon used to record the Bayeux Tapestry, with a full reproduction made in 1872. As an inducement to enable this photography for the English to take place, the fragment once held by the South Kensington Museum (now the Victoria and Albert Museum) was gifted back to Bayeux, though never refixed to the Tapestry. A copy of the photography was then used as the tracing template for the first full-sized embroidered facsimile, which was made by Elizabeth Wardle and the ladies of Leek in 1885–86. Famously, they decided to uphold late Victorian modesty by adding shorts to the naked figures in the borders, though they probably based this censorship on the already existing bowdlerization of the hand-coloured photographs in the South Kensington Museum. The Leek embroidery went on a highly successful tour, even travelling to the USA, before it was acquired by a former mayor of Reading in southern England and gifted to the town, thereafter being known as the Reading Tapestry. It is now held in Reading Museum, accessible for anyone to see. Since then, other replicas have been made, sometimes using embroidery and sometimes in different media.

Mrs Maude Geare, for example, displayed her needlework replica, made after eighteen years of research and work, at Tunbridge Wells Museum in 1950. It now resides in Monmouth School for Girls. Jason Welch, in Norfolk, devoted himself to carving a wooden replica of the Tapestry after the death of his son in 2011. Meanwhile, Michael Linton from New Zealand has spent thirty-three years creating a steel mosaic of the entire Tapestry. He not only replicated the original, but also created his own new ending to complete the story, taking it up to the coronation of King William.

Others, too, have produced their interpretations of the missing end panels of the Tapestry. In the mid-1990s, the embroiderer Jan Messent created her Bayeux Tapestry finale, showing the Norman army's advance to the strategically important site of Berkhamsted in Hertfordshire, where William met the surviving English nobles, and then on to Westminster Abbey for his coronation. In 2013, over 400 people on the island of Alderney worked on a replica of the Tapestry, which included an ending that also showed the coronation of King William and the construction of the Tower of London, incorporating some elements from Messent's designs.

There has also been a healthy tradition of embroiderers producing supplementary 'offshoots' of the main Tapestry story, filling in some of the gaps. By 2012, a group of enthusiasts had produced an embroidery devoted to the story of the Battle of Fulford, which was of course omitted from the Bayeux version. Similarly, a Battle of Stamford Bridge Tapestry was also worked on in advance of the 950th anniversary of that battle. The Battle Tapestry, stitched in 2016–17, is modelled on the Bayeux Tapestry and relates the post-Conquest history of Battle from 1066 to 1115 in eight embroidered scenes; it even includes the embroidery work of one of the present authors.

The Bayeux Tapestry has also been the inspiration for several artistic projects that have borrowed the spirit of the original to commemorate events from often entirely different times and places. The Overlord Tapestry, commissioned in 1968, retells the story of the D-Day Landings of 1944, which led to the liberation of Bayeux in the Second World War. The Quaker Tapestry, created between 1981 and 1996 and now housed in a museum in Kendal in the Lake District, tells the story of the influence of the Quakers on the modern world. More recently, in 2013, the artist Darren Cullen created a Bloody Sunday Bayeux Tapestry, which shows the events of 1972 in Derry/Londonderry, Northern Ireland, in Bayeux Tapestry style. And there is also the Game of Thrones Tapestry, made to support tourism across Ireland and produced using Irish linen – this has even been added to as the saga continued.

Beyond this, the Bayeux Tapestry's reach is global. The Keiskamma Tapestry was embroidered at the start of the twenty-first century in South Africa and recounts the history of the Eastern Cape region there. In Canada, the artist Sandra Sawatzky spent nine years creating the Black Gold Tapestry, which represents the development of the use of oil in human history. All these projects, and more, take the Bayeux Tapestry as their starting point; some are making political statements, some are telling stories, much like the original.

Afterlife

It is fair to say that the Bayeux Tapestry has become a cultural icon in broader ways too. Over the years, it has been repurposed countless times in cartoons and comics, in film and theatre, and on the covers of newspapers, books and magazines, for making political, satirical or straightforwardly comedic points. The *Sun* newspaper commissioned a Bye-EU tapestry (printed on canvas) to 'celebrate' Britain's plans to withdraw from the European Union, which was (briefly) presented to Bayeux Museum. And then there is the internet, where the Bayeux Tapestry has come alive.

Animated versions of the Tapestry provide an easy way into its story, and for those who want to interact with the narrative, there is even a website that allows people to create a parody scene based on its imagery, with the facility to wittily, or otherwise, caption it as a comment on contemporary matters. In the aftermath of President Macron of France's decision in 2018 to allow the loan of the Tapestry to the United Kingdom while the museum in Bayeux is refurbished, this tool was used to create an outpouring of internet memes that flooded social media. Suddenly anyone could produce their own image based on the Bayeux Tapestry without having to go anywhere near a piece of linen or pick up a needle and thread.

Modern photography and reproduction can also influence our view of the embroidery itself. The most likely way people come across the Bayeux Tapestry, other than by a visit to see the original, is in the form of a photograph, which will be of a specific scene of a certain length as in this book. And who decides where a scene starts and ends? The best example of modern photography potentially managing our understanding of the Bayeux Tapestry is the critical scene showing the death of King Harold at Hastings. In the excellent large-format book by David M. Wilson published in 1985, there is a full-length reproduction of the Tapestry, divided into double-page spreads. The beautiful photographs, reproduced in high quality, were taken when the Tapestry was rehung in 1983. The double-page spread of Harold's demise places the figure with the arrow in the eye at the centre, and thus emphasizes his importance in this scene and perhaps influences how we understand it. Because of the way it is cropped, the photograph only shows the left-hand side of the last stand of the English and ends with the figure being felled by the horseman. Turn the page, and the right-hand side of the English defence comes into view, with another group of housecarls trying to beat back the Normans. If the photograph had been reproduced including both sides of the English group (which is presumably how the original designer intended it to be viewed), then the character with the arrow in the eye would no longer occupy such a central position and the whole emphasis of the scene would not be so firmly focused on him. That might therefore make the viewer less inclined to recognize him as King Harold. And this is without any consideration of whether the arrow was original to the embroidery or the result of nineteenth-century restoration (the equivalent of a modern piece of Photoshopping). So in one particular photograph, both selectively manipulative framing and physical alteration are present. And that potentially completely changes our interpretation of the event.

The Bayeux Tapestry itself has, of course, been the subject of political manipulation and point-scoring over the years. Quite apart from what it said, or did not say, to the Anglo-Norman viewers in the eleventh century, it has been appropriated for political ends in modern times. Famously, in 1803, only half a century or so after the publication of Montfaucon's facsimile had made people generally aware of the Tapestry's existence, Napoleon had it moved from Bayeux to Paris and put on grand public display, at the very same time that his troops and boats were being massed in northern France for another attempt at an invasion across the Channel. The embroidery's story of a successful amphibious assault by French soldiers on English soil fitted in very well with Napoleon's ambitions at the time.

A century and a half later, the Bayeux Tapestry was appropriated by another set of expansionist ambitions, those of the Nazis (see pl. 19), who were taken with the idea that it was a product of Germanic culture. This was based on the argument that the Normans were descendants of Viking settlers, and that the Vikings were essentially Germanic peoples. Following German occupation of France early on in the Second World War, a team of German researchers undertook a rigorous study of the Tapestry. When it looked certain that the Allies were going to invade France, the Tapestry was transferred to Paris for safekeeping. Throughout this time Reichsführer Heinrich Himmler himself took a close personal interest in the Tapestry, so much so that during the liberation of Paris he ordered its removal to Germany – fortunately the message (intercepted by eavesdropping on German messages at the code-breaking centre at Bletchley Park in Britain) came too late. The Tapestry was recovered and eventually made its way back to Bayeux.

It has been a political pawn in Anglo-French relations as well. Twice in the twentieth century, requests were made for the Bayeux Tapestry to be loaned to Britain, first in 1953 for Queen Elizabeth II's coronation, and then in 1966 on the 900th anniversary of the Battle of Hastings, when both the Victoria and Albert Museum and Westminster Abbey hoped to display the Tapestry. Neither request was granted. The idea of the Tapestry returning to Britain was floated once more in an article in BBC History Magazine in 2008, in advance of an international conference on the Tapestry at the British Museum, and the views of historians and Tapestry researchers were gathered.

The latest phase in the Bayeux Tapestry's story is that it is going to be rehoused in a refurbished gallery in Bayeux Museum. This will be designed to present the embroidery in the best way to allow the public to see and understand it, and also ensure the embroidery's long-term survival. Although it was last rehoused thirty-five years ago, conservation, display and security requirements have advanced greatly since then. While the new exhibition space is being developed, there is an opportunity that the Bayeux Tapestry will finally be allowed to travel back to Britain on loan, hopefully to the British Museum. When precisely that will happen is not yet confirmed, but if it is exhibited in the UK it will no doubt draw very large crowds, and will become a cultural reference point in much the same way that the Tutankhamun exhibition at the British Museum did in 1972.

Some important questions need to be asked before any British exhibition takes place, though. How will it travel and its safety be assured? Where will it be cleaned and conserved, and what scientific and other research opportunities could that offer? How might it be displayed, which artifacts and documents will be assembled or loaned to accompany it and help tell its story? How will the Norman Conquest be commemorated, and how will it fit in with the national conversation? And will it finally be an opportunity to bring Edgar Ætheling back into the frame? The answers will not be known for a few years yet, but one thing is certain – the next key chapter in the long and ongoing story of the legacy of the Bayeux Tapestry is about to be written.

TIMELINE
OF KEY EVENTS

911

Treaty of Saint-Clair-sur-Epte – King Charles the Simple of West Frankia gifts lands that would become the Duchy of Normandy to a Norseman named Rollo.

927

England becomes unified as a single kingdom under King Æthelstan.

1013

England is invaded by Swein Forkbeard of Denmark (and his son Cnut), forcing England's king, Æthelred, with his second wife Emma of Normandy and their children, into exile in Normandy.

3 FEBRUARY 1014

Swein dies and Æthelred returns to England. Cnut is declared Swein's successor, but withdraws from England in April 1014 until 1016.

23 APRIL 1016

King Æthelred dies and is succeeded by his son by his first wife, Edmund Ironside.

18 OCTOBER 1016

Battle of Ashingdon (Assandun) – King Edmund is defeated by Cnut, and the English kingdom is divided between them, Cnut taking the north.

30 NOVEMBER 1016

Edmund dies and Cnut becomes king of the whole of England; Edmund's family flees overseas, as do the children of King Æthelred by Emma of Normandy, including Prince Edward (the future king of England).

JULY 1017

Emma of Normandy marries King Cnut, though her children by Æthelred remain in Normandy under the protection of Emma's brother, Duke Richard II, the Good, of Normandy.

6 AUGUST 1027

Robert I the Magnificent becomes Duke of Normandy on the death of his brother, Richard III; Robert's son, William, is born in about the same year.

3 JULY 1035

William becomes Duke of Normandy (aged about eight), on the death of his father, Duke Robert I.

12 NOVEMBER 1035

King Cnut dies and is succeeded by his son Harold Harefoot by Ælfgyva of Northampton at the expense of Harthacnut, Cnut's son by Emma of Normandy.

1036

Emma's sons by King Æthelred, Edmund and Alfred, travel to England; Alfred is blinded and dies, for which Earl Godwin of Wessex is later blamed.

1037

Emma flees to Normandy as Harold Harefoot asserts his hold over the English kingdom with the support of Earl Godwin.

17 MARCH 1040

King Harold I Harefoot dies and is succeeded by Harthacnut, who is also king of Denmark; on 17 June he arrives in England with his mother, Emma of Normandy.

1041
Prince Edward, son of Emma by King Æthelred, returns to England.

8 JUNE 1042
King Harthacnut dies suddenly and is succeeded by his half-brother Edward; the following year King Edward has his mother Emma deprived of all her property (briefly).

1043
Duke William of Normandy suppresses the military ambitions of Thurstan Goz (a rebel lord being supported by King Henry I of France) by capturing Falaise.

23 JANUARY 1045
King Edward the Confessor marries Edith, daughter of Earl Godwin of Wessex and sister of Earl Harold.

EARLY SUMMER 1047
Battle of Val-ès-Dunes – Duke William of Normandy, with support from King Henry I of France, defeats his cousin, Count Guy of Brionne.

25 OCTOBER 1047
King Magnus the Good of Norway dies, and is succeeded by Harald Sigurdsson Hardrada.

1049
Swein, eldest son of Earl Godwin, is banished for murdering his cousin, Beorn; this follows his abduction of the Abbess of Leominster.

LATE 1049/EARLY 1050
Odo is made Bishop of Bayeux; he is likely to have been in his early twenties, so below canonical age (thirty) for a bishop.

SEPTEMBER 1051
Earl Godwin and his family are exiled, avoiding civil war with King Edward. Soon after, Duke William may have visited England, and perhaps at this time Godwin's son, Wulfnoth, and grandson, Hakon, are handed over to him as hostages.

1052
Earl Godwin and his sons forcefully return to England. King Edward backs down to their demands, among them the expulsion of 'foreigners', including Robert of Jumièges, Archbishop of Canterbury; Stigand, Bishop of Winchester, becomes Archbishop.

15 APRIL 1053
Earl Godwin dies and is succeeded by his son Harold. About this time, Guy becomes Count of Ponthieu on the death of his brother Enguerrand II, and Duke William of Normandy marries Matilda, daughter of Count Baldwin V of Flanders.

FEBRUARY 1054
Normandy is invaded on two fronts in support of a rebellion by Count William of Arques, the uncle of Duke William. Battle of Mortemer – Duke William defeats the rebels in the north, and effects the withdrawal of King Henry I of France in the east.

1056
King Edward of England seeks out the children of Edmund Ironside, including Prince Edward, learning that they are still alive, exiled in the Hungarian royal court.

19 APRIL 1057
Prince Edward the Exile dies in England before he can meet King Edward; with him is his son, Edgar, who is recognized as *ætheling* (throne-worthy).

AUGUST 1057
Battle of Varaville – Duke William defeats King Henry I of France and Count Geoffrey Martel of Anjou; never

again is Normandy invaded during William's lifetime.

1060
Duke William of Normandy establishes a castle at Caen.

1063
Earl Harold and his brother Tostig invade Wales to deal with Prince Gruffydd ap Llywelyn. Duke William nominates his son Robert as his heir in Normandy.

LATE SPRING/EARLY SUMMER 1064
Harold crosses the Channel and is captured by Count Guy of Ponthieu. He then joins William on campaign against the Bretons, after which he makes a sacred oath; he returns to England later that year, or early 1065.

OCTOBER 1065
Northumbria rebels against its earl, Tostig, who is exiled (in a deal brokered by his brother, Earl Harold); Tostig flees to Flanders, then to Scotland and Norway.

LATE 1065
King Edward has a series of strokes. It is almost certain his wish is for Prince Edgar Ætheling to succeed him, perhaps with Harold as 'protector'.

4/5 JANUARY 1066
King Edward dies; on his deathbed he promises the kingdom (or safe-keeping of it) to Earl Harold.

6 JANUARY 1066
Edward is buried. Harold II is crowned in Westminster Abbey following his election as king by the Witan (a council of the nobility).

APRIL/MAY 1066
A 'star', now known as Halley's Comet, is visible in the skies above England; it is interpreted as a portent of change.

MAY 1066
Provided with Flemish ships, Earl Tostig lands in the Isle of Wight, and (after being seen off by King Harold II) raids parts of Norfolk and Lincolnshire en route to Scotland.

AUGUST 1066
Duke William gathers a fleet to invade England.

8 SEPTEMBER 1066
King Harold disbands his fleet on the Isle of Wight and his troops on the south coast, as provisions are low and opportunities for a seaborne attack diminish.

20 SEPTEMBER 1066
Battle of Fulford – King Harald Hardrada of Norway and Earl Tostig defeat an English army led by earls Edwin and Morcar, south of York.

25 SEPTEMBER 1066
Battle of Stamford Bridge – King Harold surprises and defeats Harald of Norway and Earl Tostig, east of York; both are killed.

27/28 SEPTEMBER 1066
Duke William's naval fleet crosses the Channel and lands at Pevensey on the south coast of England. His army harries Sussex to draw Harold into battle.

14 OCTOBER 1066
Battle of Hastings – William of Normandy's army defeats King Harold; Harold is killed, along with his brothers, Gyrth and Leofwine, and many of the leading English earls. Soon after, the Witan proclaims Edgar Ætheling as king, and London holds firm.

10 DECEMBER 1066
Edgar Ætheling and the English nobility submit to Duke William at Berkhamsted; earls Edwin and Morcar resist until January 1067.

25 DECEMBER 1066
William of Normandy is crowned King of England in Westminster Abbey.

EARLY 1069
Northumbria rises in revolt against King William I. Edgar Ætheling supports the rebels and (in the autumn) captures York with the assistance of King Swein of Denmark.

11 APRIL 1070
Stigand is deposed as Archbishop of Canterbury.

1072
Edgar Ætheling is expelled from Scotland, following an agreement between King William and King Malcolm of Scotland; Edgar flees to Flanders.

1072
Scolland (Scotland) of Mont-Saint-Michel becomes the Abbot of St Augustine's Abbey, Canterbury.

18 DECEMBER 1075
Queen Edith (wife of King Edward, and sister of King Harold II) dies.

14 JULY 1077
Consecration of Bayeux Cathedral; perhaps it was for this moment that the Bayeux Tapestry was made.

1082
Bishop Odo is imprisoned on the orders of his half-brother, King William I.

9 SEPTEMBER 1087
King William dies and is succeeded by his sons: Robert Curthose as Duke of Normandy, and William II Rufus as King of England.

EARLY 1097
Bishop Odo of Bayeux, released from prison by William before his death, dies in Sicily en route to the Holy Land; he is buried in Palermo Cathedral.

7 FEBRUARY 1161
King Edward the Confessor is canonized by Pope Alexander III.

1245
Romanesque buildings of Westminster Abbey demolished to make way for a new cathedral under King Henry III of England.

1412
Bayeux Cathedral crypt is reopened; it perhaps contained the Bayeux Tapestry.

1476
The Bayeux Tapestry is recorded in the inventory of Bayeux Cathedral.

1724
Drawing (of what we now know to be the Bayeux Tapestry) found by Antoine Lancelot among the papers of Nicolas-Joseph Foucault.

1729
Bernard de Montfaucon discovers the Bayeux Tapestry is in Bayeux Cathedral.

DECEMBER 1803
Napoleon Bonaparte has the Bayeux Tapestry moved to Paris for display prior to his planned invasion of England.

8 JULY 1816
Charles Stothard is sent by the Society of Antiquaries of London to make drawings of the Bayeux Tapestry; he also makes casts and cuts fragments from it.

1824
Honoré François Delauney
proposes that Bishop Odo of Bayeux
commissioned the Bayeux Tapestry
for the consecration of his cathedral.

1842
The Bayeux Tapestry first exhibited in a
specially made display case; before this,
it was rolled out to show people.

1870
During the Franco-Prussian War the
Bayeux Tapestry is hastily removed
from its case so that it could be stored
in a cylindrical zinc container for
safe-keeping.

LATE 1872
The first full photographic copy is made
of the Bayeux Tapestry for the South
Kensington Museum; a fragment of
the embroidery (previously owned by
Charles Stothard) is returned to Bayeux
as a gesture of goodwill, but never
refixed to the original.

1886
The Reading Tapestry completed by
the ladies of the Leek School of Art
Embroidery.

JUNE–JULY 1941
The Bayeux Tapestry is studied by a
German research team interested in
the embroidery both as an art object
and also within the context of
Germanic culture.

AUGUST 1944
Henrich Himmler orders the removal
of the Bayeux Tapestry from Paris
(where it was taken before the
liberation of Normandy), but the
order was never enacted.

6 FEBRUARY 1983
Opening of the new (current) display
of the Bayeux Tapestry in Bayeux
Museum, known at the time as the
Centre Guillaume le Conquérant.

2013
Scientific committee established to
advise on how the Bayeux Tapestry
might be reinterpreted and redisplayed;
at these meetings a loan to the UK is
first mooted.

JANUARY 2018
President Emmanuel Macron of France
announces the loan of the Bayeux
Tapestry to the UK; it is hoped it will
be displayed at the British Museum.

2020
Conservation assessment of the
Bayeux Tapestry.

FURTHER READING

The best way to discover and explore the Bayeux Tapestry is obviously to take a look at the embroidery itself. But if that is not possible, there are several useful books that allow a scene-by-scene examination, as well as myriad online resources. To study the images in detail, the large-format, full-colour reproduction of the 1982–83 photographs in *The Bayeux Tapestry* by David M. Wilson (Thames & Hudson, 1985) is still excellent. To get a sense of the full Tapestry, the fold-out facsimiles sold by Bayeux Museum are useful too. There is now also a fold-out facsimile measuring 30 m (almost 100 ft) with accompanying book, *La Tapisserie de Bayeux* by Xavier Barral i Altet and David Bates (Citadelles & Mazenod, 2019).

Lucien Musset's *The Bayeux Tapestry* (translated by Richard Rex, Boydell Press, 2005) also presents a full-colour reproduction of the embroidery at a useful size, with an extensive commentary, as does Pierre Bouet and François Neveux's *La Tapisserie de Bayeux* (Éditions Ouest-France, 2013), though only available in French. *The Real World of the Bayeux Tapestry*, by Michael Lewis (The History Press, 2008), also includes a full reproduction of the Tapestry, in black and white, again with a commentary and discussion of many of its facets. Very important, though out of print, is *Comprehensive Survey of the Bayeux Tapestry* edited by Frank Stenton (Phaidon Press, 1957), even if some of its information has been superseded by more recent works.

For developments in the potential loan of the Bayeux Tapestry to the UK, and any new research that comes out on the subject, much information is to be found in the pages of *BBC History Magazine*, or the magazine's website www.historyextra.com. A great journal to follow for continuing research into the Tapestry and all things of the period is *Anglo-Norman Studies: Proceedings of the Battle Conference*. This annual conference has been running since 1978 and the volumes of its proceedings are a rich source of Bayeux Tapestry material. Its website is http://www.battleconference.com/, and its proceedings are available in university libraries or similar.

EDITED VOLUMES ABBREVIATED BY EDITORS

Bouet et al. 2004
Pierre Bouet, Brian Levy and François Neveux (eds), *The Bayeux Tapestry: Embroidering the facts of history* (Presses Universitaires de Caen, 2004).

Carson Pastan and White 2014
Elizabeth Carson Pastan and Stephen D. White (eds), *The Bayeux Tapestry and its Contexts: A reassessment* (Boydell Press, 2014).

Foys et al. 2009
Martin K. Foys, Karen Eileen Overbey and Dan Terkla (eds), *The Bayeux Tapestry: New interpretations* (Boydell Press, 2009).

Gameson 1997
Richard Gameson (ed.), *The Study of the Bayeux Tapestry* (Boydell Press, 1997).

Henderson and Owen-Crocker 2016
Anna C. Henderson and Gale R. Owen-Crocker (eds), *Making Sense of the Bayeux Tapestry: Readings and reworkings* (Manchester University Press, 2016).

Lewis et al. 2011
Michael J. Lewis, Gale R. Owen-Crocker and Dan Terkla (eds), *The Bayeux Tapestry: New approaches* (Oxbow, 2011).

Morillo 1996
Stephen Morillo (ed.), *The Battle of Hastings: Sources and interpretations* (Boydell Press, 1996).

Owen-Crocker 2005
Gale R. Owen-Crocker (ed.), *King Harold II and the Bayeux Tapestry* (Boydell Press, 2005).

Stenton 1957
Frank Stenton (ed.), *Comprehensive Survey of the Bayeux Tapestry* (Phaidon Press, 1957).

CHAPTER 1: Putting the Conquest in Context

For a beautifully written account of the Tapestry's life and times, *The Bayeux Tapestry: The life story of a masterpiece* by Carola Hicks (Chatto & Windus, 2006) is excellent and widely available. Trevor Rowley's *An Archaeological Study of the Bayeux Tapestry: The landscapes, buildings and places* (Pen & Sword, 2016) takes the reader through the geography. For a popular introduction to the Conquest story, Marc Morris's *The Norman Conquest* (Windmill Books, 2013) is well worth a read, George Garnett's *The Norman Conquest: A very short introduction* (OUP, 2010) gives handy background, while *A Short History of the Normans* by Leonie Hicks (I.B. Taurus, 2014) has the wider story of the Norman adventure across Europe.

There are a couple of great short essays on England (by Rory Naismith) and Normandy (by Pierre Bauduin) before 1066 respectively in David Bates's edited volume *1066 in Perspective* (Royal Armouries Museum, 2018); this also includes an essay by Michael Lewis on the 'Myths and mysteries of the Bayeux Tapestry'. Bates himself wrote an instructive guide to pre-Conquest Normandy some years ago in his *Normandy Before 1066* (Longman, 1982). *Heirs of the Vikings: History and identity in Normandy and England c. 950–c. 1015* by Katherine Cross (York Medieval Press, 2018) delves deep into the question of identity and ethnicity at the time. *A Companion to the Anglo-Norman World*, edited by Christopher Harper-Bill and Elisabeth van Houts (Boydell Press, 2002), includes several interesting essays on the nature of England, Normandy and Scandinavia in the years preceding the Conquest. Indeed, there are so many books on the Normans and the Norman Conquest of England that it is hard to do justice to them all here.

A new collection of essays titled *Conquests in Eleventh-Century England 1016, 1066*, edited by Laura Ashe and Emily Joan Ward (Boydell, 2020), gives great context to the eleventh century as a whole. Emily Ward's essay, 'Child kings and the Norman Conquest', is instructive about Edgar Ætheling's claim to the throne.

There are several good choices of books to get to grips with the life of the two main protagonists in the story. The most comprehensive examination of the life of Duke William, rich in detail, is *William the Conqueror* by David Bates (Yale University Press, 2016), which supersedes David C. Douglas's great book of the same name (Eyre & Spottiswoode, 1964, and later editions); Marc Morris's William I (Penguin, 2018) in the Penguin Monarchs series is more concise. For King Harold II, Ian W. Walker's Harold: The last Anglo-Saxon king (Sutton, 1997) is a good place to start, but also useful is Frank Barlow's The Godwins (Pearson, 2002), which looks at the family as a whole. Also by Barlow, Edward the Confessor (Yale University Press, 1997) gives an in-depth coverage. A new biography, Edward the Confessor: Last of the royal blood, by Tom Licence (Yale University Press, 2020) brings Edgar Ætheling more strongly into focus as a contender for the throne after Edward's death, stressing the importance of the blood-claim for Anglo-Saxon kings, and posits that Harald Hardrada was Edgar's uncle. Trevor Rowley has written a biography of Bishop Odo, The Man Behind the Bayeux Tapestry (The History Press, 2013), but there is as yet nothing as comprehensive for Edgar Ætheling, apart from Gabriel Ronay's The Lost King of England (Boydell Press, 1989), which examines his life alongside that of his father, Prince Edward. To learn more about this elusive, missing figure in the Tapestry there is an article by Nicholas Hooper, 'Edgar the Ætheling: Anglo-Saxon prince, rebel and crusader' in the journal Anglo-Saxon England (14, 1985, pp. 197–214), as well as a good summation of his life by the same author in the Oxford Dictionary of National Biography. Taking the story back a little further, Queen Emma and the Vikings by Harriet O'Brien (Bloomsbury, 2006) looks at the life of Edward the Confessor's mother, while Levi Roach's Æthelred the Unready (Yale University Press, 2016) is

an excellent account of the life of his father, as is Ryan Lavelle's Aethelred II (Tempus, 2002).

To interrogate the contemporary written sources of the Conquest, a great starting place is the collection of documents drawn together by R. Allen Brown in The Norman Conquest of England: Sources and documents (Boydell Press, 1995). In this short book are key sections of William of Jumièges and William of Poitiers, plus the Anglo-Saxon Chronicle, Orderic Vitalis, William of Malmesbury, the Life of King Edward, John of Worcester, and a number of relevant writs, letters, laws, surveys and charters from the period. A combination of sources and essays specifically about the Battle of Hastings is also available in Morillo 1996.

The Anglo-Saxon Chronicle is available in several translations; the one used in this book is Michael Swanton's The Anglo-Saxon Chronicles (Phoenix Press, 2000). Eadmer of Canterbury is available in translation by Geoffrey Bosanquet: Eadmer's History of Recent Events in England (Cresset Press, 1964). Henry of Huntingdon is translated by Diana Greenway: Henry of Huntingdon. The History of the English People 1000–1154 (OUP, 1996). John of Worcester is translated by P. McGurk: The Chronicle of John of Worcester, vols II (450–1066) and III (1067–1140) (Oxford Medieval Texts, OUP, 1995). There are several volumes of Orderic Vitalis's Ecclesiastical History, edited and translated by Marjorie Chibnall (OMT, OUP, 1969–80). William of Jumièges is translated by Elisabeth van Houts: Gesta Normannorum Ducum of William of Jumièges (OMT, OUP, 1995), and William of Poitiers by R. H. C.

Davis and Marjorie Chibnall: *The Gesta Guillelmi of William of Poitiers* (OMT, OUP, 1998). William of Malmesbury is translated by R. A. B. Mynors, R. M. Thomson and M. Winterbottom: *Gesta Regum Anglorum: The History of the English Kings* (OMT, OUP, 1998) and the *Vita Edwardi Regis* by Frank Barlow: *The Life of King Edward Who Rests at Westminster* (OMT, OUP, 1992).

More specifically on the Tapestry itself, anything by Gale Owen-Crocker is well worth a read, as are articles by Michael Lewis. Both have researched and written on numerous facets of the Bayeux Tapestry, and many of Owen-Crocker's papers are gathered together in her *The Bayeux Tapestry: Collected papers* (Routledge, 2012); the volume edited by her, Owen-Crocker 2005, includes fascinating contributions on Harold's life and involvement with the embroidery.

Several works look at the question of why the Bayeux Tapestry does not appear to take as clear a line on the Conquest story as many of the written sources. David Bernstein's *The Mystery of the Bayeux Tapestry* (Weidenfeld and Nicolson, 1986) speculates that the designer might have inserted subversive pro-English messages, casting doubt on the legitimacy of William's claim to the throne. Richard D. Wissolik also argues for a covert pro-English code in 'The Saxon statement: code in the Bayeux Tapestry' (*Annuale Mediævale* 19, 1979, pp. 69–97). Andrew Bridgeford's *1066: The hidden history of the Bayeux Tapestry* (Fourth Estate, 2004) takes the view that the Tapestry is 'shot through with multiple layers of meaning', with the Norman story regularly undermined by veiled pro-English clues.

Richard Gameson's excellent introductory essay, 'The origin, art, and message of the Bayeux Tapestry', in the volume he edited, Gameson 1997 (pp. 157–211), summarizes many of the ideas about what messages, if any, lay in the Tapestry. Pierre Bouet's article 'Is the Bayeux Tapestry pro-English?' in Bouet et al. 2004 (pp. 197–215), considers whether the Tapestry was designed to be an 'open work, with part of its meaning left to the eye of the beholder' – whether the viewer takes a pro-English or a pro-Norman point of view – with the aim being to act as a work of reconciliation for both sides immediately after the battle.

The idea that the Tapestry was made by and for the monks of St Augustine's Abbey, Canterbury, with an 'open-textured, multi-layered account' of the Conquest is laid out in Carson Pastan and White 2014. According to this theory, the Tapestry was for display in the monks' own abbey, with an underlying message that the fall of the English was God's punishment for a nation's sins. By this reading, there are puns and double-meanings contained in the Tapestry's imagery that would have been sensible to the educated monks alone.

This is really just scratching the surface of works on the Tapestry. Shirley Ann Brown's *The Bayeux Tapestry: A sourcebook* (Brepols, 2013) is a detailed summation of the story of scholarship on the embroidery, building on her work *The Bayeux Tapestry: History and bibliography* (Boydell Press, 1989). It summarizes hundreds of contributions made by scholars and researchers, with a very useful introduction to the state of thought on many aspects of the subject.

CHAPTER 2: A Unique Embroidery

A great deal of information about how the Tapestry was embroidered, and how the linen panels may have been worked and joined, is found in Alexandra Lester-Makin's 'The front tells the story, the back tells the history: a technical discussion of the embroidering of the Bayeux Tapestry', in Henderson and Owen-Crocker 2016 (pp. 23–40). Lester-Makin is particularly informative on the likely causes of the misaligned joins. Carola Hicks in *The Bayeux Tapestry: The life story of a masterpiece* (Chatto & Windus, 2006) also goes into considerable detail about the making of the Tapestry, and Michael Lewis's PhD thesis, published as *The Archaeological Authority of the Bayeux Tapestry* (British Archaeological Report 404, 2005), looks at what we might infer about the designer and design of the Bayeux Tapestry.

Details about the studies carried out on the Tapestry when it was moved to its new display in 1983, and the nature of the various pieces of cloth that make it up today, can be found in articles in Bouet et al. 2004. Observations on the length of the Tapestry are found in David Hill, 'The Bayeux Tapestry: The establishment of a text' in that volume (pp. 383–402). Derek Renn has mulled on the same questions in his article 'How big is it – and was it?' in Lewis et al., 2011 (pp. 52–58). Recently Christopher Norton in 'Viewing the Bayeux Tapestry, now and then' (*Journal of the British Archaeological Association*, 172, 2019, pp. 52–89) has offered thoughts on the Tapestry's length, as well as the likely intended location of the Tapestry as the nave of Bayeux Cathedral.

The similarities in style between the Tapestry and the work of Anglo-Saxon manuscript artists has been noted many times, not least by Gale Owen-Crocker and Michael Lewis. Francis Wormald was most influential on this in his article 'Style and design', in Stenton 1957 (pp. 25–36), but also important is Cyril Hart's essay 'The Bayeux Tapestry and schools of illumination at Canterbury' (*Anglo-Norman Studies*, 22, pp. 117–67), and Michael Lewis 'La Tapisserie de Bayeux et l'art anglo-saxon' in a volume on the Bayeux Tapestry following a colloquium in Bayeux in 2016, *L'Invention de la Tapisserie de Bayeux* (Éditions Point de Vues, 2018, pp. 229–45), but only in French.

The case for the Tapestry being made in Canterbury has been put forward on numerous occasions. N. P. Brooks and H. E. Walker lay it out clearly in their article 'The authority and interpretation of the Bayeux Tapestry' (*Anglo-Norman Studies* 1, 1979, pp. 1–34). The idea that the Tapestry might have been made in the Loire Valley has been championed by George Beech in his *Was the Bayeux Tapestry Made in France? The case for St. Florent of Saumur* (Palgrave Macmillan, 2005). Wolfgang Grape outlines his theory that it was made in Normandy in *The Bayeux Tapestry* (Prestel, 1994).

On the patronage question, the idea of Bishop Odo's involvement has been rehearsed many times, the first being in 1824. More recently it appears, for example, in David Bates's biographical entry for Odo in the *Oxford Dictionary of National Biography* (2004), and in Michael Lewis's *The Real World of the Bayeux Tapestry* (The History Press, 2008). Katherine Keats-Rohan considers the possible role of Archbishop Stigand in 'Through the eye of the needle: Stigand, the Bayeux Tapestry and the beginnings of the *Historia Anglorum*' in David Roffe (ed.), *The English and Their Legacy*, 900–1200. *Essays in honour of Ann Williams* (Boydell Press, 2012, pp. 159–74). Richard Gameson wondered whether Abbot Scolland might have had a hand in the design of the Tapestry in Gameson 1997 (pp. 157–211), while Howard Clarke has taken the case for Scolland's role as the designer further and identified him in the embroidery in 'The identity of the designer of the Bayeux Tapestry' (*Anglo-Norman Studies* 35, 2012, pp. 119–40). Eustace, Count of Boulogne, has been proposed as patron by Andrew Bridgeford in 1066: *The hidden history of the Bayeux Tapestry* (Fourth Estate, 2004). The case for Edith, widow of King Edward, has been put by Carola Hicks in her *The Bayeux Tapestry: The life story of a masterpiece* (Chatto & Windus, 2006); see also a summary in Michael Lewis et al. 2011 (pp. 5–9) and the essay 'Where a Cleric and Ælfgyva...' by Patricia Stephenson (pp. 71–74) in the same volume.

As regards display and usage of the Bayeux Tapestry, Gale Owen-Crocker has suggested the possibility of it being made for show in square secular halls in 'Brothers, rivals and the geometry of the Bayeux Tapestry' in Owen-Crocker 2005 (pp. 109–23). In the same volume, Christopher Henige goes further, and locates it in Dover Castle in 'Putting the Tapestry in its place' (pp. 125–37). H. E. J. Cowdrey in 'Towards an interpretation of the Bayeux Tapestry' (*Anglo-Norman Studies* 10, 1988, pp. 49–65) talks about the possibility of the Tapestry being toured from place to place, perhaps with a guide or interpreter. Meanwhile, Richard Brilliant has argued that the embroidery was made for a vocal interlocutor, taking cues from visual prompts in the embroidery, to explain the story and significance of the imagery to the audience in 'The Bayeux Tapestry: A stripped narrative for their eyes and ears' (*Word & Image*, 72, 1991, pp. 98–126). For context on Anglo-Saxon embroidery more generally, *The Lost Art of the Anglo-Saxon World* by Alexandra Lester-Makin (Oxbow, 2020) is a great resource.

CHAPTER 3: The Story Begins

As the story proper begins to unfold, there are many contributions from researchers about the details of the Tapestry. 'The Bayeux "Tapestry": invisible seams and visible boundaries', by Gale Owen-Crocker (*Anglo-Saxon England* 31, 2002, pp. 257–73) is a useful guide to how the action in the Tapestry moves forward and how the scene endings are designed to work. Similarly, Michael Lewis, *The Archaeological Authority of the Bayeux Tapestry* (British Archaeological Report 404, 2005), considers how 'attributes' of individual characters are used within the Bayeux Tapestry's visual narrative structure.

For a round-up of the portrayal of clothing and dress in the Tapestry, go to Michael Lewis 'Intertextuality in the Bayeux Tapestry: the form and function of dress and clothing' in *Textiles, Text, Intertext: Essays in honour of Gale Owen-Crocker* (Boydell Press, 2016, pp. 69–84) or his 'Ecclesiastics in the Bayeux Tapestry' in Henderson and Owen-Crocker 2016 (pp. 75–92). Gale Owen-Crocker's *Dress in Anglo-Saxon*

England (Boydell Press, 2004) is a good introductory guide to the costume of the whole period, and John Nevinson's 'The costumes' in Stenton 1957 (pp. 70–75) looks specifically at those in the Bayeux Tapestry.

A helpful guide to the text on the Tapestry is 'The embroidered word: text in the Bayeux Tapestry' by Gale Owen-Crocker in Robin Netherton and Gale Owen-Crocker (eds), *Medieval Clothing and Textiles* 2 (Boydell Press, 2006, pp. 35–59). This sets out the idea that the text might have been dictated by a Norman and written down by an Anglo-Saxon, along with fascinating thoughts about how the text and the images work together. Observations by Nicholas Brooks and H. E. Walker in 'The authority and interpretation of the Bayeux Tapestry' (*Anglo-Norman Studies* 1, 1979, pp. 1–34) and Gameson 1997 are also of interest here.

Much has been written about the borders, in particular references to Aesop's Fables, over the twentieth century. Notable contributions are by Francis Wormald in 'Style and design' in Stenton 1957 (pp. 25–36). He takes the view that the Fables are purely decorative and not linked to the narrative, while Charles Dodwell disagrees in 'The Bayeux Tapestry and the French secular epic' (*Burlington Magazine*, 108, 1966, pp. 549–60), seeing them as reinforcing a pro-Norman message in the Tapestry that served to highlight the perfidy of Harold. Stephen D. White's article 'The beasts who talk on the Bayeux Tapestry: fables revisited' (*Anglo-Norman Studies* 34, 2011, pp. 209–36) provides a useful summary of Fable thought.

Ann Williams in 'How to be rich: the presentation of Earl Harold in the early sections of the Bayeux Tapestry' in Lewis et al. 2011 (pp. 66–70) provides a great commentary on the early panels of the Tapestry, offering thoughts on Harold's status, horses, Bosham, the feast scene and much else. Also worth looking at is Michael Lewis's essay 'Identity and status in the Bayeux Tapestry' (*Anglo-Norman Studies* 29, 2007, pp. 100–20). Regarding the Bosham feast, 'Lordship and lunching: interpretations of eating and food in the Anglo-Norman world, 1050–1200, with reference to the Bayeux Tapestry', by Mark Hagger in D. Roffe (ed.), *The English and Their Legacy, 900–1200. Essays in honour of Ann Williams* (Boydell Press, 2012, pp. 229–44), provides a detailed guide to the nature and significance of feasting. On the drinking vessels, Carol Neuman de Vegvar's article 'Dining with distinction: drinking vessels and difference in the Bayeux Tapestry feast scenes' in Lewis et al. 2011 (pp. 112–20) is great on tableware.

CHAPTER 4: Captive in France

For context on the nature of boats and channel crossings, Gale Owen-Crocker's '...*Velis vento plenis....* Sea crossings in the Bayeux Tapestry' in Stacy S. Klein, William Schipper and Shannon Lewis-Simpson (eds), *The Maritime World of the Anglo-Saxons* (Arizona Center for Medieval and Renaissance Studies, 2013, pp. 131–56) is very useful. But see also Carol Gillmor's study, 'Naval logistics of the cross-Channel operation' (*Anglo-Norman Studies* 7, 1984, pp. 105–31).

For links between the Tapestry's imagery and archaeological sites today, Trevor Rowley's *An Archaeological Study of the Bayeux Tapestry: The landscapes, buildings and places* (Pen & Sword, 2016) is a good introduction, particularly on the importance of the wavy lines in the Tapestry as guides to whether the action is taking place indoors or outdoors.

Richard D. Wissolik's 'Duke William's messengers: an "insoluble, reverse-order" scene of the Bayeux Tapestry' (*Medium Ævum*, 51, 1982, pp. 102–7) goes into detail about the curious case of the messengers and the scene ordering in this part of the Tapestry. Shirley Ann Brown's 'Cognate imagery: the bear, Harold, and the Bayeux Tapestry' in Owen-Crocker 2005 (pp. 149–60) has a particular focus on the reason for the bear-baiting scene in the lower border.

'The Mercian connection, Harold Godwineson's ambitions, diplomacy and Channel-crossing, 1056–1066' by Ad F. J. van Kempen (*History*, 94, 2009, pp. 2–19) goes into great detail about the plots, sub-plots and conspiracy theories that surround Harold's capture in the Ponthieu incident.

Christopher Monk has interesting observations on the reasons for the nude scenes in the borders in 'Figuring out nakedness in the borders of the Bayeux Tapestry' in Henderson and Owen-Crocker 2016 (pp. 54–74). George Garnett identified the priapic predilection of the Tapestry designer in 'The Bayeux Tapestry with knobs on: what do the Tapestry's 93 penises tell us?' (on www.historyextra.com).

Gale Owen-Crocker offers commentary on the undermining of Count Guy of Ponthieu in 'Dress and authority in the Bayeux Tapestry', in Brenda Bolton and Christine Meek (eds), *Aspects of Power and Authority in the Middle Ages* (Brepols, 2008, pp. 53–72). She adds further colour to the debate in

her online article 'Bayeux unravelled: the scenes behind the threads', for www.historyextra.com, and also sheds light on the prevalence and meaning of birds in the border scenes in her article 'Squawk talk: commentary by birds in the Bayeux Tapestry?' (*Anglo-Saxon England* 34, 2005, pp. 237–54). An important article in this respect is W. B. Yapp's 'Animals in medieval art: the Bayeux Tapestry as an example' (*Journal of Medieval History* 13, 1987, pp. 15–73).

'Turold, Wadard and Vitalis: why are they on the Bayeux Tapestry?' by Hugh M. Thomas (*Anglo-Norman Studies* 38, 2015, pp. 181–97) is a useful synopsis of thoughts on the inclusion of the Turold character, as is the study of these three characters by Hirokazu Tsurushima, 'Hic est miles: some images of three knights, Turold, Wadard and Vital' in Lewis et al. 2011 (pp. 81–91). David Wilson in *The Bayeux Tapestry* (Thames & Hudson, 1985, p. 176) notes that he is attracted to the idea that Turold is both the bearded dwarf and the designer of the Tapestry itself, though it is a theory that has gained little support.

CHAPTER 5: At the Court of Duke William

Gale Owen-Crocker's 'The Bayeux Tapestry: faces and places' in Lewis et al. 2011 (pp. 96–104) is a great review of what the Tapestry does with faces and hands, and it is worth revisiting the earlier work by Francis Wormald, 'Style and design', in Stenton 1957 (pp. 25–36).

Much of this chapter is concerned with the Ælfgyva episode. Patricia Stephenson's 'Where a cleric and Ælfgyva...' (Lewis et al. 2011, pp. 71–74) provides a very helpful summary of much of the thinking about the identity of the woman, and the reason for the inclusion of the scene. She outlines the case for Ælfgyva being one of Harold's sisters who was the Abbess of Wilton Abbey. Richard D. Wissolik also has Ælfgyva as one of Harold's sisters in 'The Saxon statement: code in the Bayeux Tapestry' (*Annuale Mediævale* 19, 1979, pp. 69–97), but in this case the sister is to be engaged to a Norman nobleman as part of a deal to free Harold's hostage family members.

J. Bard McNulty, *The Narrative Art of the Bayeux Tapestry Master* (AMS Press, 1989) identifies Ælfgyva as Ælfgyva of Northampton, the promiscuous mistress, and later wife, of King Cnut. Chris Henige in 'Putting the Tapestry in its place' in Owen-Crocker 2005 (pp. 125–37) follows that view, and concludes that the architecture in the scene is supposed to represent a Norwegian structure, with the scene aimed at undermining the legitimacy of Norwegian claims to the English throne. Suzanne Lewis's *The Rhetoric of Power in the Bayeux Tapestry* (CUP, 1998) outlines the point about the whole episode being more of a social commentary linked to clerical misdemeanours.

CHAPTER 6: The Brittany Campaign

The purpose of the interlude of the Breton campaign in terms of the narrative has caused a lot of head-scratching among academics, particularly as it is here that the Tapestry seems to diverge most from the written sources. 'The Bayeux Tapestry as original source', by François Neveux in Bouet et al. 2004 (pp. 171–95) lays out where the Tapestry differs from other texts. Lucien Musset's *The Bayeux Tapestry*

(Boydell Press, 2005) has a useful summary of the Breton campaign. Indeed, the inclusion of the Breton campaign is critical to George Beech's thesis that the Tapestry was made in the Loire Valley, as he sets out in detail in 'The Breton campaign and the possibility that the Bayeux Tapestry was produced in the Loire Valley' in Lewis et al. 2011 (pp. 10–16), following his book *Was the Bayeux Tapestry Made in France?* (Palgrave, 2005).

Jill Frederick's article 'Slippery as an eel: Harold's ambiguous heroics in the Bayeux Tapestry' in Lewis et al. 2011 (pp. 121–26) is a thoughtful account of what story the designer is trying to convey in the Couesnon rescue scene. 'Harold-as-Aeneas? The influence of the *Aeneid* on a rescue scene in the Bayeux Tapestry' by Nikki K. Rollason and Michael Lewis links Harold with Aeneas of Troy (*Greece & Rome* 67, 2020, pp. 203–29).

A good number of architectural features appear in this part of the Tapestry. 'Building stories: the representation of architecture in the Bayeux embroidery' by Elizabeth Carson Pastan (*Anglo-Norman Studies* 33, 2010, pp. 151–85) is a helpful guide to how to understand the depiction of buildings in the embroidery. But also see Michael Lewis's chapter on the Tapestry's buildings in *The Archaeological Authority of the Bayeux Tapestry* (British Archaeological Report 404, 2005), as well as Ralph Allen-Brown's important work on 'The architecture of the Bayeux Tapestry' in R. Allen Brown, *Castles, Conquest and Charters: Collected papers* (Boydell Press, 1989, pp. 214–16).

CHAPTER 7: A Sacred Oath

The oath scene is fundamental to almost all readings of the Bayeux Tapestry, so every interpretation of the embroidery touches on it at some point. H. E. J. Cowdrey's 'King Harold II and the Bayeux Tapestry: a critical introduction' in Owen-Crocker 2005 (pp. 1–15) is a good place to start. Pierre Bouet and François Neveux's article, 'Edward the Confessor's succession according to the Bayeux Tapestry' in Lewis et al. 2011 (pp. 59–65), helpfully places the oath scene within the context of the entire Tapestry narrative.

'The Bayeux Tapestry as original source', by François Neveux in Bouet et al. 2004 (pp. 171–95) includes good commentary on the oath scene, and the question of where it actually took place. Even more detail is provided by Stephen D. White in 'Locating Harold's oath and tracing his itinerary' in Carson Paston and White 2014 (pp. 105–25).

For more on the reliquaries on which the oaths were made, look at Karen E. Overbey's 'Taking place: reliquaries and territorial authority in the Bayeux embroidery' in Foys et al. 2009 (pp. 36–50).

CHAPTER 8: Harold Becomes King

To find out more about Edward the Confessor's Westminster Abbey see T. Tatton-Brown's 'Westminster Abbey: archaeological recording at the west end of the church' (*Antiquaries Journal* 75, 1995, pp. 171–88), Richard Gem's 'The Romanesque rebuilding of Westminster Abbey' (*Anglo-Norman Studies* 3, 1981, pp. 33–60), Michael Lewis's *The Archaeological Authority of the Bayeux Tapestry* (British Archaeological Report 404, 2005), or Eric Fernie's 'Edward the Confessor's Westminster Abbey' in Richard Mortimer (ed.), *Edward the Confessor: The man and the legend* (Boydell Press, 2009, pp. 139–50).

In the same volume 'Edward the Confessor and the succession question' (pp. 77–118) by Stephen Baxter is a useful review of the evidence and theories about who Edward intended to succeed him. Stephen Church takes a long view – 1066 to 1199 – helping to provide a context for the succession in 'Aspects of the English succession' (*Anglo-Norman Studies* 29, 2007, pp. 17–34). Not always was a comet seen in the sky, but it was a feature of Harold's coming to the throne, and is noted in most books on the Bayeux Tapestry.

Again in the volume on Edward the Confessor edited by Richard Mortimer, 'Edith, Edward's wife and queen' by Pauline Stafford (pp. 119–38) explores Edith's life in considerable detail, building on Carola Hicks's *The Bayeux Tapestry: The life story of a masterpiece* (Chatto & Windus, 2006) and others. Regarding women in the Bayeux Tapestry generally, there is an interesting essay by Catherine Karkov in Owen-Crocker 2005 (pp. 139–47), 'Gendering the battle? Male and female in the Bayeux Tapestry'. The same volume also contains useful essays by H. E. J. Cowdrey, 'King Harold II and the Bayeux Tapestry: a critical introduction' (pp. 1–15); Nicholas Higham, 'Harold Godwinesson: the construction of kingship' (pp. 19–34); and Ian Howard, 'Harold II: a throne-worthy king' (pp. 35–52), which explore the rights and wrongs of Harold's claim to the throne, and touch on Edgar Ætheling too. Barbara English's 'The coronation of Harold in the Bayeux Tapestry' in Bouet et al. 2004 (pp. 347–81) examines the question of the coronation or otherwise of Harold being shown in the Tapestry.

The relationship between Harold and his brother Tostig is not the focus of in-depth discussion, but Ian Walker's *Harold: The last Anglo-Saxon king* (Sutton, 1997) and Frank Barlow's *The Godwins* (Pearson, 2002) examine it in general.

CHAPTER 9: William Builds an Army
The operation to raise William's fleet is discussed by Carol M. Gillmor in 'Naval logistics of the cross-Channel operation, 1066', in Morillo 1996 (pp. 113–28); also worth a look are Bernard Bachrach's 'Some observations on the military administration of the Norman Conquest' (*Anglo-Norman Studies* 8, 1985, pp. 1–15) and Elizabeth van Houts's 'The ship list of William the Conqueror' (*Anglo-Norman Studies* 10, 1988, pp. 159–84). For shipping horses across the Channel, see Bernard Bachrach: 'On the origins of William the Conqueror's horse transports' (*Technology and Culture*, 26, 1985, pp. 505–31).

Much has been written about the relationship between the ships in the Bayeux Tapestry and vessels influenced by the Viking style. Important are the archaeological studies of the Skuldelev ships from Roskilde fjord, Denmark, by Ole Crumlin-Pedersen and Olaf Olsen (eds), *The Skuldelev Ships* (Viking Ship Museum, 2002), but also see the chapters on 'ships' in Michael Lewis's *The Archaeological Authority of the Bayeux Tapestry* (British Archaeological Report 404, 2005) and *The Real World of the*

Bayeux Tapestry (The History Press, 2008). Valerie Fenwick's book on *The Graveney Boat* (National Maritime Museum, 1978) provides information on an English ship.

On papal support for William's invasion, and the reaction to the assault in Europe, see Elisabeth van Houts 'The Norman Conquest through European eyes' (*The English Historical Review*, 110, 1995, pp. 832–53). Also worth a look is Michael Herren's translation of Baudri of Bourgeuil's poem *Adelae Comitissae* in Shirley Ann Brown's *The Bayeux Tapestry: History and bibliography* (1988, Boydell Press, pp. 167–77), which mentions a tapestry very much like the Bayeux Tapestry in the bedchamber of Duke William's daughter, Adela of Blois.

CHAPTER 10: The Lull Before the Storm
Bishop Odo of Bayeux now comes to prominence, and here the works of David Bates are relevant, particularly his article 'The character and career of Odo, Bishop of Bayeux' (*Speculum* 50, 1975, pp. 1–20), but also his unpublished PhD on *Odo Bishop of Bayeux* (University of Exeter, 1970). For Bishop Odo's place in the feast scene, read Elizabeth Carson Pastan, 'A feast for the eyes: representing Odo at the banquet in the Bayeux embroidery' (*The Haskins Society Journal* 22, 2010, pp. 83–122). By the same author, there is 'Bishop Odo at the banquet' in Carson Pastan and White 2014 (pp. 126–53). Both, like much in Tapestry studies, build on the work of others, notably Nicholas Brooks and H. E. Walker in 'The authority and interpretation of the Bayeux Tapestry' (*Anglo-Norman Studies* 1, 1979, pp. 1–34, specifically pp. 15–16).

The role of Robert of Mortain in the Bayeux Tapestry is discussed by David S. Spear in 'Robert of Mortain and the Bayeux Tapestry' in Lewis et al. 2011 (pp. 75–80). Introductions to the invasion of England by Harald Hardrada, with the support of Tostig, include *The Norwegian Invasion of England in 1066* (Boydell Press, 1999) by Kelly DeVries and *1066: The year of three battles* (Pimlico, 1999) by Frank McLynn, but also many books on the Norman Conquest of England.

The earliest Norman castles in England, as seen in the Bayeux Tapestry, have been a popular topic of discussion. Important are some archaeological explorations of these sites and their reports, notably by Philip Barker and K. J. Barton, 'Excavations at Hastings Castle, 1968' (*Archaeological Journal* 134, 1977, pp. 80–100). A general introduction to early wooden castles is Robert Higham and Philip Barker's *Timber Castles* (B. T. Batsford, 1992), and see also Michael Lewis's *The Real World of the Bayeux Tapestry* (The History Press, 2008).

CHAPTER 11: The Great Battle
A great deal has been written about the Battle of Hastings. John France's 'The importance of the Bayeux Tapestry in the history of war' in Bouet et al. 2004 (pp. 288–99) is a good summation of some key themes that have come out of research into military aspects of the battle. *Anglo-Norman Warfare*, edited by Matthew Strickland (Boydell Press, 1992), contains numerous excellent articles, as does Morillo 1996. Also see Jim Bradbury's *The Battle of Hastings* (Sutton, 1998).

Arms and armour is another popular topic. James Mann's 'Arms and armour' in Stenton 1957 (pp. 56–69) has been influential, but also worth reading is Christopher Gravett's introduction to the *Norman Knight* (Osprey, 1993) and Michael Lewis's 'The Bayeux Tapestry and eleventh-century material culture' in Gale Owen Crocker 2005 (pp. 179–94) as well as his 'Incipient armoury in the Bayeux Tapestry' (*The Coat of Arms*, 2012, 3rd ser. 8, no. 223, pp. 1–26). Other important works are Jennie Kiff's 'Images of war, illustrations of warfare in early eleventh-century England' (*Anglo-Norman Studies* 7, 1984, pp. 177–94) and Ian Pierce's 'Arms, armour and warfare in the eleventh century' (*Anglo-Norman Studies* 10, 1988, pp. 237–58).

For Bishop Odo's role in the battle, see 'The Norman Conquest: Odo of Bayeux and Geoffrey of Coutances' in *Warrior Churchmen of Medieval England, 1000–1250: Theory and reality* by Craig M. Nakashian (Boydell Press, 2016, pp. 125–57). The death of Harold's brothers in the battle receives coverage in Michael R. Davis, 'Leofwine and Gyrth: depicting the death of the brothers in the Bayeux Tapestry' in Lewis et al. 2011 (pp. 92–95).

The question of whether Harold really received an arrow in the eye that killed him is dealt with by Martin K. Foys, 'Pulling the arrow out: the legend of Harold's death and the Bayeux Tapestry' in Foys et al. 2009 (pp. 158–75). Also relevant here is David Hill and John McSween's article on 'The storage chest and the repairs and changes in the Bayeux Tapestry' in Lewis et al. 2011 (pp. 44–51) and Michael Lewis's 'Embroidery errors in the Bayeux Tapestry and their relevance for understanding the Bayeux Tapestry' in Foys et al. 2009 (pp. 130–40).

ACKNOWLEDGMENTS

As we hope is obvious throughout this book, we are building on the work found in numerous pieces of research from a wide range of Bayeux Tapestry scholars. We haven't named them in the text, in the interests of providing a smooth narrative for readers, but we have tried to refer to their work in the Further Reading section and we'd encourage the reader to have a look at these and follow the references within them to further studies on the Tapestry – it's a rabbit hole down which you will find yourself quickly and pleasurably lost.

We are particularly grateful to David Bates, Leonie Hicks, Alexandra Lester-Makin, Jean-Marie Levesque and Gareth Williams for looking at various sections of the book and making very insightful suggestions. Antoine Verney, Cécile Binet, Clémentine Berthelot and Fanny Garbe at Bayeux Museum have all been generous with their time and assistance. Robert Attar, Rob Blackmore and Howard Cuthbert also read drafts of the text and provided helpful comments.

David Musgrove would like to thank all his colleagues at BBC History Magazine. He is also grateful to his wife Caroline and daughters Caitlin, Eva and Rosie for putting up with another year of historical research and writing. Likewise, Michael Lewis thanks his wife Emma for her support, and also his children, Emily, Sophie and James, who have put up with Bayeux Tapestry talk since they were born...

SOURCES OF ILLUSTRATIONS

All images and details of the Bayeux Tapestry, eleventh century, with special permission from the City of Bayeux.

MAP Lisa Ifsits/Aman Phull; 1 Bibliothèque nationale de France, Paris; 2 Heidelberg University Library; 3 The British Library, London; 4 University of Cambridge; 5 Photo Jill Clardy; 6 La Cathédrale de Guillaume © CB - OT Bayeux Intercom; 7 The British Library, London; 8 The British Library, London; 9 Beatrice Preve/Alamy Stock Photo; 10, 12 University of Cambridge; 11 The British Library, London; 13 The Picture Art Collection/Alamy Stock Photo; 14 The British Museum, London; 15 With special permission from the City of Bayeux; 16 Bibliothèque nationale de France, Paris; 17 Cleveland Museum of Art; 18 Library of Congress Prints and Photographs Division, Washington, D.C.; 19 Coll. Musée de la Tapisserie de Bayeux, lot H. Jeschke.

INDEX

Adela of Blois 38, 51, 154

Aeneas 109

Ælfgyva 89, 98–104, 119, 135; Abbess of Wilton Abbey (sister of Harold II) 101; daughter of King Æthelred II 101; of Northampton, wife of King Cnut 101–2; of Shaftesbury (wife of King Edmund I) 100; of Wessex (sister of King Edmund I) 100; of York (wife of King Æthelred II) 101

Ælfwine, Bishop of Winchester 102

Aesop's Fables see fables

Æthelred II, King of England 15, 101, 102

Æthelstan, King of England 14, 15

Agatha, daughter of Duke William 101

Agatha, mother of Edgar Ætheling 206

agriculture 60, 80

Alderney 212

Alfred, Prince 15, 16

Alfred the Great, King of Wessex 14, 25

Amatus of Montecassino 200

Anglo-Saxon Chronicle 25, 111, 126, 134, 145, 183, 190, 203, 204

architecture and buildings 12, 50–51, 54, 61, 63, 83, 85, 92–93, 98–99, 100–1, 110–11, 119, 130, 133, 141, 174, 175–77

arms and armour 12, 71, 72, 81, 107, 114, 152, 158–59, 180, 181, 182–88, 190; pl. 14

Assandun (Ashingdon), Battle of 15

Augustine, St 41, 45, 48, 49, 116, 173, 208

axes 81, 98, 127, 140, 151, 154–55, 158, 170, 182, 186, 190–91, 193, 198, 199

Baldwin V, Count of Flanders 97, 146

Battle 82, 203, 212

Baudri of Bourgueil (Adelae Comitissae) 38, 51, 154, 156, 200

Bayeux 10, 44, 47, 52, 107, 210, 212, 214, 215; depiction in Tapestry 107, 118–19; museum 10, 213, 215; and swearing of oath by Harold 40, 119–21

Bayeux Cathedral 9–10, 40, 49, 51, 52; consecration of 39, 40, 52, 121, 208, 209; crypt 9, 10; inventory 9–10; pl. 5, 6

Bayeux Tapestry: captions/inscriptions 27, 31, 43–44, 51; chest stored in 9, 52;

cloth 31–33; colours 33, 60, 164, 172; conservation 34–36, 215–16; damage 10, 32, 35, 58, 202, 203; date of 36–39, 207–8; design 34, 36–37, 42–44, 84, 207–9; display 10–11, 39, 48–51, 209; hidden coding in 27–28, 83, 209; lettering 44, 172, 173; manuscripts, parallels with 37, 41–44, 80, 154, 173, 208; missing scenes 51, 54, 202–3, 209; mistakes in 185–86, 188; in modern media 213–14; narrator of 51, 146, 209; numbering of scenes 32, 111; organization 31; panels 32–33, 35–36, 38, 50, 89–90, 133, 161, 188, 197; photography of 211, 213–14; possible patrons 45–49; production of 31–37; purpose 49–52, 122, 208–9; rediscovery 10, 210; replicas and remakes 209–13; restorations 10, 35–36, 54, 58, 171, 196–97, 200–201, 202; seams/joins 32, 36, 89–90, 133, 161, 171, 189, 197; as source 20, 21, 26–30, 203, 204, 207; stitches 34–36; survival of 10, 51–52; technique 8, 31, 33–34; where made 40–44, 207–8; pl. 16, 18; see also borders and individual topics

BBC History Magazine 215

Beaurain (Ponthieu) 70, 76, 77, 79, 83–84, 85, 91

Benedict X, Pope 142

Beorn 16, 59

Beowulf 51, 115, 201

Berkhamsted 212

Bonneville-sur-Touques 120, 121

borders 31, 43, 81, 83, 92, 112, 115, 118, 129, 149, 165, 178, 187–88, 201; archers 197, 198; birds 80, 83, 87, 89, 92, 94, 176, 189; Byzantine textiles as source 87; fables 65, 73, 126, 127; fallen soldiers 189, 191, 198; fish/eels 108, 109; ghostly fleet 146; hunting 83; misaligned 36, 58, 89–90, 161; relation to main frieze 54, 58, 65, 66, 188, 208; wolves 63; see also fables and individual topics

Bosham 58, 59, 60–61, 62, 63, 68–69, 75, 173; church 61–62

British Museum 11, 197, 215, 216

Byrthnoth, ealdorman of Essex (hero of

the *Battle of Maldon*) 201
Byzantine textiles 87

Caen 75, 85, 161
Canterbury 24, 40–45, 49, 111, 143, 173,
    207–8; Christ Church (cathedral) 41,
    42, 43; St Augustine's Abbey 41, 42, 45,
    48–49, 116, 173, 208
Carmen de Hastingae Proelio 22–23, 193, 200
castles 83, 85, 110–11, 112–13, 114, 119, 165–66,
    175–77
Cerdic, founder of West Saxon dynasty
    19–20
Charles the Simple, King of West Francia
    13–14
Charles VI, King of France 9
Chichester 59
clothes and clothing 54, 71, 72, 81, 85–86,
    92, 94, 99–100, 175
Cnut, King of England, Denmark and
    Norway 15, 59, 101–2, 137
comet *see* Halley's Comet
Conan II, Duke of Brittany 43, 105, 106,
    110, 112–14, 116–17
Couesnon, River 105, 108, 110

Danelaw 14
Dibden, Thomas Frognal 210
Dinan 113
Dives-sur-Mer 161–62, 166
dogs 58, 73, 86, 92
Dol 43, 110–12, 113, 114
Dover 17, 122, 126, 196; Castle 48, 50, 122

Eadmer of Canterbury (*Historia
    Novorum...*) 24–25, 84, 86, 94, 122–23, 128
Ealdgyth 138
Ealdred, Bishop of Worcester and
    Archbishop of York 143–44, 203
Edgar Ætheling 19, 20, 30, 56–57, 123,
    139–40, 143, 206; absence from Tapestry
    135, 192, 206–7, 209; after the Conquest
    20, 203, 206; Edward's choice as heir to
    throne 75, 128–29, 134, 139–40, 143–44,
    149–50
Edith, Queen 16, 23, 44–45, 47–48, 56, 133,
    135–36, 137
Edith (or Eadgyth), Saint 101
Edith Swanneck 138
Edmund Ironside, King of England 15, 19,
    30, 57, 137, 206
Edward, Prince, the Exile 19; pl. 3

Edward, the Confessor, King of England
    13, 19, 57–58, 125, 161, 177; choice of
    successor 18–19, 25, 75, 122, 128–29,
    139–40, 143; conflicts with Godwin
    family 23, 56, 142; conversations with
    Harold 53–55, 127–29; death of 20, 21,
    22, 25, 48, 125, 130, 132–35, 140, 141–42;
    depiction in Tapestry 53, 54–55, 72, 95,
    127, 172; early life and reign 15–17, 54–57;
    and Harold's voyage to France 21, 23,
    24, 56, 75, 129; making Harold successor
    25, 46, 134, 143; making William
    successor 21, 22, 23, 24, 25, 56, 149–50;
    and mother 102; rebellion against 137,
    138; saintliness 13, 131; and wife 16, 23,
    56, 135, 136
Edward the Elder, King of Wessex 14,
    17–18
Edwin, Earl of Merica 137–38, 168
embroidery 8, 33–37, 51
Emma of Normandy, Queen of England
    15, 18, 101–2
Enguerrand II, Count of Ponthieu 74
Eu 88
Eustace II, Count of Boulogne 17, 23, 48,
    194, 196

fables 65–66, 73, 89, 98, 126, 127
Flanders 14, 18
food and feasting 61–63, 158–59, 169–73;
    pl. 11
Foucault, Nicolas-Joseph 9, 210; pl. 1
Fulford, Battle of 168, 212; Tapestry 212

Geoffrey Gaimar 156
Geoffrey Martel, Count of Anjou 97–98,
    114
Gilbert, Archdeacon of Lisieux 160
Godgifu 48
Godwin, Earl of Wessex 16–18, 23, 55–56,
    59, 62, 134, 136, 142, 196
Gospatric 137
Gregory the Great, Pope 41
Gruffydd ap Llywelyn, King of Wales 136
Gurney, Hudson 10, 11, 210
Guy, Bishop of Amiens 22–23, 120
Guy, Count of Brionne 97
Guy, Count of Ponthieu 68, 74–75, 76,
    81–82, 87, 93, 97, 128; and capture
    of Harold 22, 70, 73–74, 77–78, 84;
    undermining of 77, 78–79, 81, 88
Gyrth Godwinson 44, 191–92, 193

hair and faces 55, 76–77, 78, 83, 92, 93, 94–96, 119, 149, 175

Hakon 57, 124

Halley's Comet 144–46, 164

hands 54, 56, 80

Harald Hardrada, King of Norway 20, 25, 30, 102, 138, 139, 167–68, 177, 205–6, 212

Harley Psalter 42, 83

Harold I, Harefoot, King of England 15, 102

Harold II, Godwinson, King of England 7, 44, 64, 66, 97, 101, 152, 165–66, 179, 184, 205–6, 212; ambitions 20; Battle of Fulford 168; Battle of Stamford Bridge 168; becomes King of England 20, 22, 140–41, 143, 146, 149–50; and Bosham 58, 59, 61–62, 63–64; Brittany campaign 105, 106, 108, 109, 114, 116–17; coronation 46, 140, 141–42, 144, 145, 149; and Count Guy 68, 70–71, 72–73, 74–80, 84, 87–88; crossing Channel 64–65, 66–67, 68–69, 125, 126; and daughter of William 101, 121, 138; death 20, 198, 200–201, 202, 213, 214; and death of brothers at Hastings 191–93; and death of King Edward 132, 133, 141; depiction in Tapestry 20, 26–28, 59–59, 63–64, 88, 92; as Earl of Wessex 58, 170; early life 16, 18, 19–20; and Halley's Comet 144–45, 146; and hawks 59–60, 61, 64, 76, 77, 87; as hero 29, 55, 108, 109, 116, 201, 206; and hostages 24, 57, 74, 76, 94, 124, 128; and King Edward 25, 53, 55, 127–29; marriage to Ealdgyth 138; meets William 85–86, 87–88, 91, 92–94, 95, 98–99, 104; motives for visit to Normandy 20, 21, 22, 23, 24, 26, 54–58, 74–75, 76, 128–29; oath-swearing 22, 24, 26, 30, 40, 118, 119–24, 149–50; perjury 21, 22, 23, 122, 144, 147, 150, 153, 160, 205, 208; piety 62, 206; pilgrimage to Rome 24; provoked by William 178, 182; return to England from Normandy 125, 126; and Stigand 46, 141, 143–44; tactics in Battle of Hastings 182, 183, 190, 192; and Tostig 136–37, 146, 167–68, 177; pl. 4, 15

Harthacnut, King of England 15, 30

Hastings 116, 165, 169, 179, 180, 182, 187; castle 175, 176–77

Hastings, Battle of 7, 25, 29, 48, 176, 181, 205; aftermath 20, 111, 144; Anglo-Saxon shield-wall 7, 189, 191, 194; anniversary of 215; death of Harold 199–202;

death of Leofwine and Gyrth 191–92; exchange of ecclesiastical messengers 23; feigned retreat by Normans 195, 198–99; first engagement 189; Malfosse incident 193; Norman archers 188, 189, 191, 197, 198; Norman cavalry 182–83, 188, 189, 191, 198; Odo's role in 39–40, 107, 153; order of 182; reenactment 136; tactics of Harold 182, 190; tactics of William 182, 188, 189, 190, 195, 196

hawks 59–60, 87, 91–92

Henry I, King of France 74, 97–98

Henry III, King of England 130

Henry IV, King of Germany 19

Henry of Huntingdon (*Historia Anglorum*) 26, 57, 121, 137, 139

Herleva 96, 153

Herluin de Conteville 153

Himmler, Heinrich 215

horses 49, 59–60, 77, 80, 81, 82, 87, 107, 162, 163, 164, 185–86, 190, 193

Iaroslav I of Kiev 206

Isle of Wight 146, 166

John, Duke of Bedford 9

John of Worcester (*Chronica Chronicarum*) 25–26, 102, 134, 143, 165–66

Jumièges, abbey of 21, 131

Junius Manuscript 43, 67, 154; pl. 13

Lanfranc, Archbishop of Canterbury 46

Leek replica of Tapestry 37, 211

Leofwine Godwinson 191–92, 193

Life of King Edward 23–24, 47–48, 55, 121, 130, 133, 134, 135; pl. 10, 12

Loire Valley 44, 47

London 144, 146, 166, 168, 203, 209; Tower of London 212

Macron, Emmanuel, President of France 11, 213

Magnus the Good, King of Norway 15, 29–30

Malcolm, King of Scotland 167

Matilda, daughter of Henry IV 47

Matilda of Flanders 34, 47, 97, 164

Messent, Jan 211, 212

Montfaucon, Bernard de 9, 10, 47, 210, 214; pl. 2

Mont-Saint-Michel 45, 105–8, 116, 208; pl. 9

Mora 164
Morcar, Earl of Northumbria 137, 168
Mortemer, Battle of 74, 97–98

Napoleon Bonaparte 214
Nazis 215; pl. 19
Noah/Noah's Ark 43, 67, 154
nudity and sex 73, 82, 88, 98–99, 103, 181, 182, 202

Odo, Bishop of Bayeux 47, 48, 49, 50, 83, 153–54; advises William 151, 173–75; at Battle of Hastings 183, 194–95; and feasting Normans 172–73; imprisonment 39, 175; as patron of Tapestry 39–40, 45–47, 52, 115, 121, 208; role in Conquest 39, 40, 107
Old English Hexateuch 42–43, 44, 60, 80, 112, 133, 141, 190
Orderic Vitalis (*Historia Ecclesiastica*) 26, 101, 120, 153, 160

Paris 214–15
Pevensey (Sussex) 162, 164, 165, 169, 177
Philip I, King of France 19
Philip the Good, Duke of Burgundy 9
Polychronicon Ranulphi Higden monachi Cestrensis 102
Prudentius (*Psychomachia*) 170

Ralph, Earl of Hereford 190
Reading Tapestry 37, 211
reliquaries 119, 120
Rennes (Brittany) 112–13
Richard I, Duke of Normandy 15
Rivallon of Dol 106, 112
Robert, Count of Mortain 48, 174, 175, 183, 197
Robert I, the Magnificent, Duke of Normandy 17, 96–97
Robert Curthose 150, 203
Robert fitz Wimarch 177
Robert of Jumièges, Archbishop of Canterbury 21
Rochester Castle 83
Rodbert, the steward 133, 134
Rollo 14, 85
Rouen 13–14, 85, 87–88, 91, 102–3, 120

St Augustine's Gospels 173
St Bertin, Saint-Omer, abbey 23
St Florent, Saumur, abbey 44, 47

Saint-Omer 74
Saint-Valery-sur-Somme 161–62
Scolland, Abbot 45, 46, 49, 116, 208
Scotland 146, 167
shields 65, 66, 72–73, 85, 93, 110, 162, 164, 181, 191, 198
ships and shipbuilding 64–65, 66–68, 75, 98, 146, 149, 154–58, 161, 162–63
Skuldelev, Roskilde Fjord 157
Society of Antiquaries of London 196–97, 210
South Kensington Museum (Victoria & Albert Museum) 197, 211, 215
Southampton 126
Stamford Bridge, Battle of 25, 29, 168, 206; Tapestry 212
Stigand, Archbishop of Canterbury 45–47, 133–34, 135, 141, 142–44, 150
Stothard, Charles 196–97, 201, 210; pl. 17
Swein 102
Swein Forkbeard, King of Denmark 15
Swein Godwinson 16, 59
swords 78–79, 85–86, 93, 119, 141, 158, 174, 191, 193, 198

Tallefer 193
Thurstan Goz 97
Tostig Godwinson 25, 29, 139, 146, 157, 177; absence from Tapestry 139, 140, 205; banishment 20, 137; campaign in England 137, 138, 167–68; death of 168; rebellion against 125, 137–38; relationship with Harold 136–37; in Scotland 146, 167
trees 42, 61, 85, 147, 149, 154–55, 181, 184, 188, 194, 202
Turner, Dawson 10, 210
Turold 40, 82–83, 183

Utrecht Psalter 42, 83–84

Val-ès-Dunes, Battle of, 1047 97
Vikings/Viking Age 13–15, 42–43, 100, 157, 163, 168, 215
Vita Edwardi Regis see Life of King Edward
Vital 40, 183

Wace 156
Wadard 40, 170–71, 173, 183
Walter Map 62
Waltham Abbey 45
Wardle, Elizabeth 211

Westminster 55–56, 127, 142; Abbey 130, 131–32, 203, 212, 215

William, Count of Arques 97–98

William I, the Conqueror 7, 29, 46, 58–59, 64, 118, 126, 127, 128–29, 130, 139–40, 172, 205–6; brutality of 97–98, 161, 178–79; builds fleet 154–58; campaign in Brittany 45, 105–17; claim to the English throne 18–19, 20, 21–23, 24, 56, 79, 144, 205, 207; conversation with Harold 92–94, 95–96, 98–99, 104; coronation of 202–3, 209, 211; and Count Guy 74–75, 78, 81, 82, 84, 87–88; crosses Channel 161–64; daughters of 38, 101, 121, 153; early life 17–18, 96–98, 106; and English hostages 57, 96; and Eustace, Count of Boulogne 48; first meeting with Harold 85–86, 87–88, 91; first stages of Battle of Hastings 169–70, 180, 181, 182, 183, 188–89; and Harold's oath 24, 26, 40, 83, 118, 119, 120–23; heirs 150, 203; justification of invasion of England 8, 22, 29, 30, 103, 118, 150, 208; landfall in England 164–66, 167, 168; military prowess 18, 20, 28, 97, 196; and Odo 39–40, 151, 153, 173–75; papal support for invasion 40–41, 150, 159–61, 164; as possible patron of Tapestry 47; possible visit to England 17–18, 25; preparations for invasion of England 152–53, 157–58; ravages lands to provoke Harold 169–70, 177–78; receives news of Harold's coronation 148, 149–50; reign in England 20, 28, 38, 58, 85, 142, 202–3; and religion 24, 103, 150; rewards Harold 114; rumours of death in battle 195, 198; size and composition of army 169, 180–81, 192–93; tactics in Battle of Hastings 182, 183, 184, 188, 189, 190, 192–93, 195; wife 34, 47, 97, 164; pl. 7, 8

William II Rufus, King of England 203

William of Jumièges (Gesta Normannorum Ducum) 21–22, 26, 121, 129, 141, 155–56, 182, 184, 200, 204

William of Malmesbury (Gesta Regum Anglorum) 26, 74, 75, 81–82, 131

William of Poitiers (Gesta Guillelmi…) 21, 22, 23, 33, 73–74, 87, 94, 101, 123, 169, 204; on Battle of Hastings 182, 194–195; on Brittany campaign 106, 110, 112, 113, 114, 116; on death of King Edward 134, 149; on Duke William's Channel crossing 161–62, 164; on Duke William's preparations for invasion 152–53, 156, 158, 160; on Duke William's tactics 189; on Harold taking throne 140–41, 142; on Harold's character 22, 23; on Harold's oath 120, 121; on Harold's return to England 126; on message from Harold to Duke William 177

Wilton 44, 101

Winchester 44, 55, 127, 166

Witan 19, 140

women 33–34, 47–48, 99–101, 103, 135–36, 138, 178, 79

Wulfnoth Godwinson 57, 95

York 137, 168